Beyond 2012:

Planetary Cycles

and

World History

Beyond 2012:

Planetary Cycles

and World History

Thomas O. Sidebottom

CONCRESCENT

Copyright © 2013 by Thomas O. Sidebottom

All rights reserved. No part of this work may be reproduced in any form or by any means without permission from the publisher. Critics, however, are welcome to quote brief passages by way of review.

Concrescent Network LLC, *publisher*
1113 19th St SE, Cedar Rapids, IA 52403
http://www.Beyond2012Astrology.com

ISBN: 978-0-9890238-0-1

For John

Contents

1. Introduction 13
   Acknowledgments 14

Part I. Understanding Planetary Cycles 16

2. Feeling Planetary Rhythms 17
   What's a planetary cycle? 17
   Play that tune: The harmony of the spheres 18

Part II. The Uranus / Pluto Cycle and World Events 34

3. Uranus - Pluto: Shifts in the Will to Power 35
   Transformation in France 35
   Ferment in America 40
   Geopolitical anatomy of a Uranus - Pluto cycle 44

4. From Empire to Superpowers 45

5. To the present 55

Part III. Research on Planetary Cycles and World Events ... 60

6. Research Methods 61
   Assembling historical data 61
   Tagging the data 62
   Performing the analysis 62
   Issues with the data 63
   Why no studies about more 'positive' things? 63
   What about economic cycles? 63
   Understanding the graphs 63

7. Study controls 65
   Daily computation from 1200 through 2012 66
   Event controls 72

8. Armed conflict events and planetary cycles 78
   Uranus / Pluto and armed conflict events 78
   Saturn / Uranus and Armed Conflict Events: 1200-2012 ... 96
   Combining cycles 104

    Saturn - Pluto and Armed Conflict events: 1200-2012 105

9. **Civil unrest events and planetary cycles** 109
    Uranus - Pluto and Civil Unrest Events 109
    Saturn - Uranus and Civil Unrest Events: 1200-2012 117
    Saturn - Pluto and Civil Unrest events: 1200-2012 122

10. **Regime change events and planetary cycles** 127
    Uranus / Pluto and Regime Change Events: 1200-2012 127
    Saturn - Uranus and Regime Change Events: 1200-2012 132
    Saturn - Pluto and Regime Change events: 1200-2012 137

11. **US Economic downturns and planetary cycles** 140
    Deriving the data 140
    Controls 140
    Uranus - Pluto US economic downturns: 1793-2009 141
    Saturn - Uranus: US economic downturns 1793-2009 147
    Saturn - Pluto US economic downturns: 1793-2009 152
    Combining cycles 155

12. **Conclusions and implications** 157

Part IV. Projecting Forward 160

13. **Completing the cycles** 161
    Armed conflict 161
    Civil unrest 163
    Regime change 166
    Economic downturns 168

14. **Consolidating the timelines** 172

15. **A look farther out** 180

16. **References** 189
    About the author 194
    The work continues 194

Table of Figures

Figure 1. Schematic of Moon's monthly cycle 17
Figure 2. Sun-Moon-Earth relationship in the first harmonic 19
Figure 3. Sun-Moon-Earth relationship in the second harmonic 20
Figure 4. Sun-Earth-Moon relationship in the third harmonic 21
Figure 5. Sun-Earth-Moon relationship in the fourth harmonic 23
Figure 6. Sun-Earth-Moon relationship in the sixth harmonic 24
Figure 7. Sun-Earth-Moon relationship in the fifth harmonic 26
Figure 8. Sun-Earth-Moon relationship in the seventh harmonic 27
Figure 9. Sun-Earth-Moon relationship in the eighth harmonic 28
Figure 10. Sun-Earth-Moon relationship in the ninth harmonic 30
Figure 11. Combining the sixth and eighth harmonics 31
Figure 12. France and the 1710 Uranus - Pluto cycle 36
Figure 13. America and the 1710 Uranus - Pluto cycle 41
Figure 14. Historical events and the 1850 Uranus - Pluto cycle 46
Figure 15. Historical events and the 1966 Uranus - Pluto cycle 56
Figure 16. Uranus - Pluto Daily Geocentric Distribution: 1200-2012 66
Figure 17. Uranus - Pluto Daily Heliocentric Distribution: 1200-2012 67
Figure 18. Saturn - Uranus Daily Geocentric Distribution: 1200 - 2012 68
Figure 19. Saturn - Uranus Daily Heliocentric Distribution: 1200 - 2012 69
Figure 20. Saturn - Pluto Daily Geocentric Distribution: 1200 - 2012 70
Figure 21. Saturn - Pluto Daily Heliocentric Distribution: 1200 - 2012 71
Figure 22. Uranus - Pluto Geocentric Event Control Group Distribution 72
Figure 23. Uranus - Pluto Heliocentric Event Control Group Distribution 73
Figure 24. Saturn - Uranus Geocentric Event Control Group Distribution 74
Figure 25. Saturn - Uranus Heliocentric Event Control Group Distribution 75
Figure 26. Saturn - Pluto Geocentric Event Control Group Distribution 76
Figure 27. Saturn - Pluto Heliocentric Event Control Group Distribution 77
Figure 28. Uranus - Pluto: Armed conflict event distribution including World War II events, geocentric 78
Figure 29. Uranus - Pluto: Armed conflict event distribution including World War II events, heliocentric 79
Figure 30. Uranus - Pluto: Armed conflict event distribution excluding World War II events, geocentric 80
Figure 31. Uranus - Pluto: Armed conflict event distribution excluding World War II events, heliocentric 81
Figure 32. Distribution of Uranus - Pluto armed conflict with World War II events against event controls 84

Figure 33. Distribution of Uranus - Pluto armed conflict with World War II events against day controls 85
Figure 34. T-test of Uranus - Pluto armed conflict with World War II events against event controls 86
Figure 35. Distribution of Uranus - Pluto armed conflict without World War II events against event controls 87
Figure 36. T-test of Uranus - Pluto armed conflict without World War II events against event controls 87
Figure 37. Harmonic analysis: mapping first quadrant onto graph 89
Figure 38. Harmonic analysis: mapping second quadrant onto graph 90
Figure 39. Armed conflict event frequency and Uranus - Pluto separation in the fifth harmonic, including World War II events 91
Figure 40. T-test of Uranus - Pluto armed conflict including World War II events against event controls, fifth harmonic 92
Figure 41. T-test of Uranus - Pluto armed conflict excluding World War II events against event controls, fifth harmonic 93
Figure 42. T-test of Uranus - Pluto armed conflict including World War II events against event controls, by fifth harmonic intervals 93
Figure 43. Distribution of Uranus - Pluto armed conflict including World War II events against event controls by fifth harmonic intervals 94
Figure 44. Uranus - Pluto fifth harmonic areas associated with armed conflict events 95
Figure 45. Saturn - Uranus: armed conflict event distribution including World War II events, heliocentric 96
Figure 46. Distribution of Saturn - Uranus armed conflict with World War II events against event controls 98
Figure 47. Distribution of Saturn - Uranus armed conflict without World War II events against event controls 98
Figure 48. Armed conflict event frequency and Saturn - Uranus separation in the second harmonic, including World War II events 99
Figure 49. T-test of Saturn - Uranus armed conflict with World War II events against event controls, second harmonic 100
Figure 50. Armed conflict event frequency and Saturn - Uranus separation in the second harmonic, excluding World War II events 100
Figure 51. T-test of Saturn - Uranus armed conflict without World War II events against event controls, second harmonic 101
Figure 52. Distribution of Saturn - Uranus armed conflict with World War II events against event controls, second harmonic 101
Figure 53. Distribution of Saturn - Uranus armed conflict without World War II events against event controls, second harmonic 102

Figure 54. T-test of Saturn - Uranus armed conflict with World War II events against event controls, second harmonic 102

Figure 55. T-test of Saturn - Uranus armed conflict without World War II events against event controls, second harmonic 102

Figure 56. Saturn - Uranus second harmonic areas associated with armed conflict events 104

Figure 57. Saturn - Pluto: armed conflict event distribution including World War II events, heliocentric 105

Figure 58. T-test of Saturn - Pluto armed conflict with World War II events against event controls 107

Figure 59. T-test of Saturn - Pluto armed conflict without World War II events against event controls 107

Figure 60. Uranus - Pluto: civil unrest event distribution, heliocentric.................... 109

Figure 61. Civil unrest event frequency and Uranus - Pluto separation in the ninth harmonic... 113

Figure 62. T-test of Uranus - Pluto civil unrest events against event controls, ninth harmonic... 114

Figure 63. T-test of Uranus - Pluto civil unrest events against event controls, ninth harmonic, by interval.. 114

Figure 64. Distribution of Uranus - Pluto civil unrest events against event controls, ninth harmonic, by interval.. 114

Figure 65. Uranus - Pluto ninth harmonic areas associated with civil unrest events 116

Figure 66. Saturn - Uranus: civil unrest event distribution, heliocentric 117

Figure 67. Civil unrest event frequency and Saturn - Uranus separation in the fourth harmonic... 119

Figure 68. T-test of Saturn - Uranus civil unrest events against event controls, fourth harmonic... 120

Figure 69. Saturn - Uranus fourth harmonic with civil unrest events 121

Figure 70. Saturn - Pluto: civil unrest event distribution, heliocentric...................... 122

Figure 71. Civil unrest event frequency and Saturn - Pluto separation in the fourth harmonic... 124

Figure 72. T-test of Saturn - Pluto civil unrest events against event controls, fourth harmonic... 125

Figure 73. Saturn - Pluto fourth harmonic with civil unrest events 126

Figure 74. Uranus - Pluto: regime change event distribution, heliocentric............. 127

Figure 75. Regime change event frequency and Uranus - Pluto separation in the fourth harmonic... 129

Figure 76. T-test of Uranus - Pluto regime change events against event controls, fourth harmonic... 130

Figure 77. Uranus - Pluto fourth harmonic areas associated with regime change events 131

Figure 78. Saturn - Uranus: regime change event distribution, heliocentric............. 132

Figure 79. Regime change event frequency and Saturn - Uranus separation in the fourth harmonic.. 134

Figure 80. T-test of Saturn - Uranus regime change events against event controls, fourth harmonic.. 135

Figure 81. Saturn - Uranus fourth harmonic areas associated with regime change events 136

Figure 82. Saturn - Pluto: regime change event distribution, heliocentric............... 137

Figure 83. Regime change event frequency and Saturn - Pluto separation in the fifth harmonic.. 138

Figure 84. T-test of Saturn - Pluto regime change events against event controls, fifth harmonic.. 139

Figure 85. Uranus - Pluto: US economic downturn days distribution, heliocentric 141

Figure 86. Economic downturn day frequency and Uranus - Pluto separation in the second harmonic.. 142

Figure 87. US economic downturn day frequency and Uranus - Pluto separation in the twelfth harmonic 143

Figure 88. T-test of Uranus - Pluto downturn days against upturn days, twelfth harmonic by interval.. 143

Figure 89. Uranus - Pluto second harmonic areas with twelfth harmonic overlay; areas associated with economic downturn days... 145

Figure 90. Saturn - Uranus: US economic downturn days distribution, heliocentric 147

Figure 91. US economic downturn day frequency and Saturn - Uranus separation in the eighth harmonic.. 149

Figure 92. T-test of Saturn - Uranus downturn days against upturn days, eighth harmonic by interval 149

Figure 93. Saturn - Uranus eighth harmonic areas associated with economic downturn days.. 151

Figure 94. Saturn - Pluto: US economic downturn days distribution, heliocentric 152

Figure 95. US economic downturn day frequency and Saturn - Pluto separation in the fourth harmonic.. 153

Figure 96. T-test of Saturn - Pluto economic downturn days against upturn days, fourth harmonic by interval 154

Figure 97. Uranus - Pluto armed conflict timeline 161

Figure 98. Saturn - Uranus armed conflict timeline 162

Figure 99. Uranus - Pluto civil unrest timeline 163

Figure 100. Saturn - Uranus civil unrest timeline 164

Figure 101. Saturn - Pluto civil unrest timeline 165

Figure 102. Uranus - Pluto regime change timeline 166
Figure 103. Saturn - Uranus regime change timeline 167
Figure 104. Uranus - Pluto economic downturn timeline 168
Figure 105. Saturn - Uranus economic downturn timeline 169
Figure 106. Saturn - Pluto economic downturn timeline 170
Figure 107. Armed conflict timeline 173
Figure 108. Civil unrest timeline 175
Figure 109. Regime change timeline 177
Figure 110. US Economic downturn timeline 179

1. Introduction

This book examines the cyclic movement of the planets and how these cycles have impacted history: as the planets move their interrelationships touch life here on Earth. These subtle cycles play out sometimes over periods lasting many human lives. Their meaning emerges as shifts in how human cultures perceive the world, how nations behave with each other, how governments rise and fall, how economies go boom and bust.

Behind the apocalyptic predictions for the end of 2012 is a deeper story, one less mediaworthy but of greater significance. Three of the slowest moving planets – Saturn, Uranus, and Pluto – are forming unusual spatial relationships with each other. These relationships began in the early 2000's and rose to an intense peak with the global economic uncertainties beginning in 2008 and with the dramatic shifts in political life in the Arab world in 2011. This peak energy continues to play out between 2012 and 2016. This book seeks to unravel the underlying meaning of these changes – to present a roadmap of possible events and critical phases.

What is a planetary cycle? Each of us experiences the Moon's changing phases each month. *Part I* relates the fundamental Sun - Moon cycle to the deeper, longer lasting cycles of the other planets. The geometric patterns that the Sun and Moon trace reveal the underlying principles of planetary harmonies: geometric relationships that reinforce resonances that affect our lives. Each pair of planets forms a similar cycle with the Earth. Because the planets move more slowly than the Moon and because we do not relate to these slower passages in the same way we regard the Moon's changing phases in the evening sky, we are largely unaware of these more subtle tides. This book focuses on three of these deeper cycles, those formed by Saturn, Uranus, and Pluto. Their slow march creates a subtle pattern that relates in a profound way to the unfolding of human history.

Part II takes us backward so we can see forward more clearly. It begins with an historical journey concerning one of the most influential planetary cycles, the relationship between Uranus and Pluto. Uranus is the planet linked to dramatic change, to mutation, to the new, and to the breakdown of old, established structures that we rely on to be comfortably unaware of our contingent milieu. Pluto is a deeper energy, tied with mass communication, propaganda, political movement and unrest. Uranus and Pluto move slowly. The geometric patterns that they weave unfold over many years – as much as a century and half. Between 2012 and 2016 these planets once again fall into significant relationship with each other. To understand the potential for this upcoming encounter, we look backward at how the story has played out in the past, starting with the French and American Revolutions, then from the zenith of the British Empire to its decolonialization and the rise of superpowers, and finally on to the present.

Part III presents original research that shows how the Saturn, Uranus, and Pluto cycles relate to four different types of historical events: armed conflicts between nations, civil unrest within a nation, major changes in governance, and economic downturn cycles in the United States. This research begins with a database of thousands of historical events from 1200 CE to 2012. It presents detailed evidence for the impact of the planetary cycles on these events, and yields a new understanding of how planetary cycles relate to human events.

This research effectively turns the narrative of Part II on its head. Rather than beginning with astrological interpretations, it starts with historical data and derives the significance of the planetary cycles freshly. This is not astrology as it is typically practiced. You will seek in vain for mention of zodiacal signs. The exposition in this section is technical, delving into the underlying harmonics of planetary cycles and using terms and approaches which may not be second nature to astrologers. The results from this research confirm a profound link between planetary cycles and human events, but they accent the importance of a systematic, data-driven approach to planetary cycles, one less tied to zodiacal signs and more closely aligned with harmonic astrology.

Part IV takes these results and creates detailed timetables of critical periods unfolding over the next few years. These periods accent when geopolitical and economic events are most likely to occur. It closes by returning to the archetypal symbolism that makes astrology so lively: it presents strategies for resilient living drawn from the archetypal meaning of Saturn, Uranus, and Pluto.

Acknowledgments

As will be painfully obvious to any serious historical scholar, I am no historian. I have approached this material as an outsider, as an astrologer deeply interested in historical trends, but one who is completely dependent on basic sources to understand these trends. I have relied on these:

- *Cassell's Chronology of World History* [112][1], a timeline of historical events wonderfully compiled and presented by Hywel Williams.

- A large number of articles about historical timelines, events, and trends from Wikipedia.org. The research presented in Part III relies completely on a large database of historical events drawn entirely from Wikipedia.org sources.

I began this work long before becoming acquainted with the seminal contributions of Richard Tarnas in his groundbreaking book, *Cosmos and Psyche* [95]. His work on the Uranus - Pluto cycle dovetails neatly with the work in this book. The historical narrative

---

1   All references for works cited in this book appear in Chapter 16. Each reference is numbered; the reference number appears in the body of the work between square brackets.

in Part II embellishes Tarnas's broader sketches, adding greater detail about the Uranus - Pluto cycle and showing how the shifts in the global Zeitgeist relate to the different phases of this cycle.

I have studied astrology since I was ten, having picked up a pocketbook about astrology just before I rode on vacation in the back of my family's old red Ford Fairlane from Illinois to Florida in the mid-1960's. Since that time my astrological perspectives have transformed, largely through the transformational work of Reinhold Ebertin on cosmobiology and by John Addey's seminal work on harmonic astrology. This book depends deeply on their work, and, I hope, strengthens the evidence for their approaches.

I have been deeply fortunate to have worked closely with astrological colleagues over many years and to have exchanged astrological ideas with some of my friends in the life and social sciences and in business management. Many thanks to Brian Bowman, Lee Rowen, David Taylor, Phoenix Wang, and Jacquelyn Wheeler. Meredith Karns and Eileen Nauman spent hours in sessions with me reviewing the ideas presented here: my thanks to them.

Minerva Books in Palo Alto, California during the 1980's and 1990's was a unique environment for metaphysical study. I was able to teach astrology in classes at Minvera's, and I am deeply indebted to the store and its founder, Robert Clark, for the networking that happened there. Robert Clark and Kathleen Jacoby, my friends from Minerva's, have been co-workers and confidants for many years. Their careful reading of this work and their comments helped me in countless ways. My special thanks to them.

Finally, my enduring thanks to John Schwartzkopf, artist-in-wood, philosopher and anthropologist, my partner in life.

Part I. Understanding Planetary Cycles

2. Feeling Planetary Rhythms

What's a planetary cycle?

There is a rhythm to the unfolding of human events. Astrology describes this rhythm as the cyclic movement of the Earth and the other planets. As the planets move, they create geometric patterns with other planets that change in a predictable way. These changing geometries are the basis for the planetary cycles that influence life.

All of us intimately know one planetary cycle. It unfolds every month: the Moon's changing relationship with the Sun and the Earth.

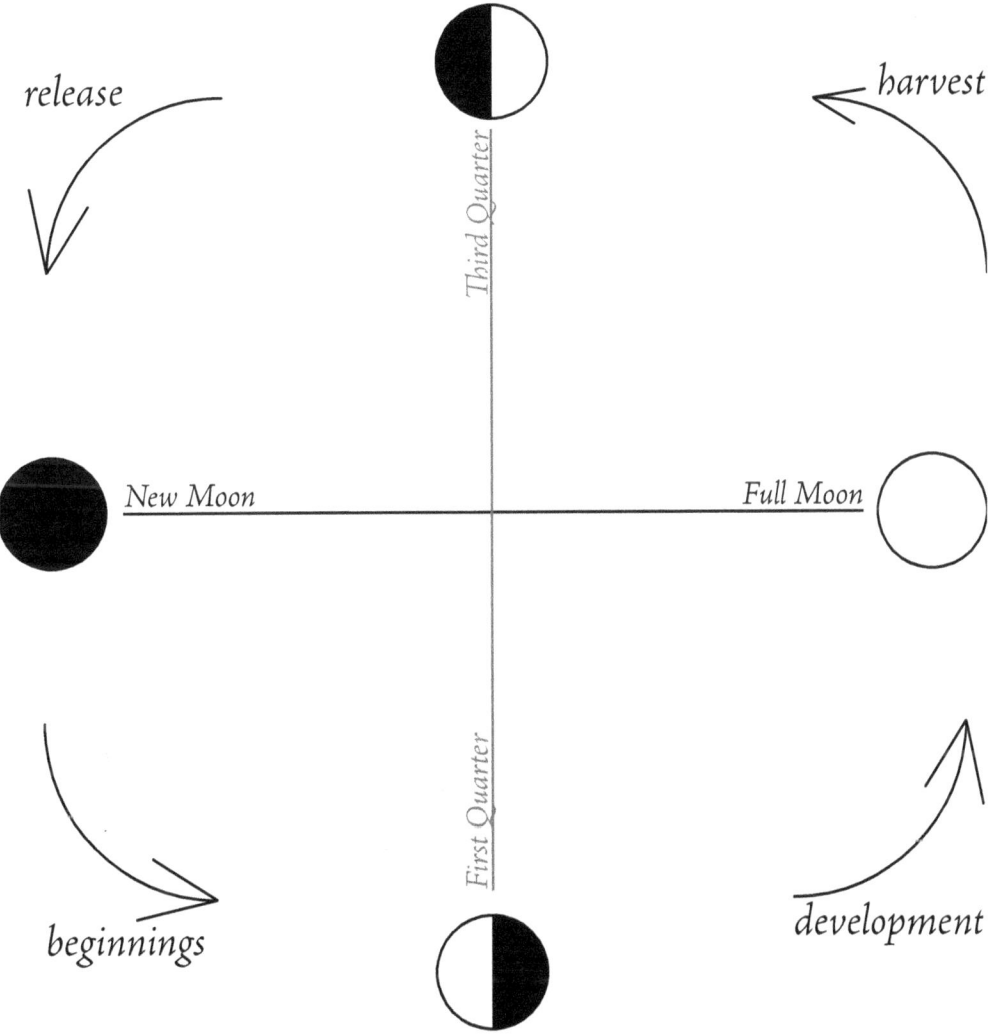

Figure 1. Schematic of Moon's monthly cycle

As the Moon moves around the Earth it goes through phases. The variable light of the Moon's phases inspires poetry and romance and intimately affects life on Earth. At the physical level, the changing relationship of the Earth, Moon, and Sun affects tides and the growing of plants. At a subtle level, this same cycle touches us emotionally. This subtle influence is the subject of astrology.

At the New Moon, the Sun, Moon, and Earth are aligned. At that moment we here on Earth can see no sunlight reflected from the Moon. The Moon's disk is dark. This moment begins a new lunar cycle. Over the next twenty-nine days or so, the Moon gradually moves around the Earth. As it does it begins to reflect more and more light back to us. The Moon waxes, beginning with a narrow crescent, through the First Quarter when the Moon's disk is half-lit. The Moon's reflected light grows night by night until the evening when the Moon is on the opposite side of the Earth from the Sun. That is the Full Moon. Then the Moon's illumined disk shrinks. At the Third Quarter the Moon's disk is again half-lit. Just about seven more nights brings a sliver crescent Moon, and then the next lunar cycle begins with the following New Moon.

Humans respond to the Moon's phase, too. On my last visit to my doctor's office the receptionist muttered under her breath that the day would be a bit crazy: the Moon was Full. She followed the lunar cycle each month as a guide to the patient load and intensity that the clinic would experience.

Play that tune: The harmony of the spheres

Harmony and rhythm aren't idle words when describing planetary cycles. Planetary cycles derive from much the same principles that musical intervals and harmonies do, by dividing a whole into a fixed number of intervals.

Musical pitches relate to each other by taking a vibrating string and dividing the string in half, in thirds, or by other whole numbers. These divisions give rise to the musical harmonic series. Combinations of different harmonic series gives complexity to the harmony. Changing these harmonic emphases over time creates a feeling of rhythm.

First harmonic: 360° / 1 = 360°

All planetary cycles work in the same way. By dividing the circle of the sky by a series of whole numbers, a harmonic series results. There are 360 degrees in a circle. To begin, if we divide 360 by one, we get 360 back.

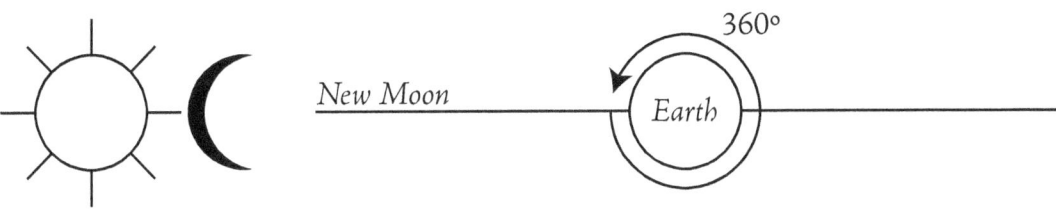

Figure 2. Sun-Moon-Earth relationship in the first harmonic

The first harmonic is a spacing of 360°, which is the same as going completely around the circle and returning back to the starting point. Being 360° apart means the planets are in the same place in the sky. Astrologers term this connection a *conjunction* aspect, and it represents a strong blending of the energies of the planets involved. The New Moon is the conjunction or first harmonic connection between Sun and Moon.

A conjunction begins a cycle between two planets and is special because it unifies the planetary energies. That's the energy felt at the New Moon, when the Sun's nature of growth and energy blends with the Moon's emotional flow. What happens at the New Moon becomes the lunar cycle's theme. In the same way, what happens when two planets are conjunct becomes the theme for the following planetary cycle.

Second harmonic: 360° / 2 = 180°

Dividing 360 degrees by two gives us 180 degrees for the second harmonic spacing. Drawing the cycle in the second harmonic looks like this:

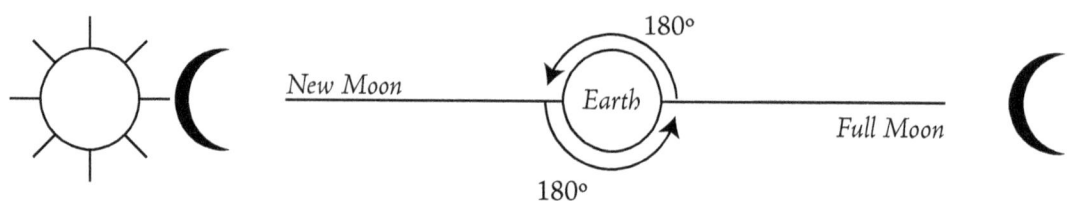

Figure 3. *Sun-Moon-Earth relationship in the second harmonic*

When the Moon moves around the Earth so that it appears to be 180° from the Sun, we have the Full Moon. Astrologers term this an *opposition* of the Sun and Moon. An opposition – a second harmonic connection – contrasts the energies of the two planets. They are related but pulling in opposite directions. At the Full Moon, the dynamic relationship between the different energies is at its peak. The polarity between the two viewpoints is at its greatest strength. The Moon's emotions run high: they are opposed to the Sun's nature of energy and growth. Both sides assert themselves. There is a potential for conflict. The dynamic nature of the opposition encourages a *synthesis* to occur, a blending of the two energies that is stronger than either one alone. So while conflict may arise there is the potential for increased depth and awareness. This same quality of polarity, difference, and potential synthesis occurs in every planetary cycle.

Things return home

When the Moon moves so that it appears to be 180° from the Full Moon, the next New Moon occurs. The second harmonic – a division of the circle by 180° – also contains the first harmonic – a division of the circle by 360°. A harmonic cycle consists of continuing by the harmonic spacing until we come around full-circle to the beginning of the next cycle. The conjunction aspect, the first harmonic contact, is implicitly part of every harmonic cycle.

Third harmonic: 360° / 3 = 120°

Dividing the circle by three gives us something completely different. When we divide 360° by three, we get 120°. Tracing around the circle by 120° brings us one-third of the way around. If we go another 120°, we wind up at 240°, which is 120° from the starting point of the circle going the other way around. Connecting the points gives us an equilateral triangle around the circle of the sky.

Often we do not realize when the Moon is 120° from the Sun, informally terming those phases waxing and waning Gibbous Moons. This angle is important to astrologers, though. Planets separated by 120° are in *trine*.

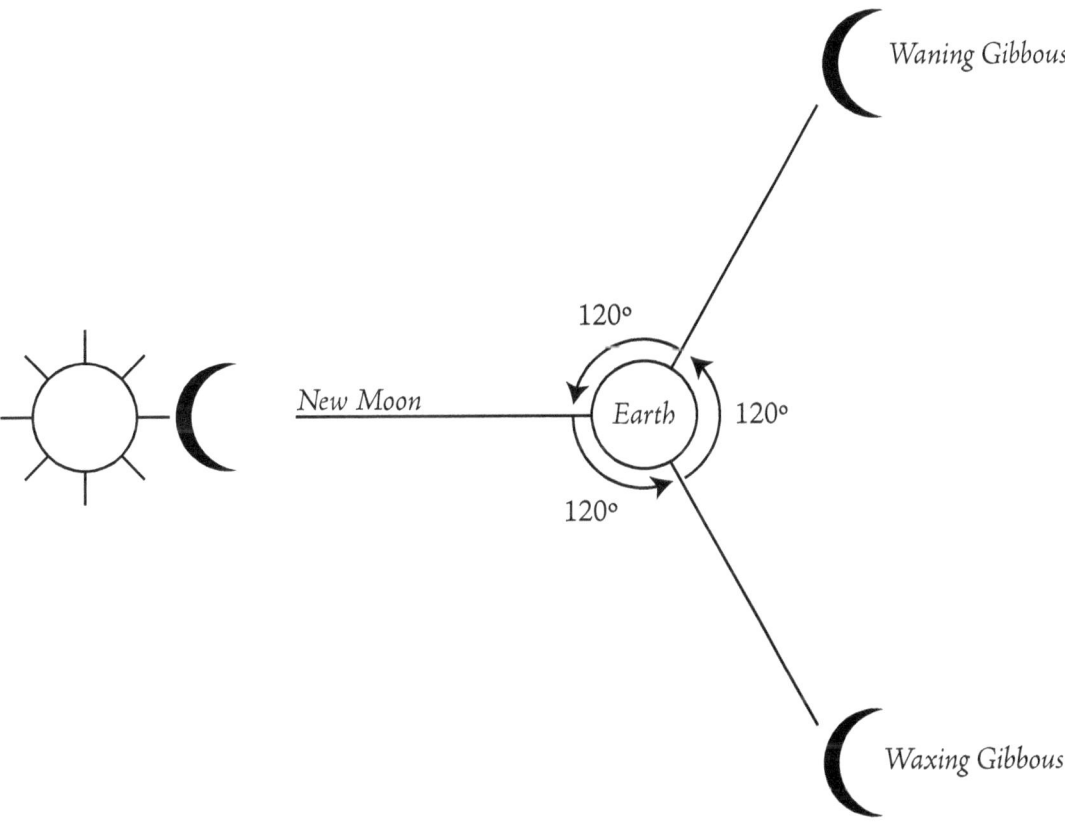

Figure 4. Sun-Earth-Moon relationship in the third harmonic

A third harmonic connection – a trine – combines the energies of the planets in an harmonious way. Astrologers traditionally consider this relationship to be smooth and flowing. Think of a relaxing, easy afternoon off: that's the energy of a trine.

At the waxing gibbous phase (120° from the New Moon) all energies are combined for growth and development. At the waning gibbous phase (240° from the New Moon and 120° from the next New Moon) the drive is toward harvest and completion.

Fourth harmonic: 360° / 4 = 90°

Every harmonic so far started with a prime number. With the fourth harmonic we leave the realm of prime numbers. Why does this matter? A prime number cannot be divided by any other number. Prime numbers other than two cannot be even. The second harmonic – the number two – relates to opposition and polarities. *Harmonics based on prime numbers other than two do not contain the opposition.* These harmonics do not contain the potential for reflection, for polarity, and for growth through synthesis of opposites. We saw this in the third harmonic: the 120° aspect series does not include the opposition.

Harmonics based on even numbers implicitly contain the opposition. The fourth and eighth harmonics, being powers of two, are more fine divisions of the second harmonic, of the opposition. Each of these express a more subtle variation of polarity.

The number *four* is *two times two*. The fourth harmonic contains a double polarity. When we divide 360° by four, we get 90°. As we trace around the circle 90° from the starting point, we arrive at the first square aspect. The square is 90° between two planets. In the lunar cycle, the first square happens at the First Quarter.

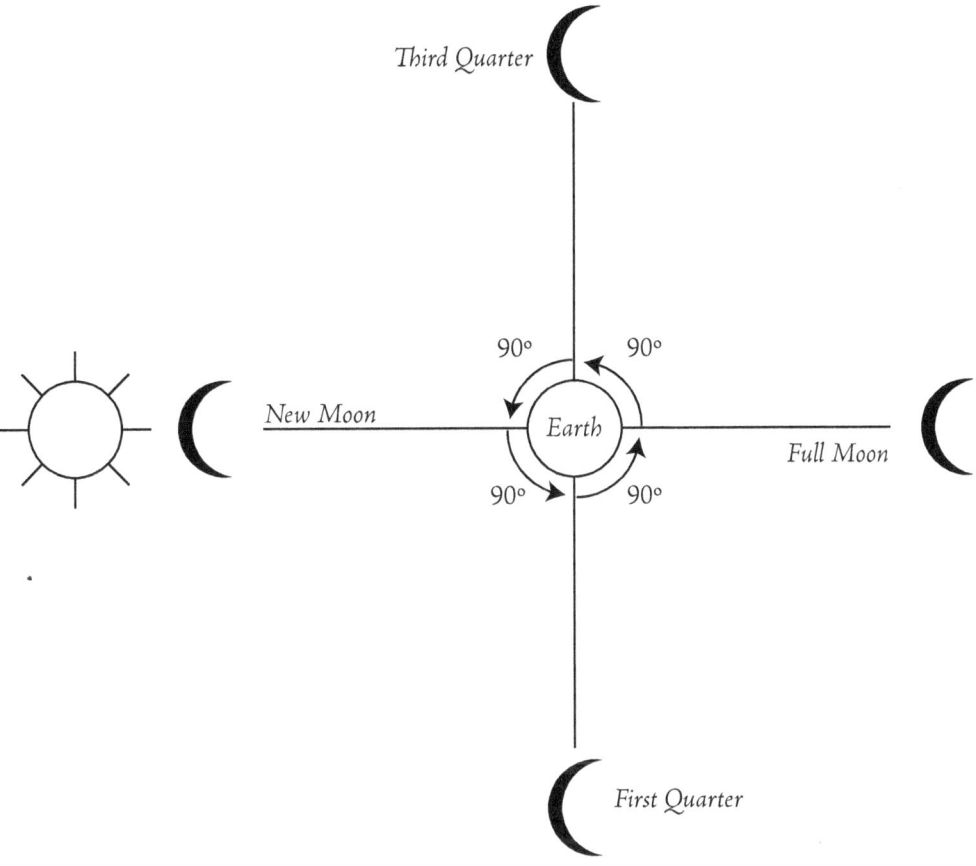

Figure 5. Sun-Earth-Moon relationship in the fourth harmonic

Tracing around another 90°, we come to the opposite point from where we started. The fourth harmonic contains the opposition, the symbol of polarity. As we continue to trace around another 90°, we are 90° from the original point tracing around the opposite way. In the lunar cycle, this is the Third Quarter. So the fourth harmonic contains the conjunction, the opening and closing squares, and the opposition.

The opening square at the First Quarter is a time for critical evaluation and judgment. *Is the current direction the right approach? Does the strategy need an adjustment?* The opposition takes place at the Full Moon, with all the drive and conflict created by the polarity of energies. The closing square at the Third Quarter is again a time for evaluation: this time to determine what is worth keeping from the current cycle and what needs to be discarded to make way for the next cycle of development.

This four-fold cycle forms a fundamental framework to analyze life. These aspects – conjunction, square, opposition – create a dynamic that brings new things into the world. The new arrives through conflict with the existing state of things. The evolving nature of the world proceeds through examination, polarity, conflict, and synthesis.

Sixth harmonic: 360° / 6 = 60°

Six is two times three. Six combines the energy of polarity – two – with the flowing, harmonious energy of three. When we divide 360° by 6 we get 60°:

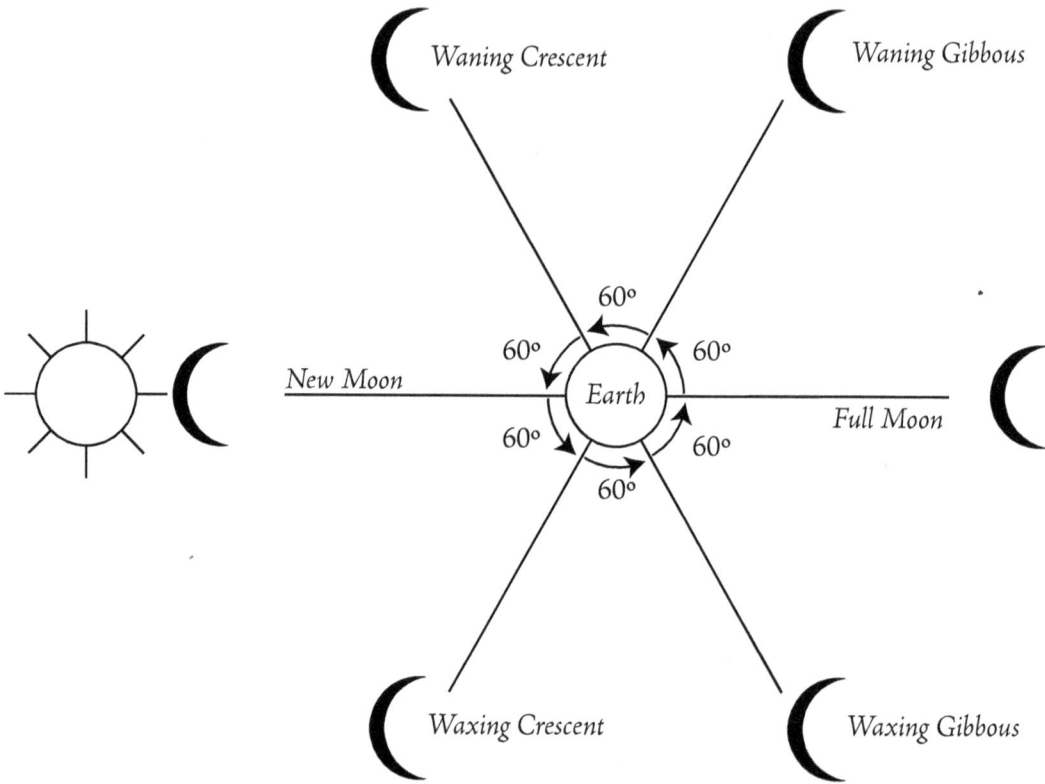

Figure 6. Sun-Earth-Moon relationship in the sixth harmonic

Tracing around the circle 60° we arrive at the first *sextile* aspect. In the lunar cycle, the sextile is part-way to the First Quarter but not quite there yet. This is the Waxing Crescent.

Continuing on another 60° we reach the first trine, the 120° aspect described above. This is the Waxing Gibbous Moon. Going another 60° we reach the opposition at the Full Moon. Because six is two times three, the opposition aspect of the second harmonic appears in the sixth harmonic as well. Continuing to move in 60° arcs, we reach the closing trine, the closing sextile and finally back to the beginning of the next cycle.

A sixth harmonic connection combines the flowing energy of the third harmonic with the awareness of polarity of the second harmonic. Traditionally astrologers view the sextile as a smoothly flowing combination of planetary energies.

Beyond traditional astrology: other harmonics

Traditionally astrology has mostly paid attention to harmonics based on two or three: the second / fourth harmonic series, and the third / sixth harmonic series. Fundamental to traditional astrology is dividing the circle into twelve, creating the twelve signs. *Twelve* is *three times four* or *two times six*; twelve brings together the second, third, fourth, and sixth harmonics.

The next few sections look at divisions of the circle that are not often used by astrologers. The fifth and seventh harmonics are based on prime numbers that divide the circle uniquely. The other two harmonics are higher divisions of existing ones. The eighth harmonic is a division of the fourth harmonic into two, while the ninth harmonic is a three-fold division of the third harmonic.

All aspects derived from these harmonics are difficult to find without the help of a computer, because the aspect's angle is not easily spotted by eye.

Fifth harmonic: 72°

Dividing the circle's 360° by 5 gives 72°: the *quintile* aspect.

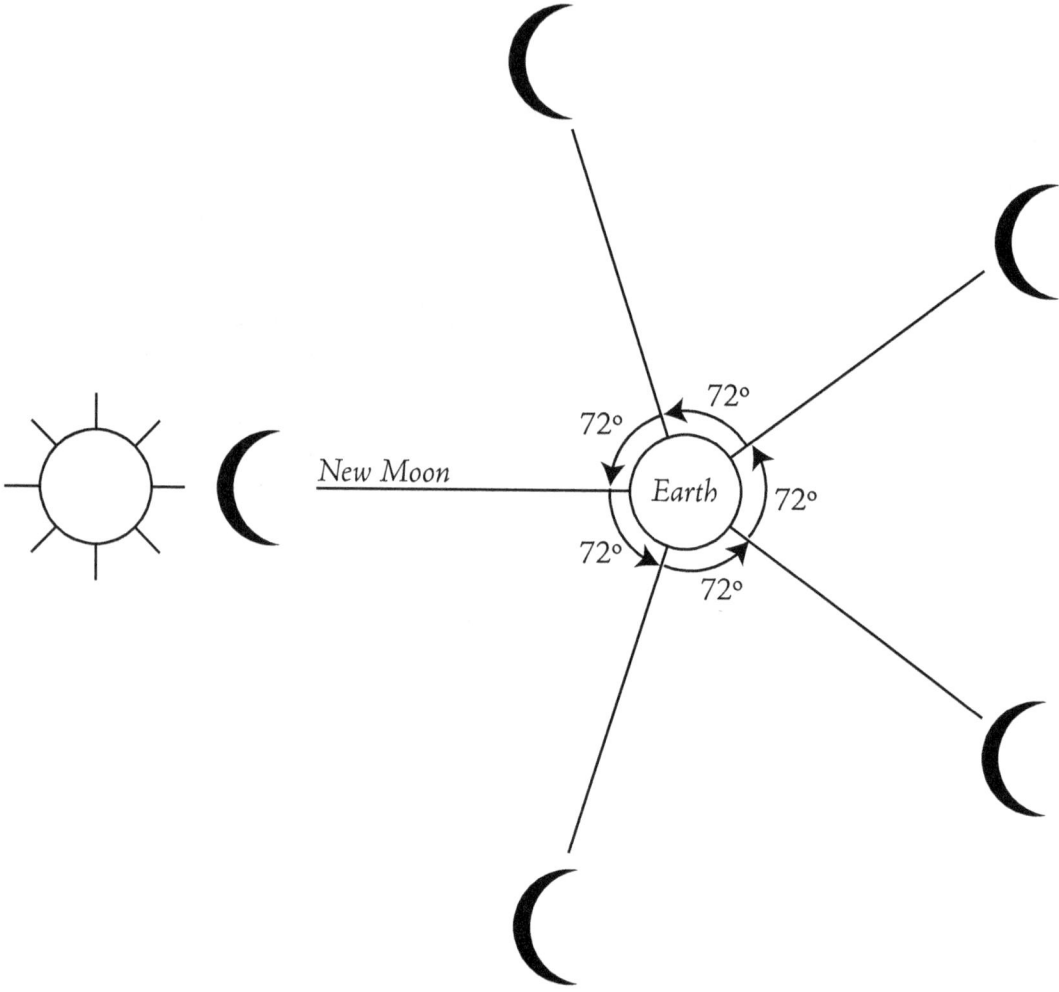

Figure 7. Sun-Earth-Moon relationship in the fifth harmonic

The quintile series (0°, 72°, 144°, 216°, 288°) deals with *arranging the world in a purposeful way*[42]. Purpose manifests in many ways: as art, with an arrangement based on aesthetic values; as engineering and technology, with an arrangement based on useful result. Purpose relates to *creativity*. Because five is not even, the fifth harmonic series does not contain the opposition or square. Further, because five is prime, the fifth harmonic series does not contain the trine or sextile aspects, making this relationship different from any we have worked with so far.

Seventh harmonic: about 51.2°

Dividing 360° by 7 gives us a bit over 51.2°: the *septile* aspect.

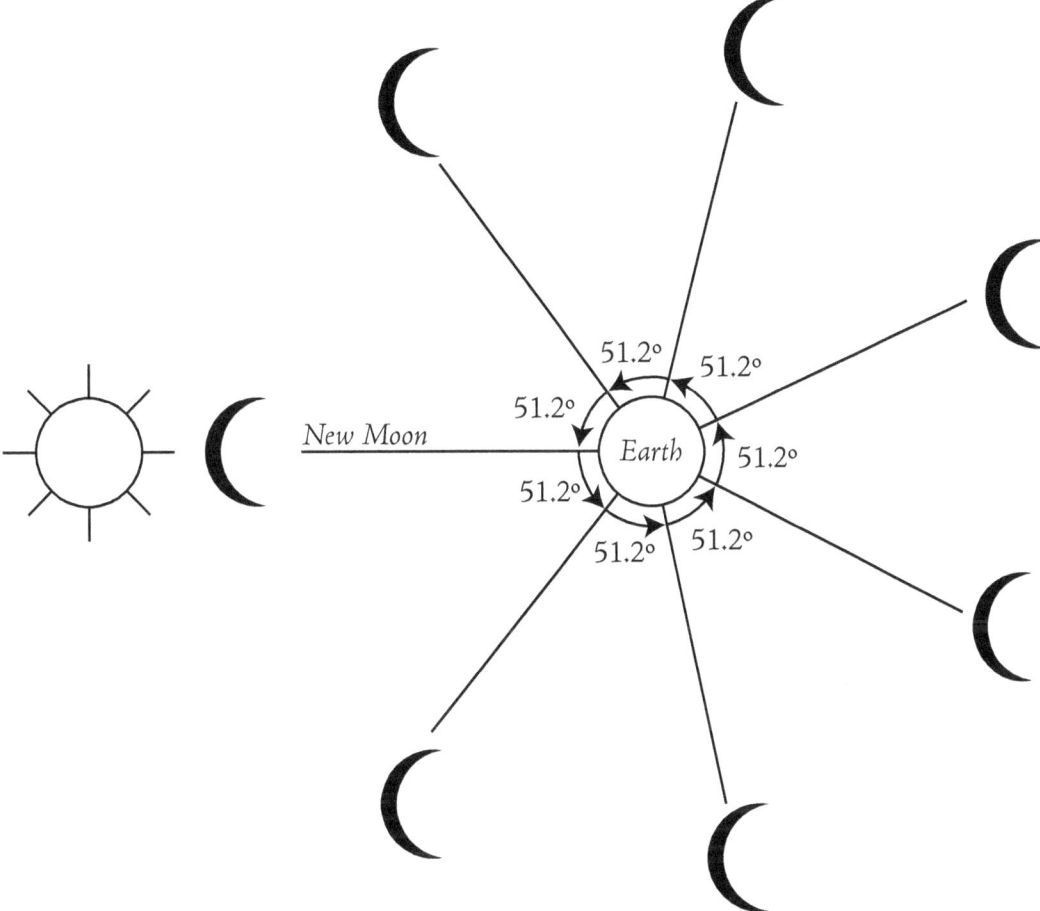

Figure 8. Sun-Earth-Moon relationship in the seventh harmonic

360° does not divide evenly by seven, so the harmonic interval is not an even number of degrees. The septile aspect is almost impossible to find without a computer. Astrologers have given the seventh harmonic aspects very little attention, but it appears to relate to *inspiration* and *imagination*[43].

Eighth harmonic: 45°

Four is *two times two*. If we multiply four by two, we get *eight: two cubed*. Once again we augment the energy of polarity, comparison, conflict, and synthesis. Eight is the basic polarity cubed.

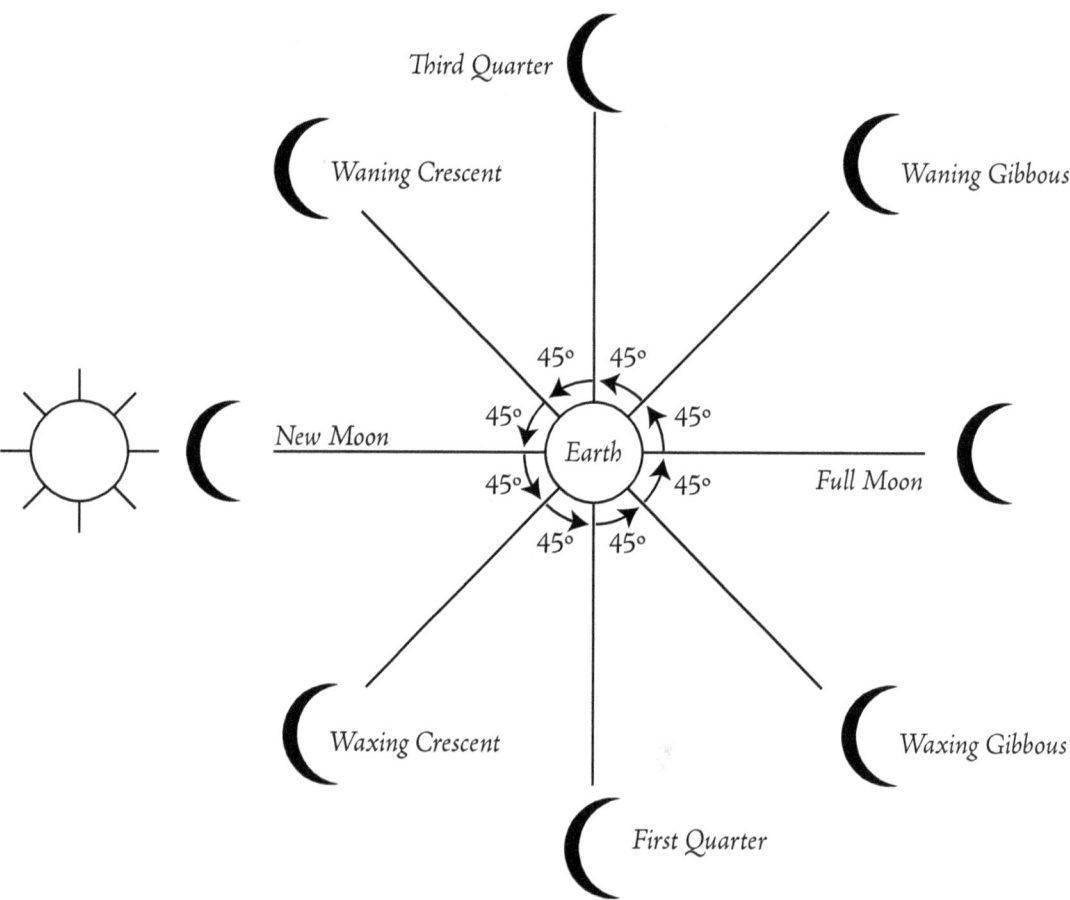

Figure 9. Sun-Earth-Moon relationship in the eighth harmonic

When we divide 360° by eight we get 45°. Most western astrologers regard the 45° and 135° aspects as 'minor' aspects that deserve relatively little weight in analysis. This historical attitude probably arises from the difficulty in spotting them without assistance of a computer or other special graphical device. From another perspective, twelve does not divide evenly by eight; the 45° and 135° aspects in the eighth harmonic play no role in the twelfth harmonic that underlies traditional astrology with its emphasis on dividing the circle into twelve signs of thirty degrees.

Reinhold Ebertin, the developer of cosmobiology, incorporated the eighth harmonic as an essential part of chart analysis and forecasting. His research found that the eighth harmonic aspects strongly relate to physical events.

From a harmonic astrological perspective the 45° and 135° aspects are potent. Tracing around the circle by 45° we arrive at a *semisquare* aspect. Trace around another 45° and we arrive at the 90° square. Tracing around another 45° brings us to the 135° aspect, the *sesquiquadrate*. Continuing on another 45° we arrive at the 180° opposition. We can continue tracing around 45°, bringing us to another sesquiquadrate, then to the closing square, and finally to the closing semisquare. The sequence is 0°, 45°, 90°, 135°, 180°, 225°, 270°, 315°.

Looking at the lunar cycle, the semisquare (45°) aspect represents the time just after birth at the New Moon when growth is moving into high gear. The initial small growth steps give way to more pronounced movement. The sesquiquadrate (135°) aspect is the time between the opening square at the First Quarter and the opposition at the Full Moon. At the 135° aspect growth is at its peak and maturity approaches with vigor.

After the Full Moon the cycle enters the phase harvest and release. The closing 135° aspect is the peak of harvest. The closing 45° aspect is the time of maximum release. These same critical points occur in every cycle. The eighth harmonic is the harmonic of dynamic change.

Ninth harmonic: 40°

Dividing 360° by 9 gives us 40°: the *novile* aspect.

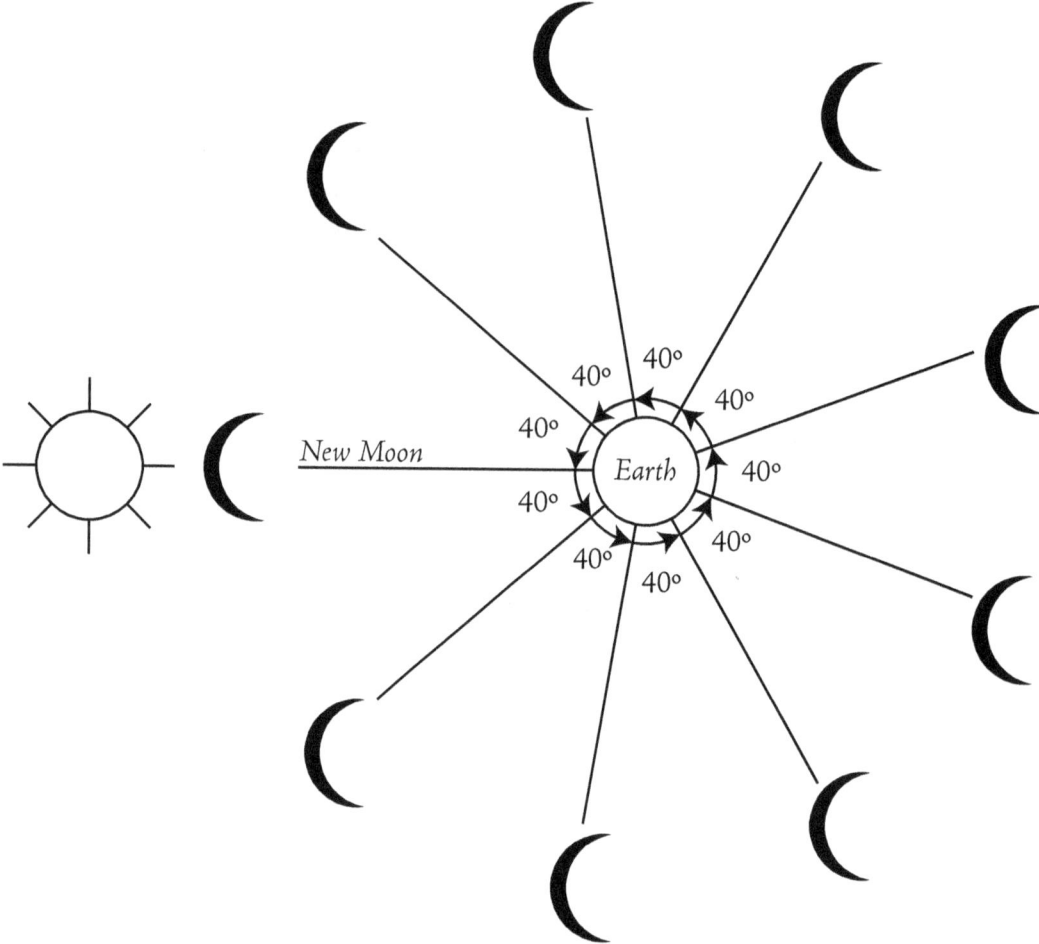

Figure 10. Sun-Earth-Moon relationship in the ninth harmonic

The ninth harmonic is a three-fold division of the third harmonic. Three novile aspects in a row is a trine (3 x 40° = 120°). This harmonic emphasizes the harmonious nature of three, and relates to the *higher mind*, to *insight*, and to *inner development*[44].

Combining harmonics

Part II presents a detailed look at how one of the most important long-term planetary cycles relates to major historical events over the centuries. The basic interpretive framework combines the sixth and eighth harmonics to give this view of a planetary cycle:

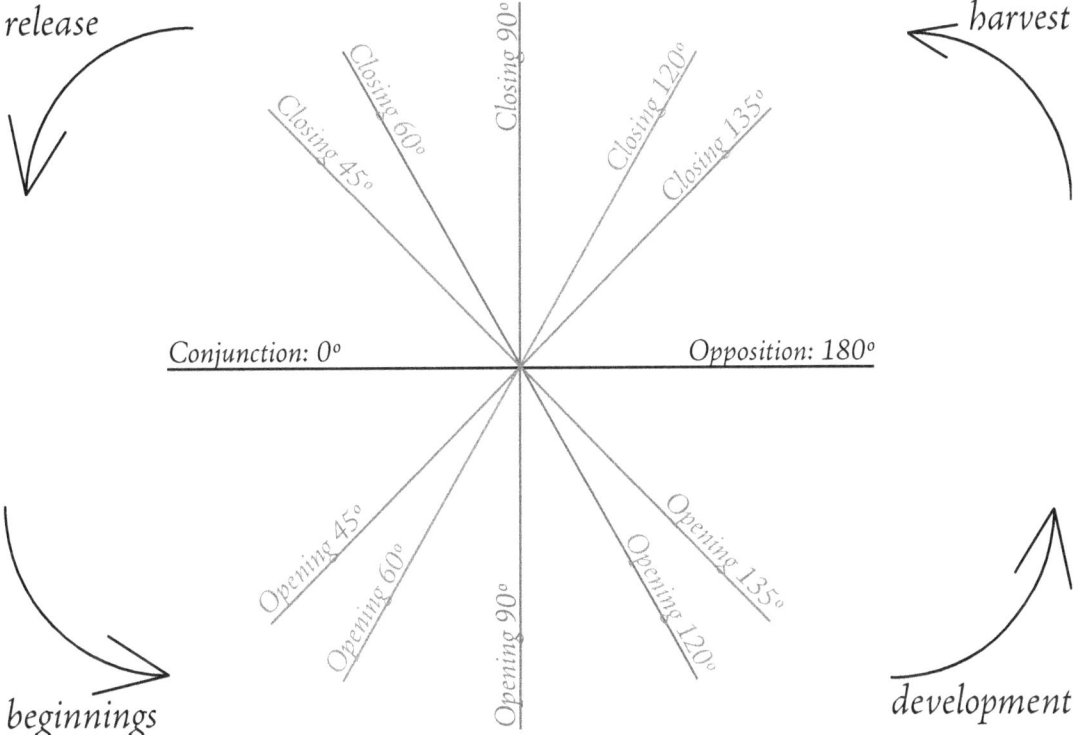

Figure 11. Combining the sixth and eighth harmonics

This blending of the sixth and eighth harmonics strikes a balance between the more dynamic combinations of the eighth harmonic with the more flowing combinations of the sixth harmonic. The four quadrants relate to the cycle's unfolding:

+ The *cycle's beginning sets the stage, defining the theme and the major actors.*

+ The *development phase begins with tensions between the actors* becoming more clear and the push for growth, change, and potential conflict arising.

+ The *harvest phase solidifies the changes* in the cycle.

+ The *cycle's closing is the release phase: discarding things no longer needed* and preparing to plant the seeds for the following cycle.

Each pairs of planets form a unique cycle

The lunar cycle relates the position of the Sun, the Moon, and the Earth. The other planetary cycles are not so familiar, but every pair of planets has the same kind of cyclic relationship with each other. Because the planets move so much more slowly than the Moon does, these cycles unfold over months or years – sometimes even centuries.

A cycle's meaning comes from the planets involved. Because we live on the Earth, not on the Sun, astrologers often look at planetary motion from an geocentric perspective. Astronomers do the same when computing where to point an Earth-based telescope. In *geocentric* astrology, the Sun appears as a planet along with the other traditional planets. The Sun represents the physical life, energy, growth. The Moon represents emotion, relationship, change. Combining the Sun and Moon relates the energy that invigorates all life with the emotional charge that creates and breaks relationships. The Sun and the Moon are at the core of life.

In *heliocentric* astrology, the Sun takes center stage. Many financial and mundane astrologers find a heliocentric viewpoint makes it easier to focus on worldwide trends, rather than on events of a personal nature.

Each pair of planets creates a planetary cycle. The outer planets, Jupiter, Saturn, Uranus, Neptune, and Pluto, move much more slowly and create a more sustained effect. The slowest moving planets, Uranus, Neptune, and Pluto, are so slow that their effects have an influence over an entire generation.

A question of inexactness

Planets may spend only a day or two in precise angular relationship. These are the times that an aspect is exact. Experience shows an influence that extends around the time of exactness, however. The degree of inexactness in an aspect where the influence is still effective is the aspect's *orb of influence*. Astrologers differ in how large an orb may be.

Retrogradation and the timing of cycles

In a geocentric view, a planetary cycle involves three points: the two planets representing the cycle, and the Earth itself as a point of reference. Because the Earth itself moves around the Sun, computing the placement of a planet is complex. There are periods where the relationship between the Earth's position and those of the planets causes planets to appear to move backward through the sky. This is *retrograde* motion. When the planet again appears to move forward through the sky, the planet returns to direct motion.

All planets have periods of retrograde motion in the geocentric view. The Luminaries (the Sun and the Moon) do not, however. The outer planets can spend as much as half of the time in retrograde motion.

Retrograde motion makes the timing of planetary cycles more complex. Two planets may come to an exact aspect with each other only for one or both of the planets to enter retrograde motion. During retrograde motion the planets may form another exact aspect. When the planets return to direct motion, another exact aspect may occur. One major cycle happening between 2011 and 2015 actually occurs six times because Uranus and Pluto planets make repeated retrograde and direct passes over each other. From a heliocentric perspective, however, each aspect occurs only once: there is no retrograde motion.

Part II. The Uranus / Pluto Cycle and World Events

3. Uranus - Pluto: Shifts in the Will to Power

The Uranus - Pluto cycle forces a shift in the *Zeitgeist*, the spirit of the times that reverberates through public events. Often it represents a shift in the *will to power*: how power is perceived, how rulers wield it, how the masses respond to it. A key aspect of the Uranus - Pluto cycle is that the incumbent in power at the beginning of the cycle is rarely still at the peak of power by the end of the cycle.

The Uranus - Pluto cycle unfolds over more than a century: nominally about 130 years. Because Pluto's orbital motion is the most eccentric of any of the planets, there can be a variability in each particular cycle's length.

The years from 2011 through 2015 bring Uranus and Pluto to the opening square, a critical turning point in the cycle's development. Astrological reference books provide some insight into this cycle's meaning, but to understand the forces at play we must turn backward to see forward. By looking at how this cycle relates to major historical shifts over the past few centuries, we can anticipate the challenges and opportunities at play right now.

In this chapter we examine the Uranus - Pluto cycle and the events leading up to the French and American Revolutions.

Transformation in France

The cycle begins with Louis XIV, France's greatest king, on the throne at the peak of his power. His successor, Louis XV, was born; no other incident for the French monarchy occurred. By the time the cycle is half-way complete, however, the monarchy was abandoned with the beheading of Louis XVI and Marie Antoinette and the proclamation of the First Republic in France.

The cycle is not yet complete. The First Republic lasted but a few years. Napoléon I rose to power and took over much of Europe as Emperor of France. His dominion endured not even one quarter of the Uranus - Pluto cycle. As the cycle closed, the last of the House of Bourbon to reign over France was deposed and France became a republic.

The following figure shows the Uranus - Pluto cycle beginning in 1710 and ending in the mid-1800's:

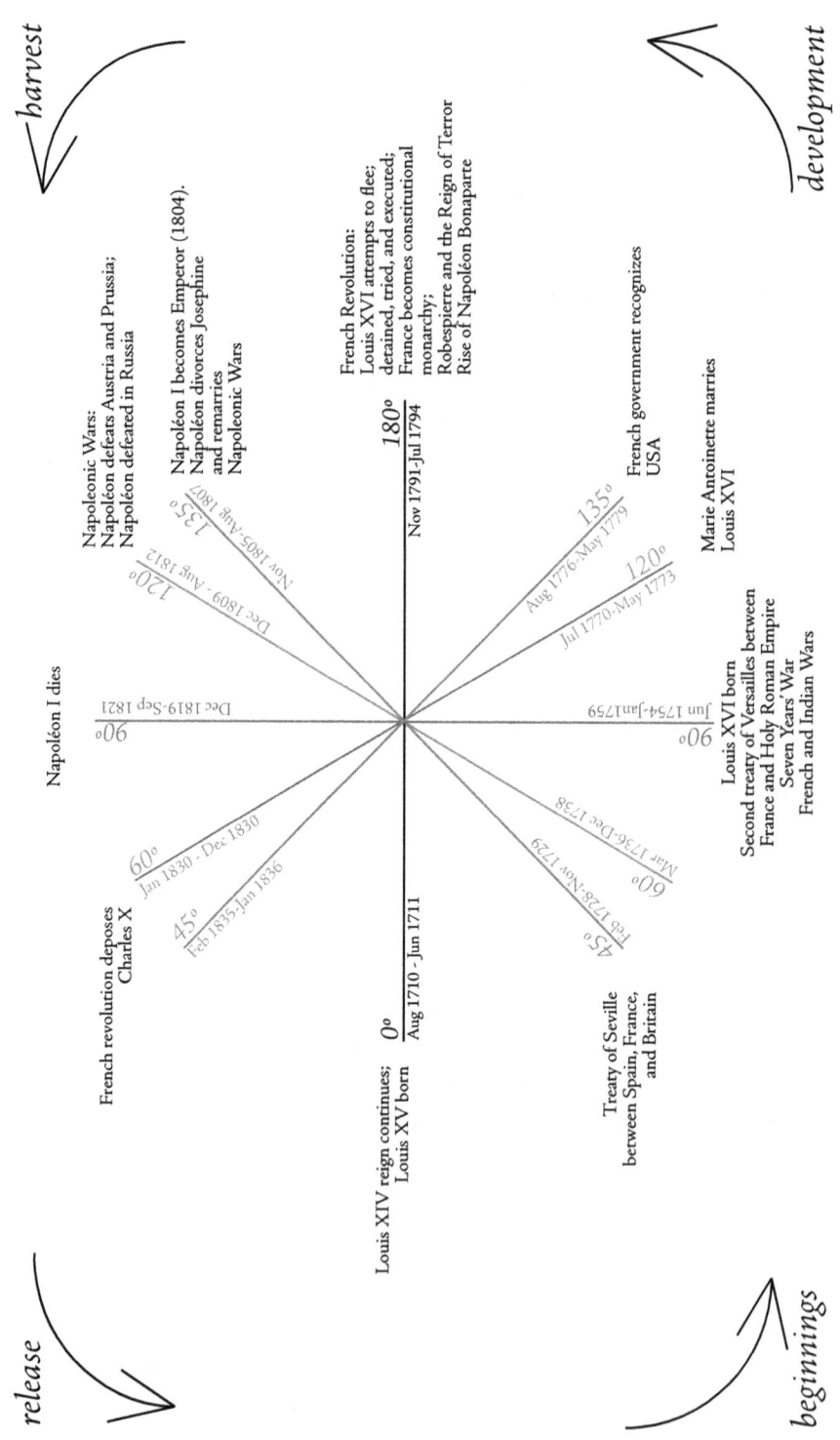

Figure 12. France and the 1710 Uranus - Pluto cycle

Uranus-Pluto conjunction: 1710-1711

The opening conjunction between Uranus and Pluto occurred between 1710 and 1711. Two questions are important to ask at the beginning of a Uranus - Pluto cycle:

- Who is the incumbent in power when the cycle begins?
- What are the structures of power and the assumptions that underlie the execution of power?

Uranus and Pluto mutate and transmute how power works as the cycle unfolds. During the cycle power tends to flow away from the incumbent, and the way of wielding political and economic power changes.

Uranus and Pluto conjoined between 1710 and 1711. At that time Louis XIV, the *Roi-Soleil* (Sun-King), ruled France, having been on the throne sixty-seven years. Looking back one Uranus - Pluto cycle, Louis XIV ascended to the throne at the closing trine of the previous cycle.

By 1710 Louis XIV had outlived his son. As this cycle begins his grandson, Louis XV, was born. A few years later, Louis XIV passed away.

Opening semisquare: 1728-1729

During the opening 45° aspect, England, France, and Spain signed the Treaty of Seville ending the Anglo-Spanish war. War broke out when England attempted to blockade a Spanish port while Spain sought control over Gibraltar. The war achieved neither side's aims and a stalemate resulted. The treaty returned things to the *status quo*.

Opening sextile: 1736-1738

No significant events involving France occurred during the opening sextile.

Opening square: 1754-1759

The opening square is often a critical development time for the unfolding cycle. Questions begin to arise about basic power structures. New political alliances and treaties often come into being, leading to the eruption or ending of active conflicts.

Just as Louis XV was born when the cycle began, one quarter of the cycle later Louis XVI was born.

Power was shifting throughout Europe. Alliances shifted between the major parties of the day: France, Prussia, England, and Austria. Historians refer to the Diplomatic Revolution of 1756 when old alliances between France and Prussia and between England and Austria mutated into new, diametrically-opposed alliances. The old partnerships changed hands with two new treaties. The Second Treaty of Versailles between Austria and France called for France to assist Austria against Prussia. Frederick II of Prussia negotiated the Treaty of Westminster with England, completing the switch-over of diplomatic alliances. The hope was to prevent future war in Europe.

The Seven Years' War erupted, proving these hopes groundless. In 1757 Frederick II of Prussia launched a preemptive attack on the Kingdom of Bohemia. Initially things looked very grim for Prussia, but Frederick reversed the situation and defeated the French at Rossbach.

The Seven Years' War evolved into the first truly world war, with active campaigns being waged between French and English colonies throughout the world: between the French and English forces in North America (the French and Indian Wars), and confrontations between the British East India Company and French trading interests in India (the Third Carnatic War).

The Uranus - Pluto square passed long before the Seven Years' War ended in 1763 with the Treaty of Paris. The French lost Louisiana to Spain and the remainder of New France to the British. This ended French power in North America.

The British returned French trading posts in India, but the French were effectively unable to maintain them as military bases. This ended the French power in India and paved the way for the British to control the Indian subcontinent.

Frederick II controlled Silesia and parts of Austria by the war's end. Napoléon Bonaparte regarded Frederick II as a tactical genius. Napoléon used Frederick's tactics to great effect in later phases of this cycle during the Napoleonic Wars.

Opening trine: 1770-1773

Marie Antoinette, originally Archduchess Maria Antonia of Austria, married Louis XVI, becoming the Dauphine of France during the opening trine. Initially popular because of her engaging nature and beauty, she was eventually regarded as an outsider by the French people, who suspected her of having sympathies for the Austrians.

Just after the trine completed, in 1774 Louis XVI was crowned King of France and Marie Antoinette became Queen.

Opening sesquiquadrate: 1776-1779

Revolution was in the air by 1776 in America during the opening sesquiquadrate. The French were informally involved in the revolution on the American side, supplying goods and armaments. By 1778 France signed the Treaty of Alliance with the new American government: a direct result of Benjamin Franklin's negotiations with the French court. The French navy gradually entered the war, evening out the imbalance in naval power between the British Fleet and the fledgling American navy.

Opposition: 1791-1794

The opposition marks the half-way point in a cycle's evolution. The original state of affairs at the start of the cycle often begin to unwind and to destabilize. The secure power structures at the cycle's beginning now become increasingly tenuous.

The cycle's opposition coincided with the French Revolution. The French populace stormed the Tuileries in 1792, demanding the abolition of the monarchy. Louis XVI and Marie Antoinette first attempted to flee France, but were detained and imprisoned. They were eventually executed as the First Republic was proclaimed.

The First Republic assembled the National Convention to draft a new constitution, but the Convention failed. As the situation worsened the Convention created several Committees to administer affairs of state. The Committee of Public Safety (*Comité de salut public*), under the control of Maximilien Robespierre, took control domestically. It executed thousands during the Reign of Terror. At the same time, however, France's external military efforts improved through Napoléon Bonaparte's tactics.

Uranus - Pluto aspects open existing power structures to the influence of new ideas. Even though the National Convention failed in its constitutional efforts, it founded a system of public education which endures to the present and abolished slavery throughout the French Empire.

By the end of the opposition in 1794, Robespierre was seized and executed without trial, ending the Reign of Terror. This also marked the beginning of Napoléon Bonaparte's rise to power.

Closing sesquiquadrate: 1805-1807

Just before the sesquiquadrate aspect came to exactness Napoléon Bonaparte declared himself Napoléon I, Emperor of France, and crowned Joséphine Empress, ending the First Republic. During the aspect, Napoléon I divorced Joséphine and remarried.

The Napoleonic Wars began with dramatic success for Napoléon's forces. French troops routed Austrian forces. They defeated the Prussians at Jena-Auerstädt and French forces entered Berlin. With most of continental Europe under French control, France began the Continental Blockade (*blocus continental*), an embargo against British trade which lasted until Napoléon's defeat.

At the end of this aspect French forces attacked Russia, and engaged Russian and Prussian forces at Eylau.

Closing trine: 1809-1812

Napoléon I continued to consolidate his power and to expand his conquests during the closing trine. He annexed the Kingdom of Holland.

Finally Napoléon's forces crossed the Niemen River into Russia. Initially they saw success, but eventually were forced to retreat with disastrous consequences. This defeat began a series of reversals that led to Napoléon's defeat at Elba in 1813 and his abdication in 1814 after the trine had faded. After Napoléon abdicated, the House of Bourbon returned to the throne of France with Louis XVIII becoming king in 1815.

Closing square: 1819-1821

Napoléon I died in exile on Saint Helena during the closing square.

Closing sextile: 1830

Charles X was the last of the House of Bourbon to reign in France. With the closing sextile in 1830 a mob of fourteen thousand prepared to attack the royal family in Rambouillet. Charles X went into exile in Britain.

Ending the cycle

Louis-Philippe I became king on Charles X's departure. He remained king until the end of the cycle in 1848. By the beginning of the next cycle in 1850, the Second Republic was declared, which lasted only until 1852 when Napoléon III became Emperor.

Ferment in America

Now let us reexamine this same cycle, this time detailing events in North America leading up to and following the American Revolution.

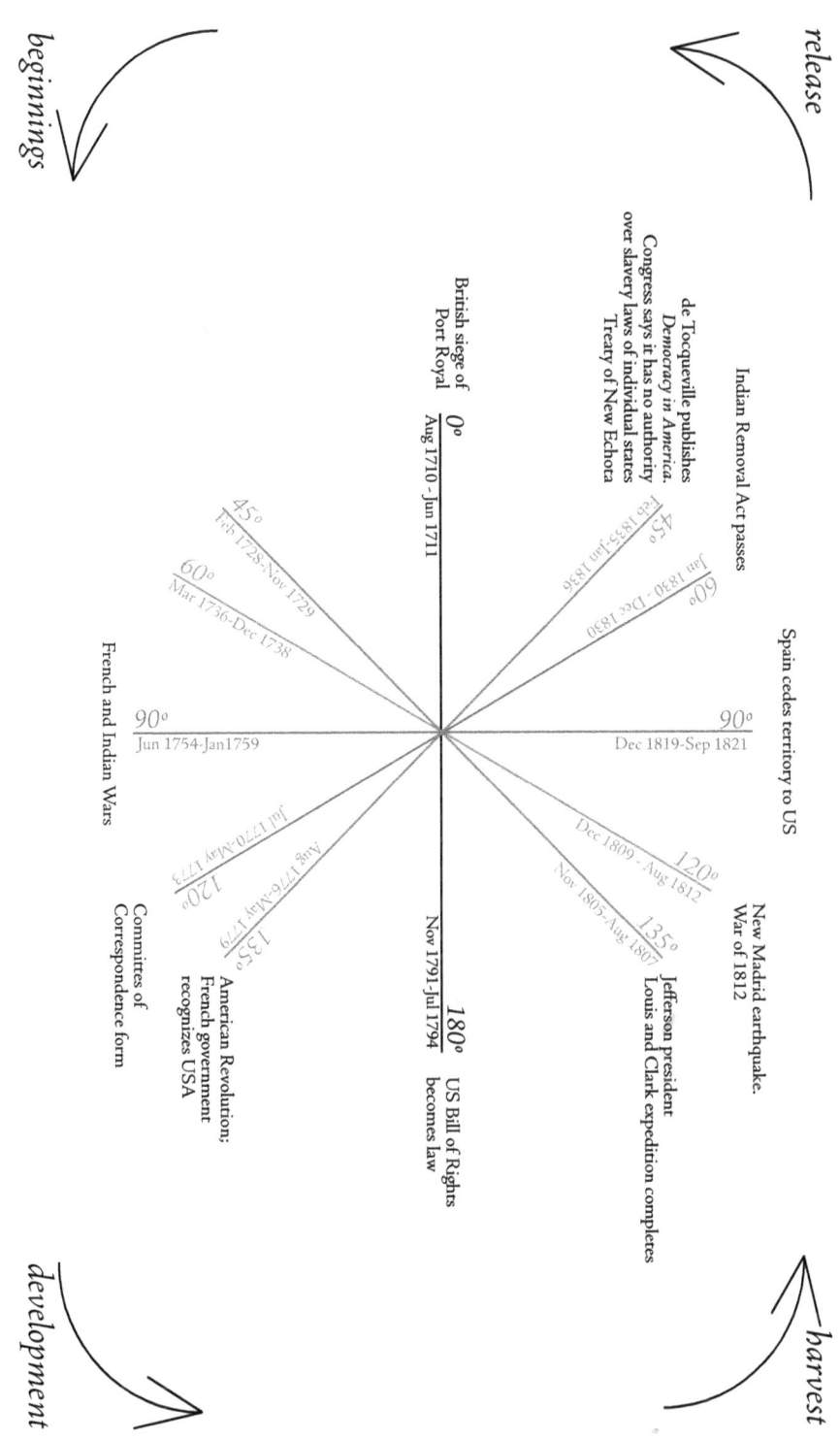

Figure 13. America and the 1710 Uranus - Pluto cycle

Conjunction: 1710-1711

The cycle opened in North America with jockeying for power between France and Britain. France, Britain, and Spain controlled virtually all of North America east of the Mississippi River.

The Siege of Port Royal marked the first time the British conquered a French colonial possession. The takeover of the Acadian garrison led to Britain renaming the settlement Nova Scotia. British successes framed the French-British negotiations beginning in 1711.

Opening square: 1754-1759

The Seven Years' War in Europe became a world-wide war. Within the North American theater the Seven Years' War is sometimes known as the French and Indian War. It was fought between the royal French forces and their Native American allies against British colonists supported by units from Britain.

British campaigns in 1757 were disastrous and the British government fell. William Pitt came to power and dramatically increased British military forces in North America. France was unable to match the British escalation because of their commitments in the European theater of the war.

By 1760 after the transit completed the British penetrated into New France – modern-day Canada – and took control of Montréal. Fighting ended in North America, while in the European theater the Seven Years' War continued for some time. France ceded Louisiana to Spain and the remainder of New France to Britain.

Opening trine: 1770-1773

Committees of Correspondence formed in various American Colonies against British rule. These committees became shadow governments, eventually superseding the colonial legislature and British officials. They determined the war effort at colonial and local levels.

Opening sesquiquadrate: 1776-1779

The American Revolutionary War unfolded at the opening sesquiquadrate. The battle of Lexington and Concord took place in 1775 before the aspect became exact. By July 1776 the revolutionaries had control in all colonies. France and Spain aided the revolutionaries, at first in secret. Benjamin Franklin negotiated a permanent military alliance with France in 1778.

Hostilities ended at Yorktown in 1781 after the aspect had faded.

Opposition: 1791-1794

The US Bill of Rights was ratified as constitutional amendments in 1791 during the opposition. The Bill of Rights is key in American government and law. It encompasses many of John Locke's ideas originally proposed in his work *Two Treatises of Government*; Locke published this work during the closing sextile of the previous Uranus - Pluto cycle.

Closing sesquiquadrate: 1805-1807

The closing aspect occurred during Thomas Jefferson's second term as president. Uranus - Pluto symbolizes restless change which manifested as American desire to press westward. This period included the Lewis and Clark expedition (1804-1806), which brought considerable knowledge about western North America by exploring lands acquired by the Louisiana purchase in 1803.

Closing trine: 1809-1812

The New Madrid earthquake occurred during the closing trine. This earthquake was the strongest recorded in central North America. Its force caused the Mississippi River to flow backwards for a time.

The War of 1812 began as the trine was closing. The United States declared war for a variety of reasons, including on-going trade disputes and British support of Native American tribes against American expansion. The Napoleonic Wars in Europe were more important to British interests than the War of 1812; for a period of time, the British fought primarily a defensive game. The war ended in 1814 with the Treaty of Ghent.

Closing square: 1819-1821

The closing square unfolded during the signing of the Adams-Onís treaty between the United States and Spain. In this treaty the United States purchased Florida from Spain and fixed a border between the United States and New Spain (now Mexico). John Quincy Adams negotiated the treaty for the United States.

Closing sextile: 1830

The closing phase of the cycle increased the desire for American expansion westward. 1830 brought the passage of the Indian Removal Act. The United States began to negotiate with Indians for their removal to west of the Mississippi River. In most cases these negotiations were coercive, and the forcible removal of Indians to lands west of the Mississippi River began.

Closing semisquare: 1835-1836

Slavery and expulsion of Native Americans from tribal lands occurred during the closing semisquare. These themes continued into the next Uranus - Pluto cycle.

This period found increased forced transport of slaves across state lines as Congress passed a resolution that it had no authority over state slavery laws. Congress also passed the Treaty of New Echota, in which the Cherokee Nation agreed to cede all territory in the Southeast and to move to the West. The Cherokee Nation never ratified this treaty. Nonetheless, it became the legal basis for forced removal of all Native Americans from east of the Mississippi River: the *Trail of Tears*.

Geopolitical anatomy of a Uranus - Pluto cycle

A Uranus - Pluto cycle lasts for more than a century, and its impact is generational rather than personal. The cycle describes major shifts in political, economic, and military power, but these changes often result from a fundamental shift in thinking about power.

- *During the cycle, power shifts away from the incumbents at the cycle's start.* Looking at France, this cycle saw the fall of the House of Bourbon, an unthinkable prospect considering Louis XIV's power and majesty at the cycle's beginning. In North America, European colonial powers largely lost control of their colonies.

- *Diplomatic and legal shifts are critical.* Both in France and in North America many critical changes began not with overt military efforts but with diplomatic or legal changes. In Europe the shifting diplomatic ties directly led to the Seven Years' War. In North America the cycle brought about the US Bill of Rights and important treaties establishing and expanding the US borders and in wresting control of Native American lands.

- *A cycle's meaning is different in different locations.* The same cycle manifested differently in Europe and in North America.

- *Cycles beget cycles.* Each cycle sets the stage for the subsequent one, establishing a new incumbent and locus for change. In North America, the end of this cycle set the stage for increasing conflict in the following cycle both over slavery and over control of land held by Native American peoples.

4. From Empire to Superpowers

The Uranus - Pluto cycle beginning in 1850 marked the beginning of four dynamic trends:

- The British Empire was at the peak of its power in 1850. The first half of the cycle continues British dominance. By the end of the cycle, Britain had largely decolonialized following two world wars.

- China was in civil war for much of the cycle, from the Taiping rebellion at the cycle's beginning, through the Boxer revolution at the cycle's midpoint. By the end of the cycle, Mao Zedong proclaimed the People's Republic of China.

- Marx entered his most productive period of thought as the cycle began. By the cycle's end, Marxist-Leninist theories had profoundly changed life in Russia and China.

- As the cycle began the United States struggled with internal issues: slavery and the continued quest to control much of North America. By the cycle's end, the United States was locked in strategic Cold War games with the Soviet Union.

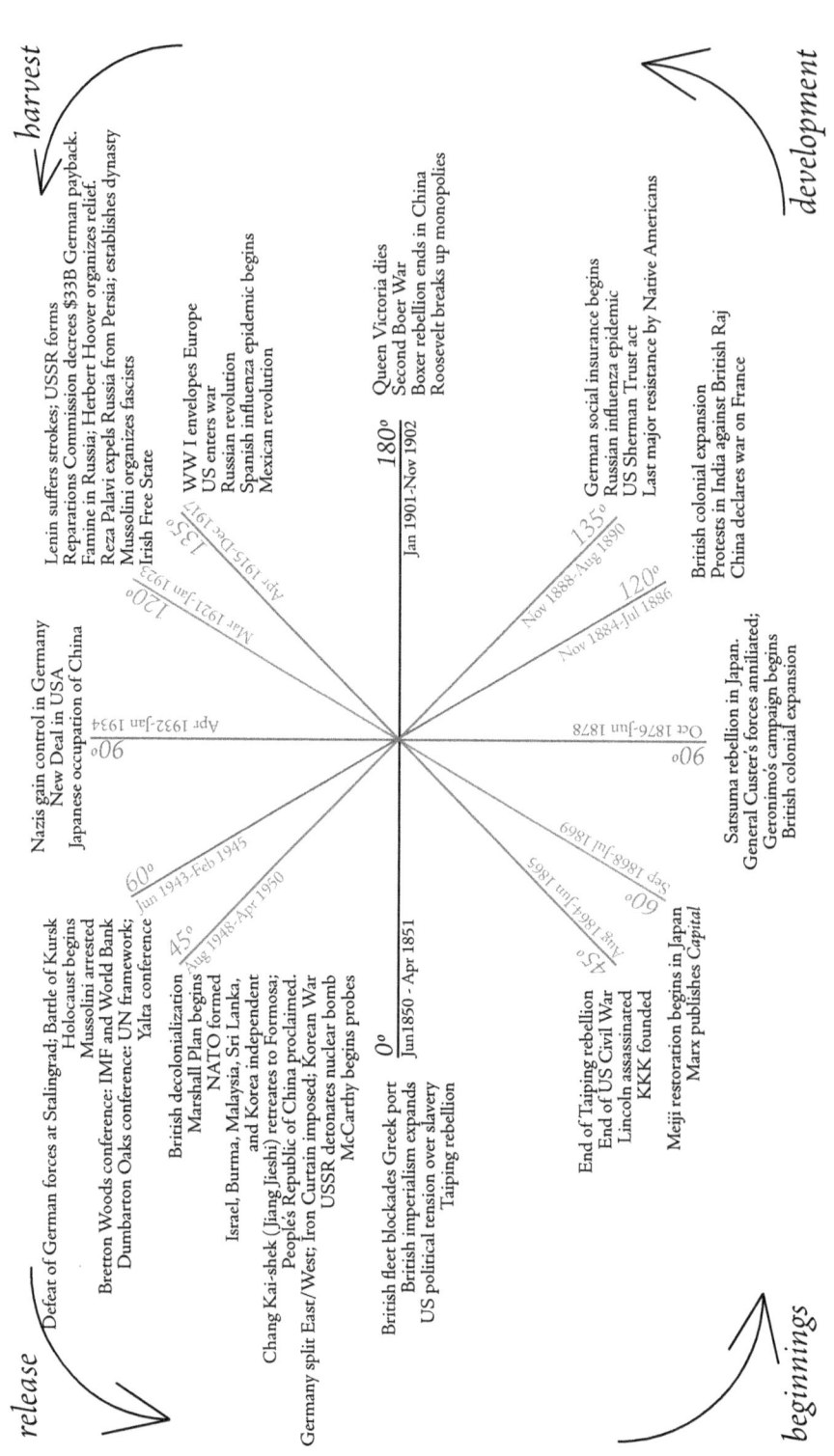

Figure 14. Historical events and the 1850 Uranus - Pluto cycle

Conjunction: 1850-1851

The Uranus - Pluto conjunction in 1850 took place during the middle of what some historians refer to as Britain's imperial century. An example of increased British imperialism at the conjunction was the blockade of the Greek port of Piraeus by the British navy in response to the Don Pacifico affair: a British citizen's property was plundered by a Greek mob while the Greek police took no action.

In the United States, political tension over slavery increased. The Compromise of 1850 was Congress's attempt to quell confrontation between slave and free states with a package of five bills. Neither side was happy with the compromise, which eventually led to the American Civil War.

The Taiping rebellion began in southern China. This civil war was led by a Christian Chinese convert who claimed to receive visions against the Qing Dynasty. Between the conjunction in 1850 and the end of the rebellion in 1864 during the opening semisquare aspect almost twenty million people died, mostly civilians.

Two years after writing *The Communist Manifesto*, Karl Marx in London began work on his concepts of historical materialism, transitioning from his early Hegelian thought to his more mature analysis and critique of capitalism and class struggle. This work led directly to *Capital*, his masterwork.

Opening semisquare: 1864-1865

The opening semisquare aspect brought two major armed conflicts to an end: the American Civil War and the Taiping rebellion in China.

In the United States, the Civil War began in 1861. By 1864, Ulysses S. Grant was given control of all Union armies. He organized Union armies to attack the Confederacy from all directions, eventually resulting in General Robert E. Lee's surrender at Appomattox. Abraham Lincoln was assassinated just days after the war ended. While open hostilities ended, tensions remained high: this period was the founding of the first Ku Klux Klan in Tennessee by Confederate Army veterans.

The Taiping rebellion in China ended with the entry of British and French troops on the side of the Qing Dynasty and the fall of Nanjing to imperial forces.

Opening sextile: 1868-1869

The Meiji restoration began in January 1864, with Mutsuhito, Emperor Meiji, declaring his restoration to power against the supporters of the Tokugawa Shogunate. This triggered the Boshin War, with the eventual unification of the country under imperial rule in Tokyo, replacing feudal society and leading to the development of modern Japan. The Meiji restoration marked the most dramatic economic modernization of any nation yet seen.

Marx published the first volume of *Capital*, his analysis of capitalist production. Marx's trenchant diagnosis of structural problems in capitalism still commands respect even if his socialist prescriptions have failed. (from Nouriel Roubini):

> *So Karl Marx, it seems, was partly right in arguing that globalization, financial intermediation run amok, and redistribution of income and wealth from labor to capital could lead capitalism to self-destruct (though his view that socialism would be better has proven wrong). Firms are cutting jobs because there is not enough final demand. But cutting jobs reduces labor income, increases inequality and reduces final demand.* [82]

Opening square: 1876-1878

The opening square saw the expansion of the British Empire and attempts by the United States government to consolidate its position against Native American land holdings.

After the Mughal Emperor was deposed by the British East India Company, Queen Victoria was proclaimed Empress of India. The British were very active in Africa as well, attempting to create a single unified state in southern Africa to control trade routes around the Cape of Africa and to possess massive gold and diamond reserves. British annexation led to the Boer Wars.

The American Indian Wars date from this same period. General Custer's forces were annihilated at the Battle of Little Bighorn. Subsequent US retaliation against Cheyenne forces was intense, culminating in the Battle of Wolf Mountain. While the battle was fought to a draw, Crazy Horse surrendered to US forces.

The Satsuma rebellion in Japan marked the last significant resistance of ex-samurai against the new Meiji government.

Opening trine: 1884-1886

The opening trine brought additional British imperialist expansion along with the beginnings of resistance to British rule in India. Following the Third Anglo-Burmese War, the province of Burma was created as part of British India.

The India National Congress (often known as the Congress Party) was founded by Indian and British members of the Theosophical Society. While not initially opposed to British rule, over time the party became more radicalized.

China rejected a French protectorate in Indochina and declared war against France. The war ended in 1885.

Opening sesquiquadrate: 1888-1890

The opening sesquiquadrate occurred with significant changes in thinking about governmental power. Germany created the modern welfare state, while the United States Congress acted against monopolistic business practices.

Germany under Otto von Bismarck[72] created the welfare state by providing social insurance to the elderly. German Kaiser Wilhelm I stated that *"those who are disabled by age and invalidity have a well-grounded claim to care from the state."* von Bismarck pioneered the idea to stave off calls for more socialist alternatives. The idea of a welfare state proved very controversial and led to von Bismarck being dismissed from his position as Chancellor.

The Constitution of the Empire of Japan (Meiji constitution) was adopted. This created a constitutional monarchy with broad imperial powers which remained in control until the end of the World War II as this cycle closed.

The Wounded Knee massacre of Lakota occurred just after the aspect ended in December 1890. It was the last battle of the American Indian Wars.

The United States Congress adopted the Sherman Antitrust Act. The act prohibits business practices that reduce competition and allows the government to break up prohibited business trusts. The act remained largely unused until Theodore Roosevelt's presidency in 1901 when Uranus and Pluto were in opposition.

The Russian influenza pandemic took place under this aspect. The epidemic spread rapidly from the index case in St. Petersburg, Russia, reaching the United States in only seventy days. This epidemic had about one-tenth the fatality rate of the 1919 Spanish influenza epidemic.

Opposition: 1901-1902

The Uranus - Pluto opposition brought great changes for the British Empire: Queen Victoria passed, ending a reign of over sixty-three years.

This was also the end of the Second Boer War, but residual guerrilla actions continued for some years in southern Africa. The British created concentration camps for Boers and black workers; around 100,000 individuals were incarcerated. These camps saw catastrophic death rates, eventually leading to British public opposition to the concentration camps.

The Boer Wars focused international attention on the British Empire. The scorched earth policy dramatically changed agriculture in southern Africa. Irish nationalists sided with the Boers; this may have accelerated the Irish Civil War and the eventual Irish Free State. Modern insurgency and counter-insurgency warfare techniques begin with the history of this war.

In China, the Boxer rebellion ended. The rebellion was a nationalist movement against the influence of foreign powers and Christianity. In early 1900 just before the opposition, the Dowager Empress Cixi supported the rebellion. After attacks on foreign diplomats, an international alliance of eight Western powers put down the rebellion. The Qing Dynasty was forced to pay reparations to the alliance. Japan gained international prestige through its military efforts in the war. Japan's increasing international confidence probably led to the Russo-Japanese war two years later.

In the United States, Theodore Roosevelt became president. His administration used the Sherman Antitrust Act for the first time to break up trusts and monopolists.

Closing sesquiquadrate: 1915-1917

The closing sesquiquadrate coincided with revolution and war throughout the world. World War I enveloped Europe. Imperialistic policies of many of Europe's great powers largely caused the war and fostered its spread throughout the colonies of the warring European powers. By the beginning of the aspect, the western front became a war of attrition that ended only as the aspect ended in 1917. The United States entered the War as the aspect ended in 1917 in response to sustained German attacks on US merchant vessels.

Close troop quarters and large-scale movements of personnel probably led to the Spanish influenza epidemic of 1918 and 1919. The index cases of the epidemic occurred as the aspect ended in 1917.

The Russian Revolution began with the deposing of the Tsar in February 1917. The provisional government fell during the October 1917 Bolshevik revolution as the aspect ended.

In India, Mohandas Gandhi returned from South Africa and began organizing peasants to protest excessive taxation. His influence in the Congress Party increased.

In Mexico, the Mexican revolution intensified with conflicts between Pancho Villa's and Venustansio Carranza's forces. Incursions by Villa's forces into New Mexico led to US involvement. Carranza's attempt at enforcing the new constitution failed with continued conflict with insurgent forces led by Emiliano Zapata. The revolution largely ended in 1920 just before the trine.

In China, Sun Yat-sen moved the Kuomintang's operations to Guangzhou.

Closing trine: 1921-1923

The closing trine occurred during the systemic economic consequences of World War I and the rise of fascism and communism in Europe and China.

The victorious Allies forced the German government to pay substantial reparations for World War I. The resulting hyperinflation in Germany accelerated to unprecedented levels, destabilizing the Weimar Republic.

In Italy, Mussolini organized the Fascists and marched on Rome. Mussolini became Prime Minister, holding this position until 1943 during the closing Uranus - Pluto sextile.

The Soviet Union formed by uniting the Russian Socialist Federative Soviet Republic with former territories of the Russian Empire. Stalin became General Secretary of the Soviet Communist Party after Lenin suffered a series of strokes. Agricultural mismanagement led to widespread, severe famine throughout Russia; in the US, Herbert Hoover organized a large, effective hunger relief effort.

In Ireland, the Irish Civil War took place, which led to the establishment of the Irish Free State as an entity independent of the United Kingdom.

In the Middle East, the British Mandate for Palestine was confirmed by the League of Nations. Following the fall of the Ottoman Empire, the mandate created an British administration for Palestine and Transjordan which lasted until the proclamation of the State of Israel in 1948 under the closing semisquare aspect.

In Iran, Reza Khan drove out both Russian and British forces which occupied Iran. This established the Pahlavi Dynasty in Iran.

In India, government forces arrested Mohandas Gandhi for sedition.

China was in civil war. An assassination attempt on Sun Yat-sen failed. With Jiang Jieshi (Chang Kai-shek), Sun Yat-sen regained control of Guangzhou. In Shanghai, the Chinese Communists organized.

Closing square: 1934-1934

During the closing Uranus - Pluto square, the Nazi party attained power in Germany while economic issues trumped all others in the United States.

In Germany, the government dropped bans against activity by the *Sturmabteilung* (SA, Storm Detachment, Brownshirts paramilitary forces) and *Schutzstaffel* (SS, Protection Corps). 1934 saw the founding of the *Geheime Staatspolizei* (Secret State Police, Gestapo). During the *Nacht der langen Messer* (Night of the Long Knives), Gestapo and SS forces killed SA leaders, consolidating support for Hitler within the Reichswehr (professional armed forces). Hermann Göring was elected chairman of the German Senate. The Reichstag Fire occurred; the subsequent Reichstag Fire Decree reduced civil liberties. Finally the Enabling Act passed, making Hitler dictator.

In the United States the worldwide Great Depression focused the nation's attention on economic policy. Franklin Delano Roosevelt was inaugurated. The First New Deal began with landmark legislation in FDR's first one hundred days of power, including:

- significant changes in fiscal policy and banking reform (including a bank holiday and the start of the Federal Deposit Insurance Corporation),

- monetary reform (ending the gold standard which suspended convertibility of fiat currency into gold),

- domestic public works (including establishing the Public Works Administration) and farm programs,

- increased government industrial planning (National Recovery Administration), and trade policy liberalization.

Closing sextile: 1943-1945

The closing sextile aspect coincided with turning points in World War II and with international agreements on post-war political, diplomatic, and economic matters.

The German defeat at Stalingrad, the battle of Kursk, the Japanese defeat at Guadalcanal, and the surrender of the German Afrika Corps were decisive turning points against the Axis powers. Mussolini was deposed in Italy. At the same time, however, the holocaust began.

Josip Broz Tito declared the provisional Yugoslav government.

Three major conferences took place under the closing sextile which attempted to redefine the international order after the war.

- The Yalta conference between Stalin, Roosevelt, and Churchill attempted to govern post-war Germany and to define the European order. With Russian troops less than 100 km from Berlin at the beginning of the conference, Stalin felt he could dictate terms, including the partitioning of Germany. Roosevelt wanted Stalin to enter the War in the Pacific theater, so he agreed to Stalin's terms, setting the stage for Cold War developments after the War's end.

- The United Nations Monetary and Financial Conference at Bretton Woods took place in 1944. It established the International Bank for Reconstruction and Development (IBRD, subsequently known as the World Bank), International Monetary Fund (IMF), and General Agreement on Tariffs and Trade (GATT). These organizations were designed to regulate worldwide monetary and financial affairs after the end of the War. Internationally open markets were the goal of these agreements: to reduce the risk of future conflict through free trade.

- The Washington Conversations on International Peace and Security Organization occurred in Dumbarton Oaks to establish a new international organization to replace the League of Nations. The conference set down proposals which eventually resulted in the organization of the United Nations.

Closing semisquare: 1948-1950

The years following World War II were filled with geopolitical realignments. The British Empire entered a period of decolonialization:

- India and Pakistan were partitioned in 1947, a year before the aspect began. Partitioning ended the British Indian Empire and the British Raj. Mohandas (Mahatma) Gandhi was assassinated just before the aspect came into full force. The aftermath of political partitioning on the Indian subcontinent during the aspect was the forced migration of more than fourteen million people: Hindus moved to the new State of India; Muslims migrated to the new State of Pakistan. War broke out almost immediately between Pakistan and India over disputed territory in Kashmir. A UN-mediated cease-fire began in 1948, but territory there remains disputed to the present.

- The State of Israel was proclaimed in May 1948 just before the aspect formed. The proclamation followed the United Nations partition plan of Mandatory Palestine, replacing the British administration of Palestine.

- The Republic of Ireland was proclaimed in 1948, severing remaining governmental ties with the United Kingdom.

- In South Africa, apartheid was officially proclaimed in the Group Areas Act.

The Cold War alignment of Western democracies against Eastern communist countries solidified:

- In China, the end of World War II led to open civil war between the Kuomintang under Jiang Jieshi (Chiang Kai-shek) and the communists under Mao Zedong. Jiang became the President of the Republic of China, but communists refused to recognize the new constitution. Jiang and the Kuomintang evacuated to Taiwan. Mao proclaimed the People's Republic of China in 1949.

- The Bundesrepublik Deutschland (Federal Republic of Germany, West Germany) was created in 1948 from the Allied Occupation Zones held by the British, French, and United States. The Soviet Union created the Deutsche Demokratische Republik (German Democratic Republic, East Germany) from the Soviet-occupied German territories a year later.

- Stalin began the Berlin blockade in 1948, leading to a hardening of tensions between the eastern and western blocs in Europe. A consortium of western powers provided airlifts to provide provisions for West Berlin. A sustained program of political propaganda on both sides began, including Radio Free Europe.

- The North Atlantic Treaty Organization (NATO) was founded in 1949. It focused more directly on military purposes in 1950 with the beginning of the Korean War: Kim Il Sung's forces invaded South Korea as the aspect ended.

- Communist nations recognized the Democratic Republic of Vietnam based in Hanoi, while non-communist nations recognized the French-based State of Vietnam, based in Saigon. Strategists in the US became convinced that Indochina was another example of communist expansionism.

- The Marshall Plan was underway providing reconstruction support for war-torn European countries.

- The Soviet Union tested the atomic bomb; the United States began development of the hydrogen bomb.

- In the United States, government probes into communist activities began.

5. To the present

The current Uranus - Pluto cycle began in 1965 and continues until 2089. At the time of this book's writing Uranus and Pluto are in their opening square, marking the first quarter of this cycle's development.

As the cycle began, Cold War and massive centralized state politics directed events around the world:

- China began the Cultural Revolution, convulsing the nation in waves of purges and forced relocation.

- In the United States, civil rights demonstrations and legislation and Great Society programs increased the welfare state and attempted to address continuing racial issues.

- Cold War tensions escalated with increased involvement of the United States, China, and Soviet Union in developing countries like Vietnam.

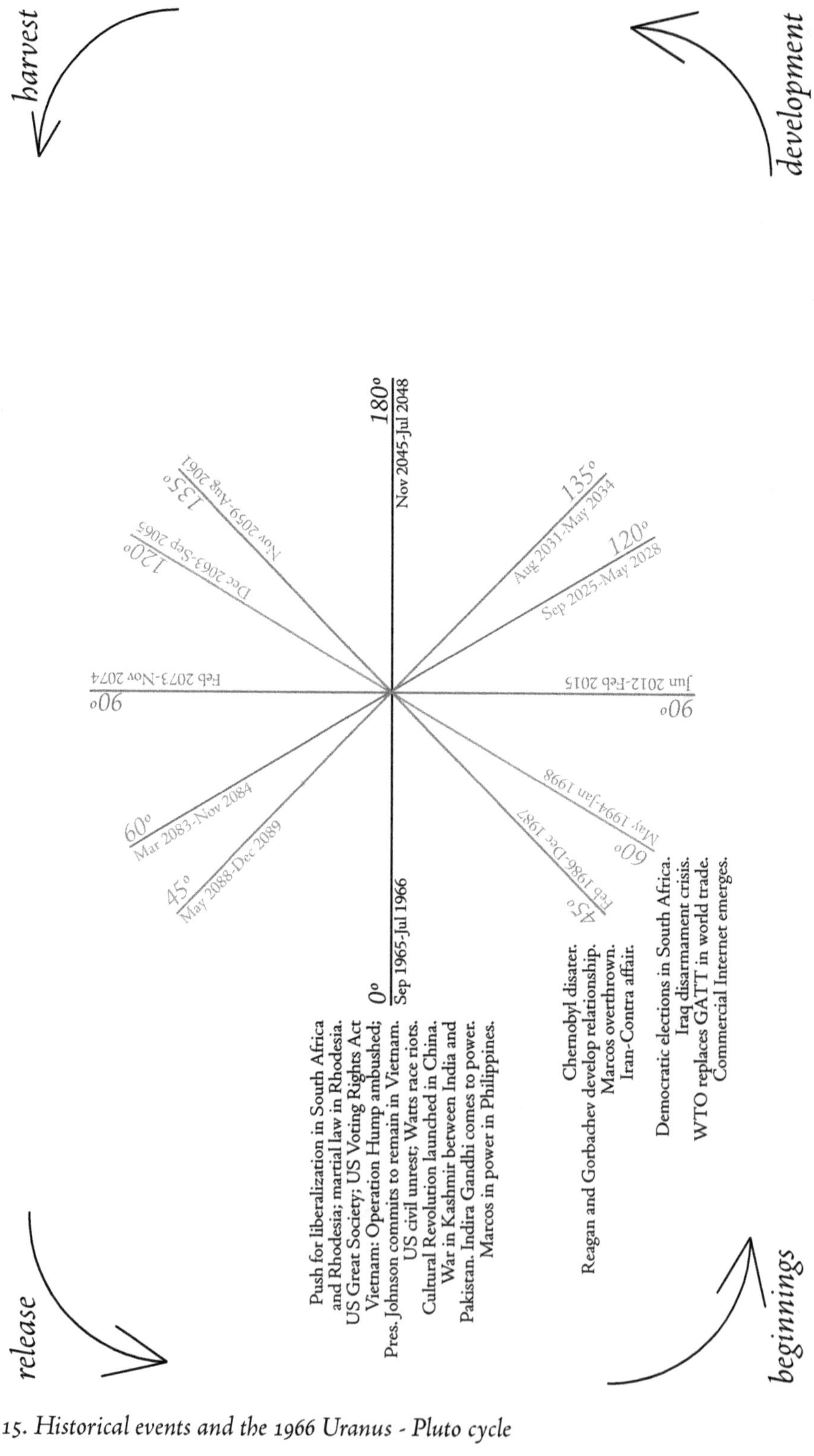

Figure 15. Historical events and the 1966 Uranus - Pluto cycle

Conjunction: 1965-1966

The cycle began at a time filled with worldwide civil rights issues, increasing Cold War interventions in developing nations, and major changes in the welfare state.

Mao's Cultural Revolution in China enveloped the nation with wave after wave of purges and forced relocation and economic restructuring. The Chinese education system effectively halted. Maoist thought became central to all activity in China.

Major civil rights conflicts emerged in the United States and in southern Africa:

- The Watts riots occurred in Los Angeles, flaring racial tensions throughout America.
- In Rhodesia, the conservative Rhodesian Front pushed for unilateral independence from the British Empire without majority rule. International action against the new regime was swift, including UN Security Council resolutions.

Domestic policy in the United States changed greatly under President Lyndon Johnson. Johnson's Great Society programs were shaped by a number of presidential task forces. By the time the cycle began in 1965 the Civil Rights Act was in force. The legislative sessions in 1965 and 1966 produced a wide range of results:

- The Voting Rights Act assured minority registration and voting.
- The War on Poverty appropriated $2 billion for many programs, including the Job Corps and the Model Cities Program for urban development.
- Social Security payments increased.
- In education, the Elementary and Secondary Education Act provided significant federal aid, including Project Head Start.
- In health, the Social Security Act of 1965 established Medicare. In 1966 legislation created Medicaid.
- In the arts, legislation created the National Endowment for the Arts. Just after the conjunction ended, legislation created the Corporation for Public Broadcasting.
- In environmental affairs, legislation provided a variety of acts aimed at controlling pollution and reversing industrial encroachment on natural resources.

The Cold War escalated into a number of developing countries:

- US forces invaded the Dominican Republic in 1965, just before the aspect came into full effect.

- Just before the aspect came into full effect, Congress approved the Gulf of Tonkin resolution allowing US military operations in Vietnam to continue absent a formal declaration of war. President Johnson escalated US involvement significantly during the conjunction, changing the US's role from that of military advisor to full combatant with many ground troops. General Westmoreland predicted victory by the end of 1967.

Ferdinand Marcos came to power in the Philippines.

Indira Gandhi came to power in India. She would serve as prime minister for three successive terms. Open war resumed with Pakistan over Kashmir.

Opening semisquare: 1986-1987

The opening semisquare applied worldwide pressure for political reform of repressive regimes:

- Mikhail Gorbachev became the General Secretary of the Communist Party of the Soviet Union about a year before the aspect began. By the time the aspect came into force Gorbachev started his *perestroika* movement for political reform. The Chernobyl nuclear disaster occurred, forcing the Soviet Union into greater international cooperation. When Matthias Rust, the unauthorized German pilot, landed his plane next to the Kremlin, Gorbachev swept opponents of reform out of office citing their incompetence, and launching perestroika. Gorbachev and President Reagan began to develop a working relationship.

- In the Philippines, Ferdinand Marcos was overthrown, eliminating his political dynasty which began at the Uranus - Pluto conjunction.

- In Pakistan, the repressive military regime of General Zia-ul-Haq came under increasing international pressure. Benazir Bhutto returned to Pakistan during this transit. General Zia died in a plane crash shortly after the aspect ended in 1988.

- In South Africa, Desmond Tutu became Archbishop of Cape Town. During this period, continued international economic forces pressured the South African government toward reform. Tutu organized massive peaceful marches in Cape Town.

- The Iran-Contra affair also came to light in the United States. The Reagan administration secretly sold arms to Iran, which was under an arms embargo. The administration then attempted to divert the funds to fund the Nicaraguan Contras. The affair caused a temporary drop in public support for the Reagan administration. Internationally, the United States's reputation fell severely, calling into question US-based criticism of negotiating with terrorists.

Opening sextile: 1994-1998

The opening sextile coincided with economic treaties, disarmament pacts, and mostly an increase in civil liberties:

- The United States, Mexico, and Canada signed the North American Free Trade Agreement. The World Trade Organization (WTO) replaced the General Agreement on Tariffs and Trade (GATT), changing international trade policy established during the closing sextile of the previous Uranus - Pluto cycle.

- Presidents Clinton and Yeltsin signed the Kremlin accords, ending programmed targeting of US and Russian targets and allowing for dismantling of nuclear assets.

- The first elections open to all occurred in South Africa. Nelson Mandela became the President of South Africa.

- Israel and Jordan signed a treaty ending a state of war.

Several major conflicts and flash points caused international action:

- The genocide in Rwanda began.

- There was continued conflict in the Balkans: mortar attacks on Sarajevo and UN tribunal charges of genocide against Serbian commanders.

- The Iraq disarmament crisis began.

- In the United States, domestic terrorism occurred with the Oklahoma City bombing.

The United Kingdom transferred sovereignty of Hong Kong to the People's Republic of China, ending British colonialism in Asia.

The widespread use of the Internet began. The first conference about commercial nature of the Internet occurred in San Francisco; the first commercial web browser became available. A dramatic rise in the US stock market coincided.

Opening square: 2011 - 2015

With the opening square we move from history to forecasting. Part III presents original research on the Uranus - Pluto cycle as well as the Saturn - Uranus and Saturn - Pluto cycles. Based on these findings, Part IV proposes a timetable of forecasts for the these cycles.

Part III. Research on Planetary Cycles and World Events

6. Research Methods

Part II relates the Uranus - Pluto cycle to major geopolitical events. Part III takes the opposite approach. Rather than beginning with an framework based on traditional astrological theory, it starts with a database of thousands of historical events and seeks correlation between the historical data and planetary cycles. The larger goal is to understand how well traditional astrological theory holds up in a broad historical retrospective study, and what changes to traditional astrological approaches might be needed to develop more sound forecasting techniques.

Assembling historical data

Ten years ago this study would have been impossible. This study uses a rich historical database of events stretching back over hundreds of years that can be classified into broadly similar categories. This makes possible planetary cycle correlation studies with large numbers of events. Creating such a database from scratch is a mammoth undertaking.

This database used here originates from the open and publicly available programming interface that the Wikimedia Foundation provides to the data underlying their Wikipedia.org site. I created a program using these web services interfaces to extract summary information of historical events occurring in each year from 1200 CE through 2012. Wikipedia.org has pages containing a summary of historical data for every year. This program tours these summary pages and extracts information about events in a standardized way.

The program splits each historical entry apart to retrieve the event's date and the textual content for the event. Where exact date information is available, the program uses it. Where only information about the event's month is available, the program uses the first day of the month as the event's date. Where only seasonal information is available, the program uses as the event's date the fifteenth day of February, May, August, and October as the date for the seasons Winter, Spring, Summer, and Fall, respectively.

Original entries frequently contain specially coded internal hyperlinks to other Wikipedia articles. The text for such links usually represent a keyword tag or summary term for the item. The program extracts the text from each hyperlink and builds a database of these keywords. It then relates each keyword to all historical events having that hyperlink. For example, many Wikipedia entries describing World War II events contain the hyperlink [[WWII]]. The program extracts this hyperlink, creates a keyword named *WWII*, and links the keyword with the event. All events having the same Wikipedia hyperlink text automatically connect to the same keyword.

The program then writes the extracted date, event description, and keyword tags to a database. The resulting database contains more than forty thousand entries.

Tagging the data

While tremendously helpful, the keywords derived from the original Wikipedia entries do not classify historical events to facilitate studies of long-term event cycles. I created a number of standardized keywords for the study and then applied these keywords to events in the database:

- *Armed conflict*: an increase or decrease in conflict between nation-states. This keyword excludes armed conflict within a state, like insurrections or civil war. For early dates where the constitution of nation-states is unclear, I have tagged all conflicts as armed conflict.

- *Civil unrest*: increase or decrease in civil unrest or civil war within a nation-state.

- *Regime change*: creation or destruction of a nation-state or significant change in the state's rulership.

I created a specialized application to facilitate browsing the historical event database and updating keywords for specific events and for groups of events.

Wikipedia entries relating to a particular historical event usually have related keyword tags derived from the original hypertext links. For example, *WWII*, *Thirty Years' War*, and *Napoleonic Wars* are Wikipedia-defined keywords that apply to many individual events. The program permits associating a standardized keyword with all the events having another, well-defined keyword. Using this approach, I tagged a large number of events fairly quickly. For example I tagged all events having the *WWII* keyword with the *armed conflict* keyword in a single step.

I also reviewed events individually from 1200 through 2012 and assigned standardized keyword tags.

Performing the analysis

Custom analysis software computes the planetary positions for events in the database. The software plots the frequency of event occurrence for planetary phases between any two planets for events having any selected tag along with a list of all actual events for review. It provides both geocentric and heliocentric views of the data.

The software is efficient. Generating a plot for the armed conflict study for a planetary pair based on over two thousand event dates takes less than a second on an Intel Core i7-based computer.

Issues with the data

There are roughly 2200 historical events in the armed conflict study; there are fewer events in the other studies. In every instance more recent major events have correspondingly more complete event reporting than earlier events do. For example, the fall of Constantinople and the Byzantine Empire in 1453 has no more than five historical events in the original Wikipedia data while World War II has more than four hundred associated events.

The studies below present two sets of armed conflict data: one with and one without World War II-related events. The plot of data without World War II events shows important trends that are less obvious when plotting the complete data set. Similar skewing occurs to a lesser extent in the civil unrest study where the number of events related to the American Civil War is large.

The analysis below looks for trends repeated across planetary cycles. In some cases I have deliberately discarded possibly interesting results where the supporting data comes from only a single planetary cycle.

Why no studies about more 'positive' things?

I attempted to tag events related to events related to major advancements in philosophy, science, the arts, health, and civil liberties. The original data for such events is spotty and the number of available events is too small to compute good correlations between planetary cycles and these events. I continue to seek better sources for such historical data.

What about economic cycles?

Chapter 11 examines correlations between economic data and planetary cycles. Again, the Wikipedia-based data for economic cycles is spotty. For example, Wikipedia event information usually focuses on the dates for a specific bank failure, but does not depict the broader range of time over which an economic downturn evolves. Fortunately there are lists of well-defined economic cycles that serve as the basis for study. Rather than have sparse dates of specific economic events, the economic cycle data uses ranges of dates during which a downturn occurred.

Understanding the graphs

The following studies show how the number of events tagged with a single keyword varies with the *phase angle* – the number of degrees – separating two given planets at the time of the event. Two planets in sextile, for example, have a phase angle of 60°. Most astrologers ignore phase angles that do not match a known astrological aspect. These studies, however, examine *every possible degree of separation, not just the angles that astrologers have traditionally thought to be significant*. Lines radiating from the center on each graph mark the standard astrological aspects used throughout this book so far.

The bold line wrapping around the graph represents the how many events occurred at a particular phase angle between the two planets. The distance the bold line is from the center of the plot represents the percentage of historical events that occurred when the two planets were that number of degrees apart. The line moves farther out from the center when more events occur at that phase angle, and moves closer to the center when there are fewer events. The bold horizontal line on the right side of the graph indicates the plot's scale in the percent of the total number of study entries in a given degree of separation.

Except where noted all graphs use a three-degree moving average to smooth the signal. Without smoothing the plot is noisier but has the same general shape. All statistics and harmonic analyses, however, use raw, unsmoothed data.

Each graph has highlighted zones to draw attention to areas of particular interest. These *ad hoc* zones highlight areas where historical events repeat over a broad range of years; in most cases such zones represent correlations that have endured across more than one planetary cycle. Each zone is numbered to make easy reference to tables that follow with detail about the major historical events that occurred within that zone. *Every row in each table includes the first year when the particular sequence of events began; in many cases, events continue for a considerable time after the first event.*

7. Study controls

Before exploring the relationship between planetary cycles and historical events, this section first presents two controls for this study. The controls compute the three planetary cycles in two different ways:

- *Daily controls.* This control group consists of daily computation of the planets's places for dates from the beginning of 1200 CE through the end of 2012. This control group comprises almost 300,000 days.

- *Event controls.* This control group contains more than 34,000 events in the Wikipedia.org database that are unrelated to armed conflict, civil unrest, regime change, and economic downturn.

Daily computation from 1200 through 2012

Here is a distribution graph showing the daily geocentric frequency of the Uranus - Pluto phase angle over the eight hundred year study interval.

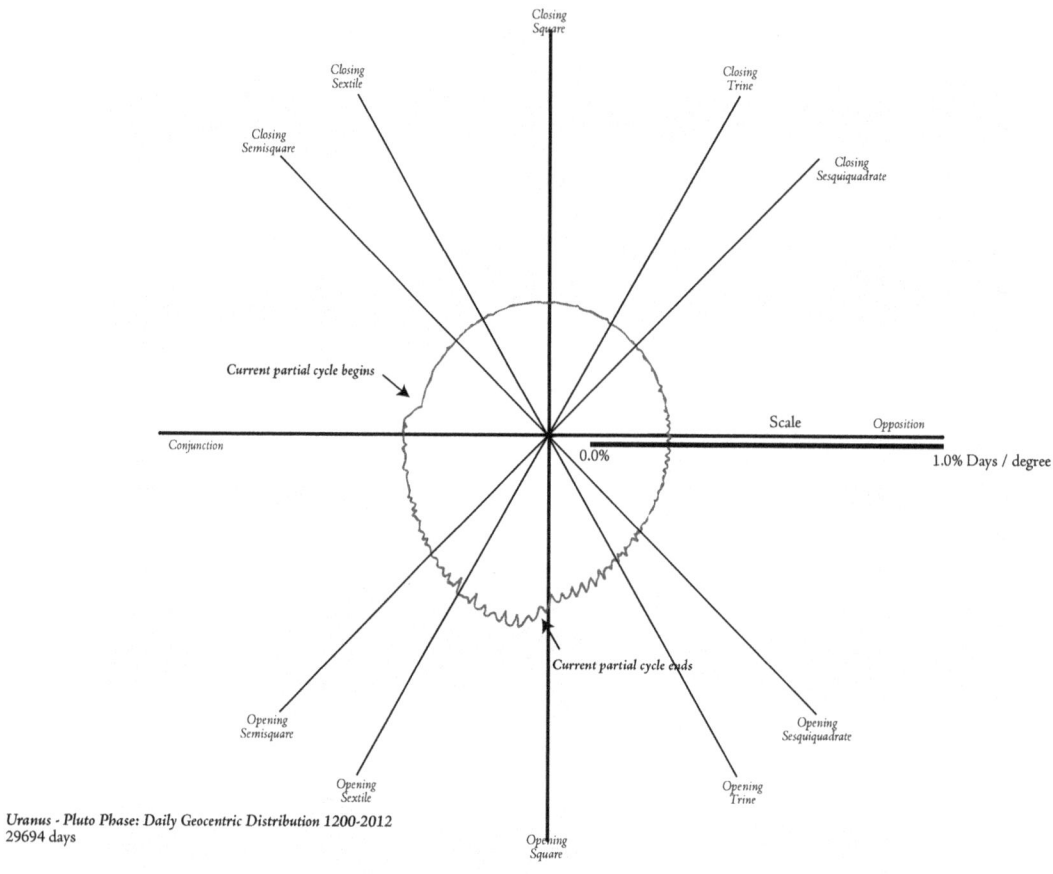

Figure 16. Uranus - Pluto Daily Geocentric Distribution: 1200-2012

The lines radiating from the center mark the standard astrological aspects. Examining the top half of the curve we see that Uranus and Pluto are roughly equally likely to be at any location between the opposition and just before the conjunction. This means that any of the aspects from the opposition through the closing semisquare are equally frequently observed.

Arrows mark the beginning and ending of the current Uranus - Pluto cycle, which is not yet complete. The Uranus - Pluto cycle is around 130 years long. Over the eight hundred years of this study the cycle completes an uneven number of times. During the current incomplete cycle the graph shows a higher frequency of occurrence due to the extra partial cycle's positions, creating a bump up in frequency between the arrows.

Retrogradation produces the saw-toothed appearance of the geocentric graph. Graphing the same data with heliocentric positions reveals a smooth appearance:

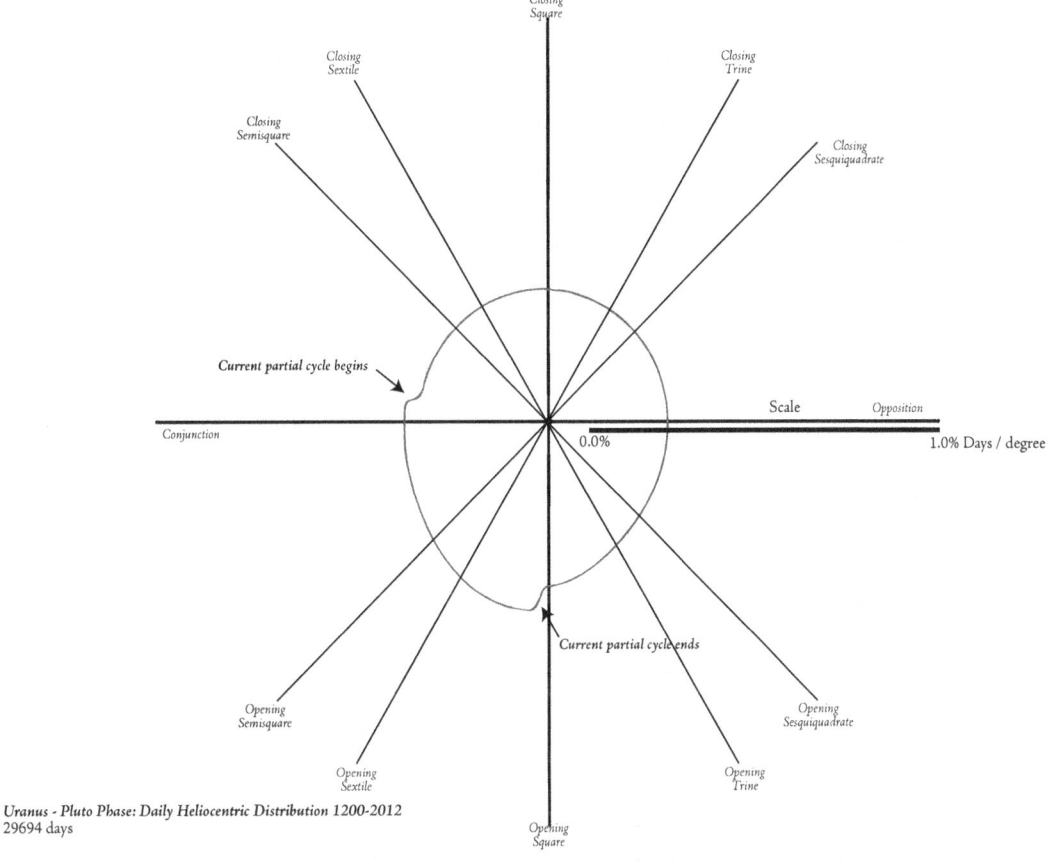

Figure 17. Uranus - Pluto Daily Heliocentric Distribution: 1200-2012

The wave-like peaks in the geocentric distribution show that there are angular relationships between the Earth, Uranus, and Pluto that are more frequent than others. These peaks appear even more strongly in the distributions of other planetary cycles.

Note that the graph is slightly egg-shaped. The frequency of the Uranus - Pluto separation is slightly higher in the first half of the cycle between the conjunction and the opposition – between the beginning of the cycle and the half-way point – than it is in the second half of the cycle. Pluto's highly eccentric orbit causes this uneven distribution, along with the effect that Uranus's position has on Pluto's orbit.

67

The graph of the Saturn / Uranus distribution is much less eccentric:

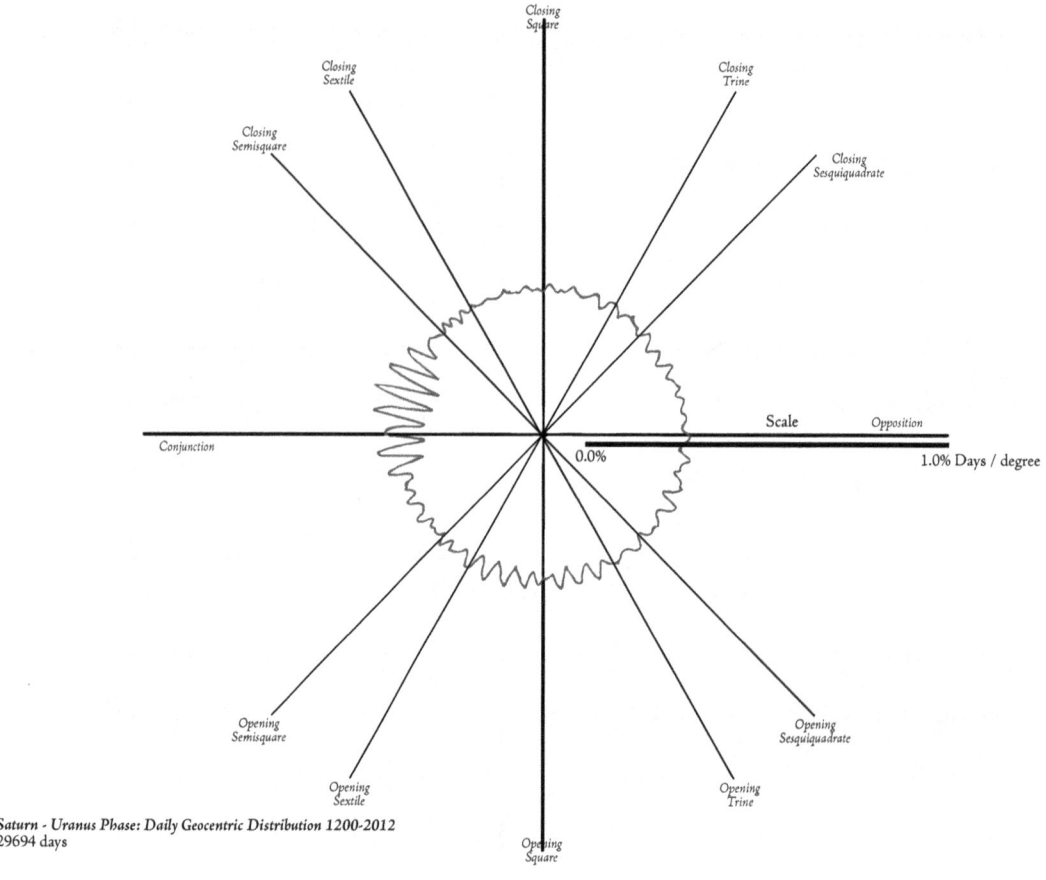

Figure 18. Saturn - Uranus Daily Geocentric Distribution: 1200 - 2012

The Saturn - Uranus cycle is about four times shorter than the Uranus - Pluto cycle, meaning there are four times as many cycles during the eight hundred years in this study. The missing partial cycle is not apparent in the geocentric data because the larger total number of cycles causes the missing data to be averaged out. In the heliocentric data the bump from incomplete cycles does appear, but is of small magnitude.

Retrogradation in the geocentric values causes the saw-toothed pattern; the wave-like pattern is stronger here than in the Uranus - Pluto case. These waves show that there are certain angular relationships near the Saturn - Uranus conjunction that are more frequent than others. Plotting the data as heliocentric values shows a completely smooth graph:

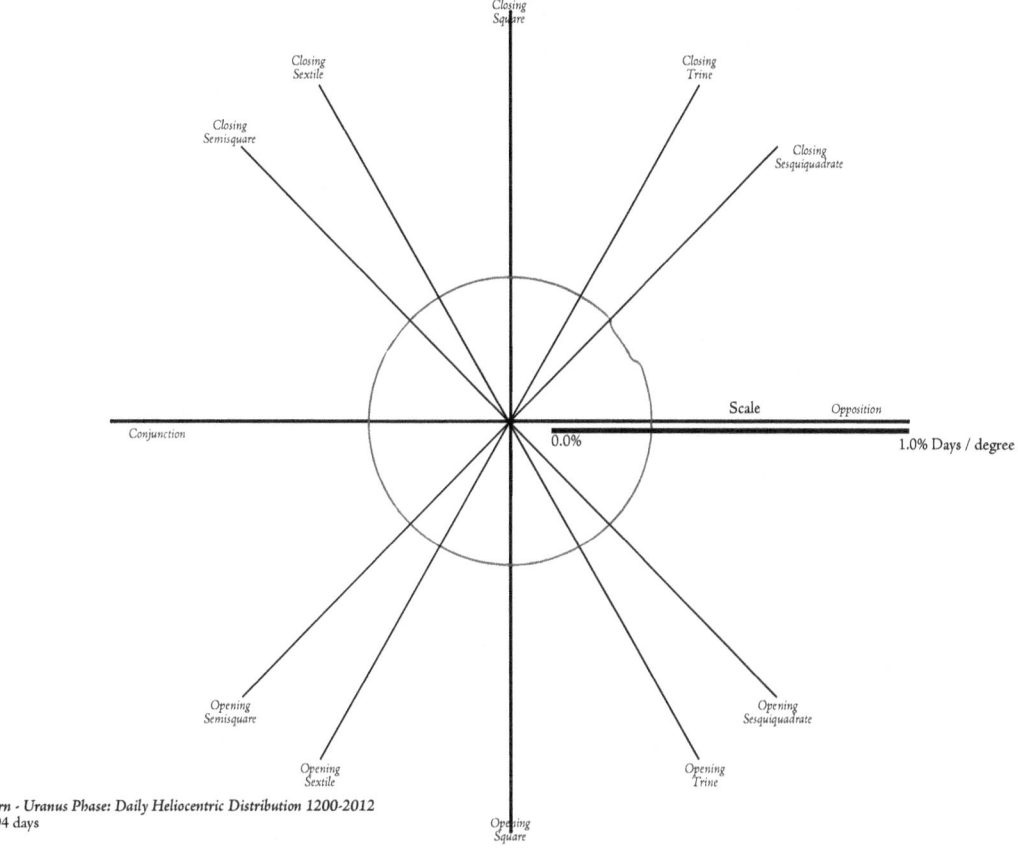

Figure 19. Saturn - Uranus Daily Heliocentric Distribution: 1200 - 2012

The notch that appears just before the closing sesquiquadrate comes from a partial planetary cycle. Effects of retrogradation in the geocentric plot are so large that they completely mask this notch.

The graph of the Saturn - Pluto cycle is also uniformly distributed:

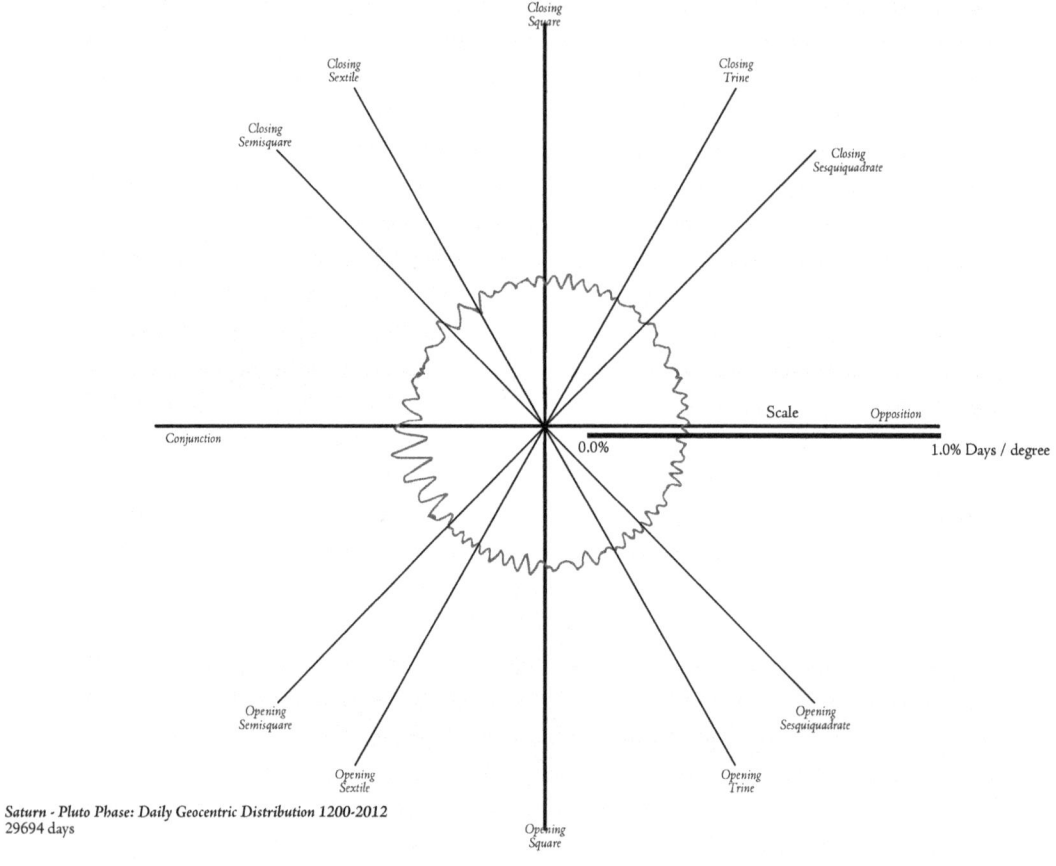

Saturn - Pluto Phase: Daily Geocentric Distribution 1200-2012
29694 days

Figure 20. Saturn - Pluto Daily Geocentric Distribution: 1200 - 2012

The bump from incomplete cycles does not appear in this plot. Again, the Saturn - Pluto cycle is about four times shorter than the Uranus - Pluto cycle, resulting in four times as many cycles during the eight hundred years in this study. The missing partial cycle does not show in the geocentric data.

In the heliocentric data the bump from incomplete cycles does appear, but is again of small magnitude:

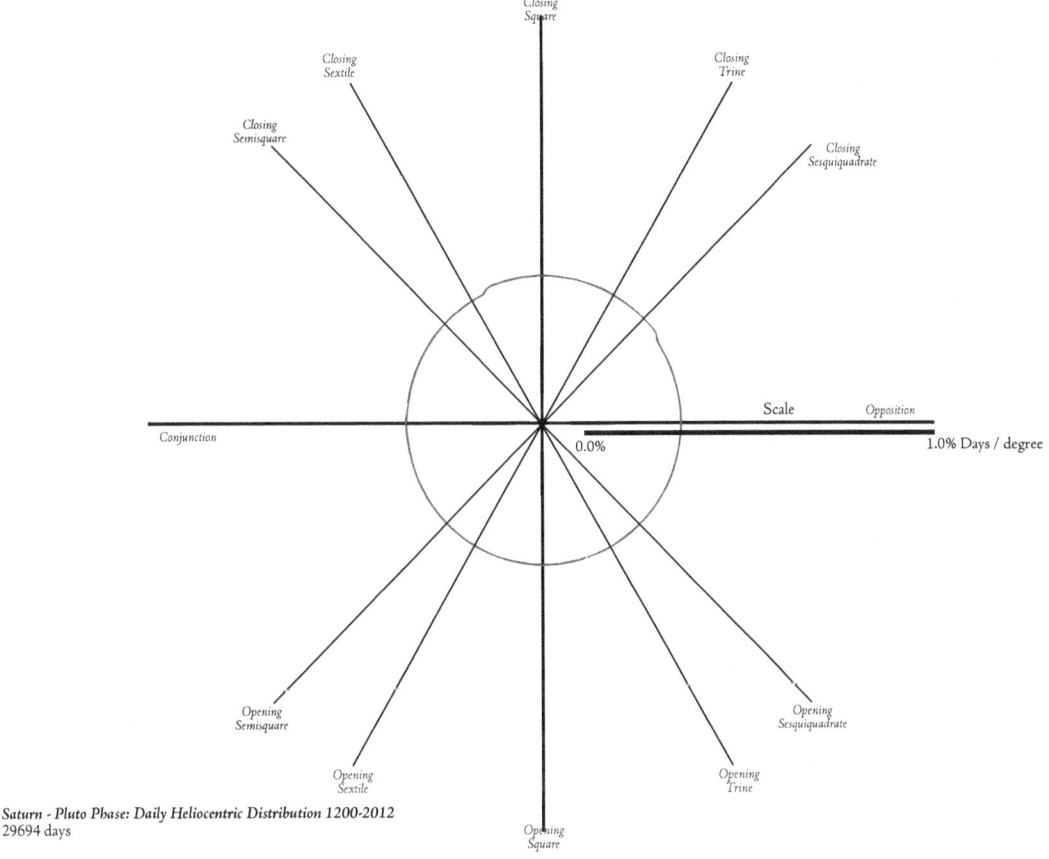

Figure 21. Saturn - Pluto Daily Heliocentric Distribution: 1200 - 2012

Event controls

Here is a distribution graph showing the geocentric frequency of the Uranus - Pluto phase angle for charts in the event control group:

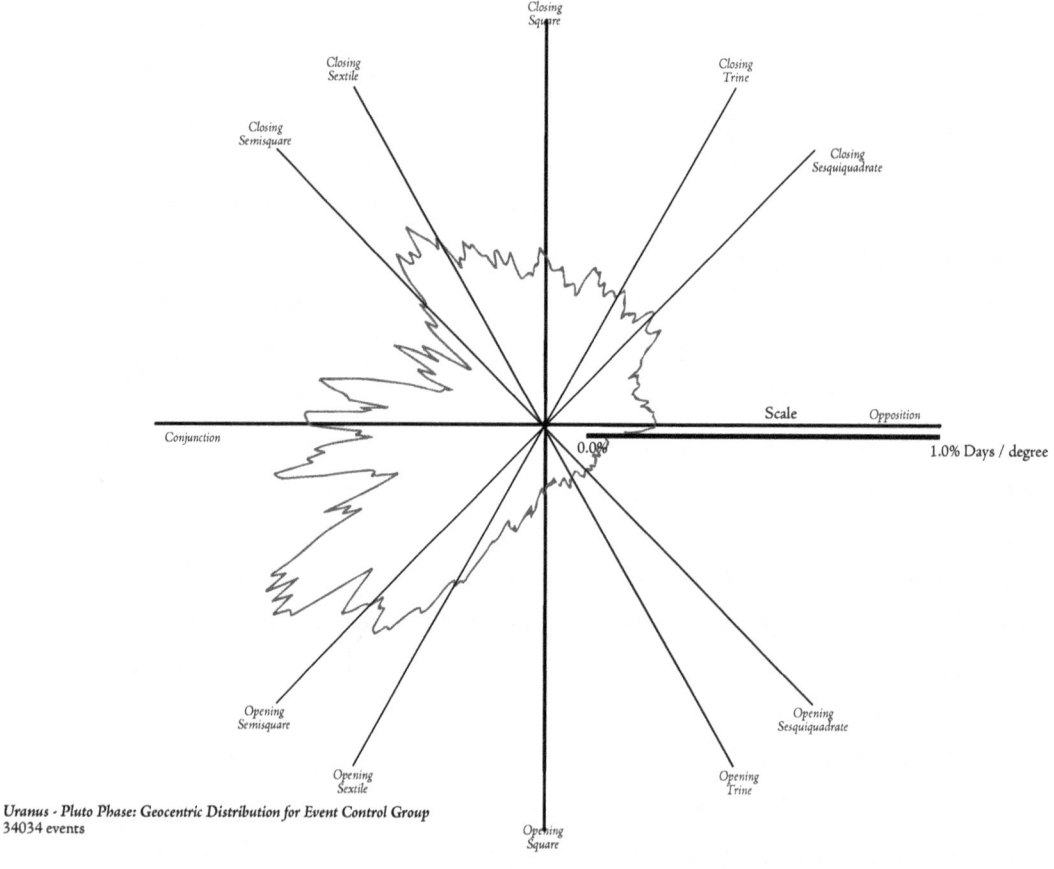

Figure 22. Uranus - Pluto Geocentric Event Control Group Distribution

The uneven distribution pattern comes from date biasing in the original Wikipedia.org event data. Events that occur in more recent years are more likely to be reported as entries in the database. These more recent entries appear most often in the early part of the current Uranus - Pluto cycle than in previous cycles, so there is an overall emphasis in the distribution plot from the conjunction to the opening sextile.

This same bias appears in the heliocentric graph:

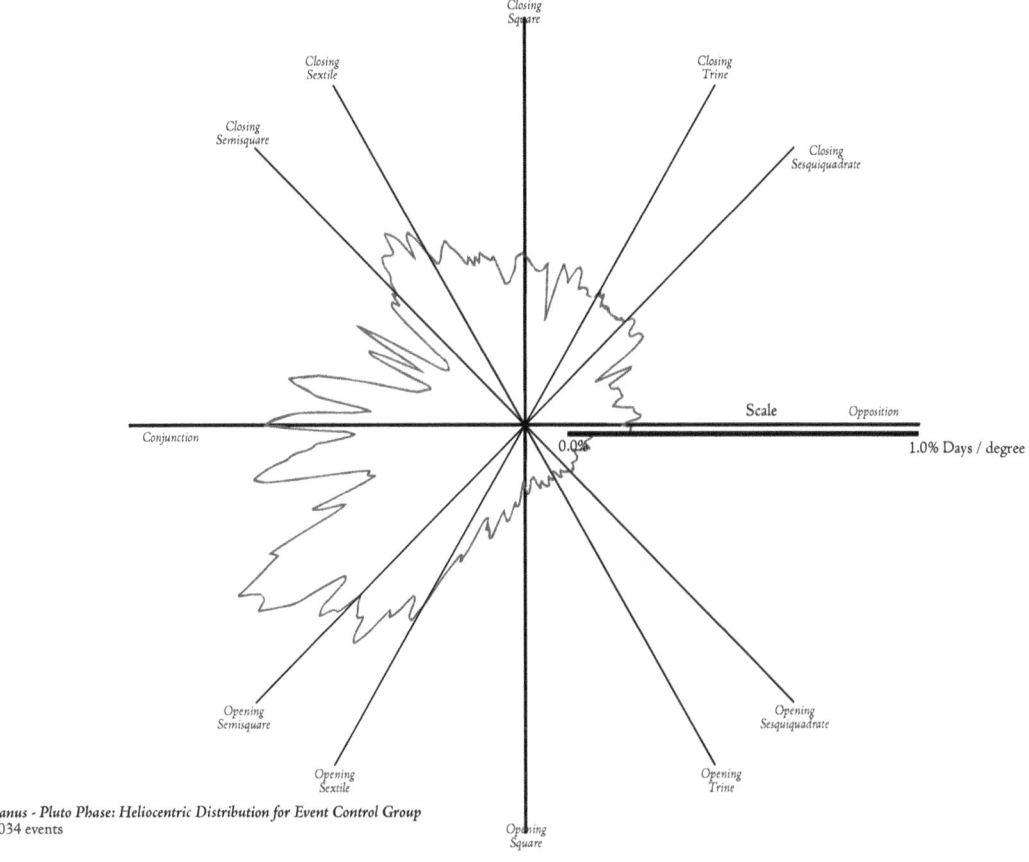

Figure 23. Uranus - Pluto Heliocentric Event Control Group Distribution

The Saturn - Uranus distribution graphs, however, show a more even distribution. Here is the geocentric distribution:

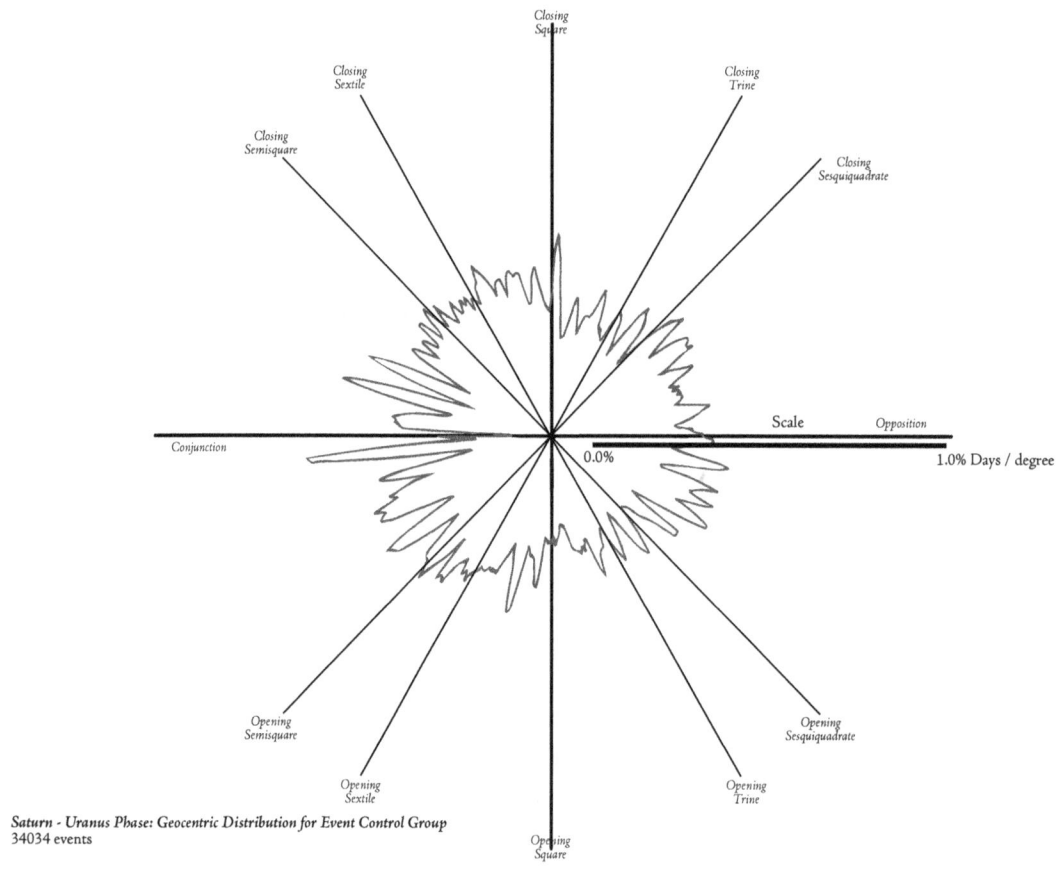

Figure 24. Saturn - Uranus Geocentric Event Control Group Distribution

Here is the heliocentric distribution:

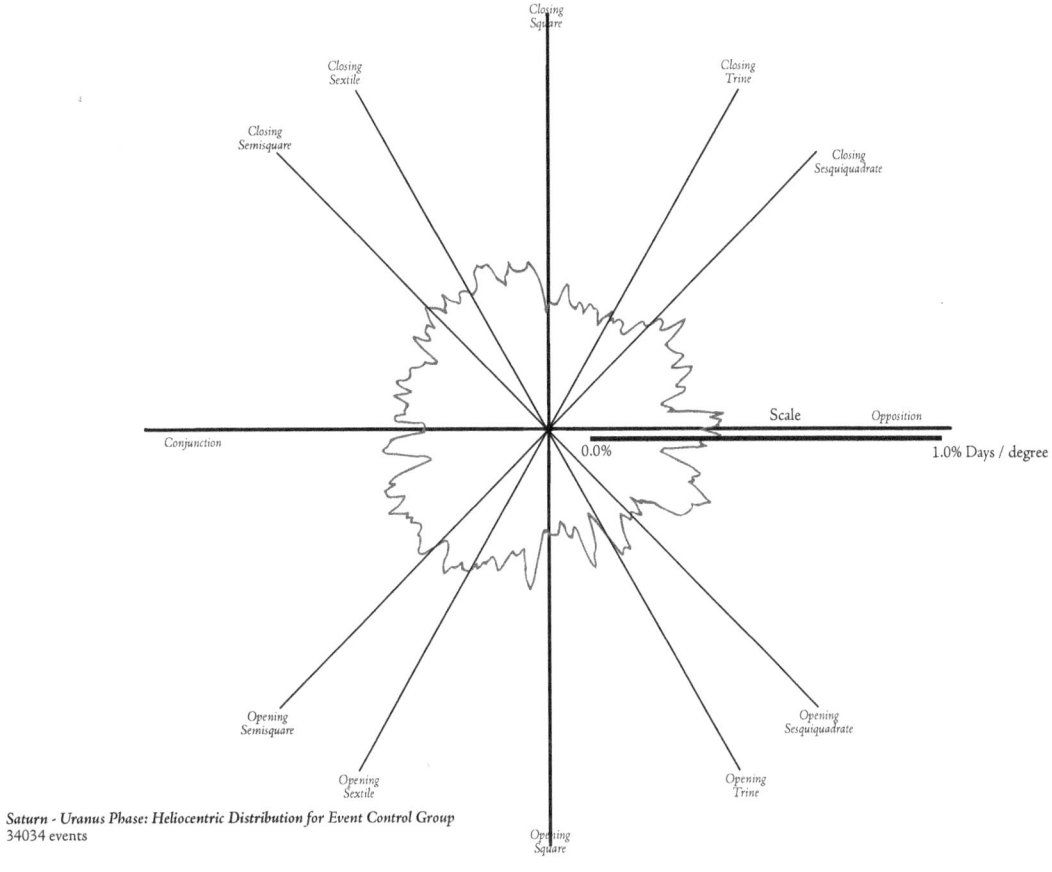

Figure 25. Saturn - Uranus Heliocentric Event Control Group Distribution

While more evenly distributed than the Uranus - Pluto case (Figure 23), the Saturn - Uranus distribution for the event control group is not as smooth as the daily values (Figure 19), which represent almost ten times more samples evenly distributed over 800 years. Retrogradation in the geocentric study accounts for the differences between the geocentric and heliocentric graphs.

Similar results appear in the Saturn - Pluto event control group geocentric distribution:

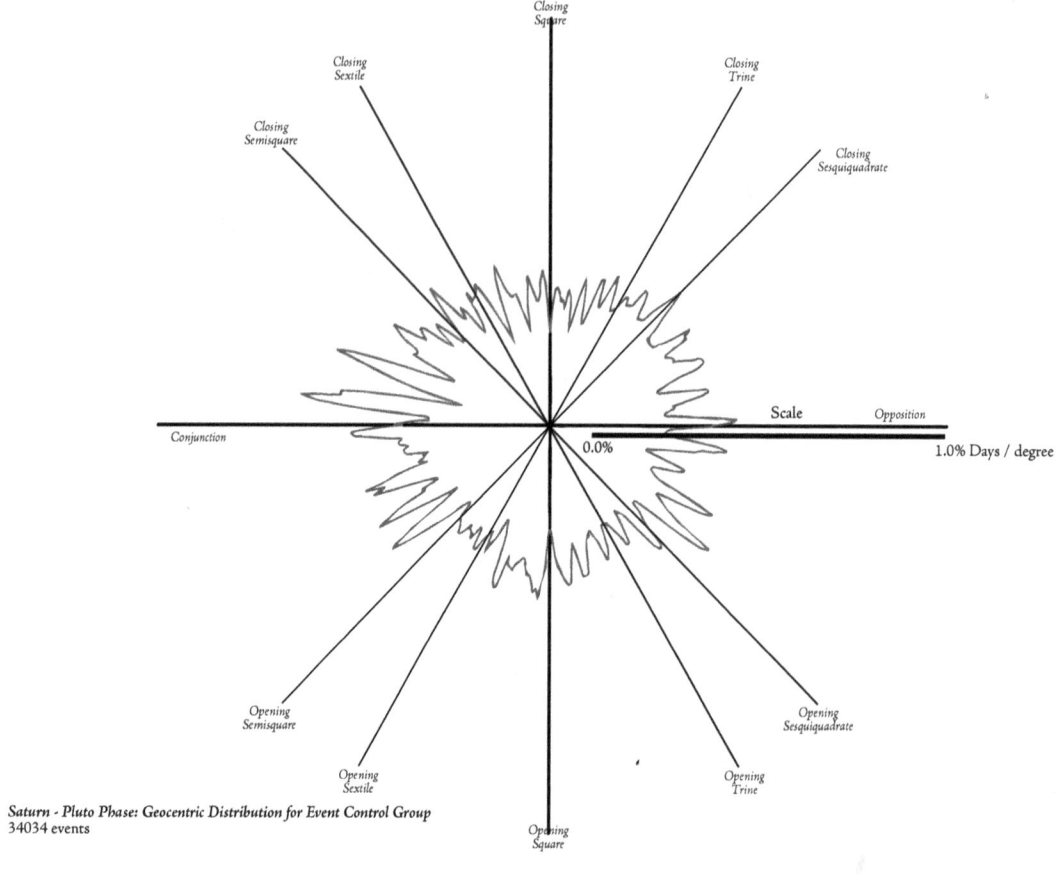

Figure 26. Saturn - Pluto Geocentric Event Control Group Distribution

This graph is similar in shape but less smooth than the daily control group (Figure 20).

Like the Saturn - Uranus case, the heliocentric data are less evenly distributed than the daily control case.

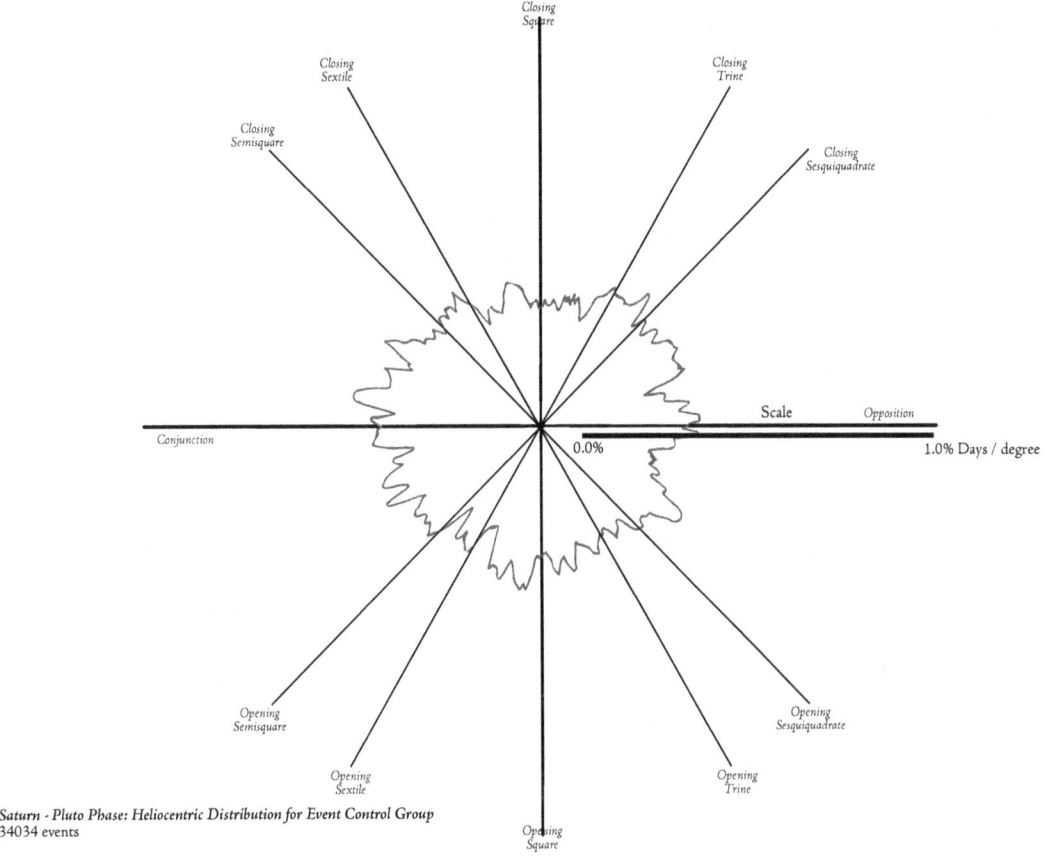

Figure 27. Saturn - Pluto Heliocentric Event Control Group Distribution

These controls are critical to determine the statistical significance of the findings below.

8. Armed conflict events and planetary cycles

Uranus / Pluto and armed conflict events

The graph below shows the distribution of 2286 historical armed conflict events, including all World War II events, with respect to the phase angle between Uranus and Pluto. Comparing these graphs with the Uranus - Pluto controls (Figure 16 and Figure 23) shows striking differences. The large number of World War II events dominates the graph's scale with a massive peak in Zone 5. The scale of this graph is twice that of the other figures.

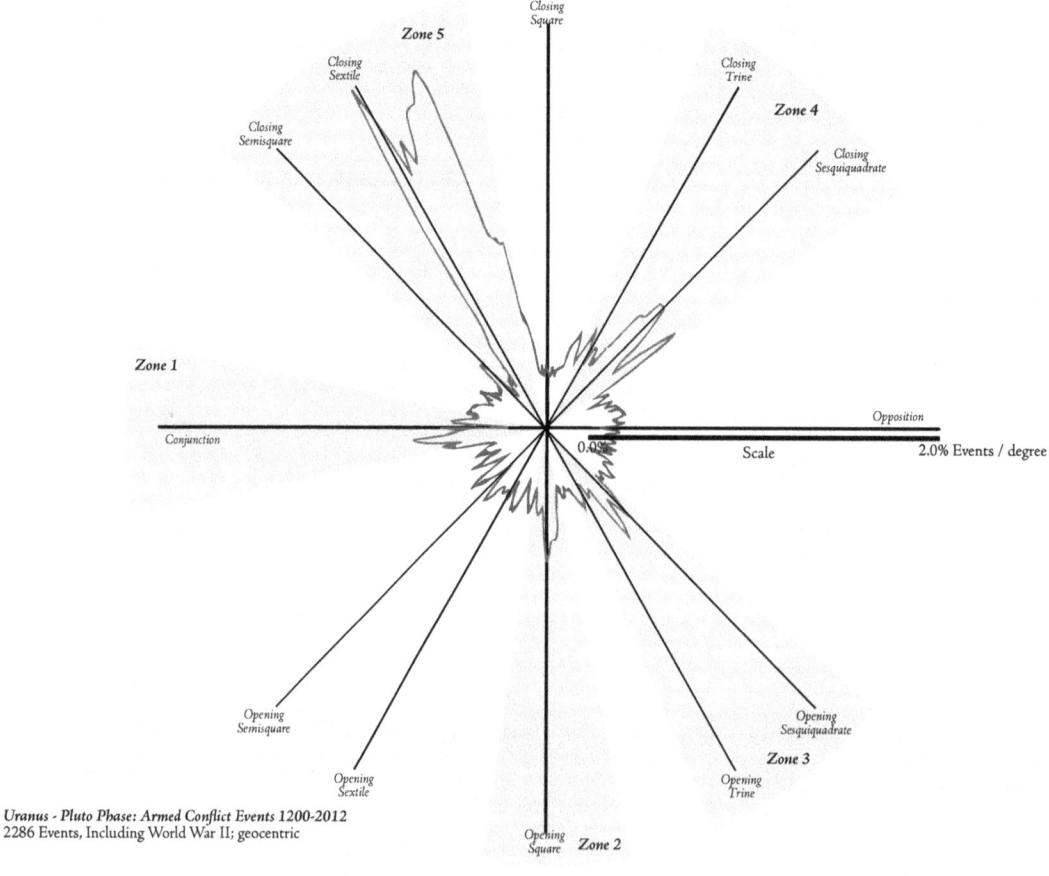

Figure 28. Uranus - Pluto: Armed conflict event distribution including World War II events, geocentric

The large peak in Zone 5 reaches a maximum at a Uranus - Pluto phase angle of about 290°: about twenty degrees past the closing square and ten degrees before the closing sextile.

Redrawing the graph using heliocentric values yields largely the same results:

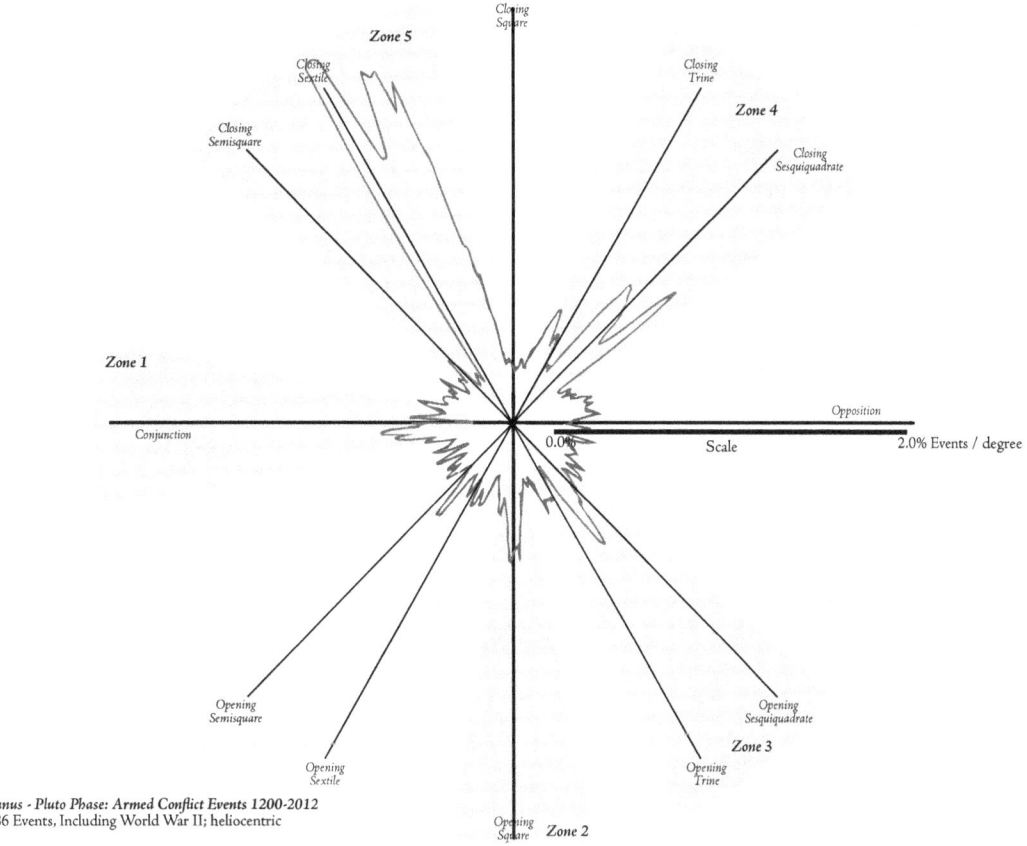

Figure 29. Uranus - Pluto: Armed conflict event distribution including World War II events, heliocentric

The following graphs shows the data redrawn and rescaled by removing World War II events; the remaining 1714 events are the same as in the previous graph. The scale for the following graphs is half that of Figure 28 and Figure 29. The rescaling makes clearer the fine structure within the other emphasis zones. Here is the geocentric result:

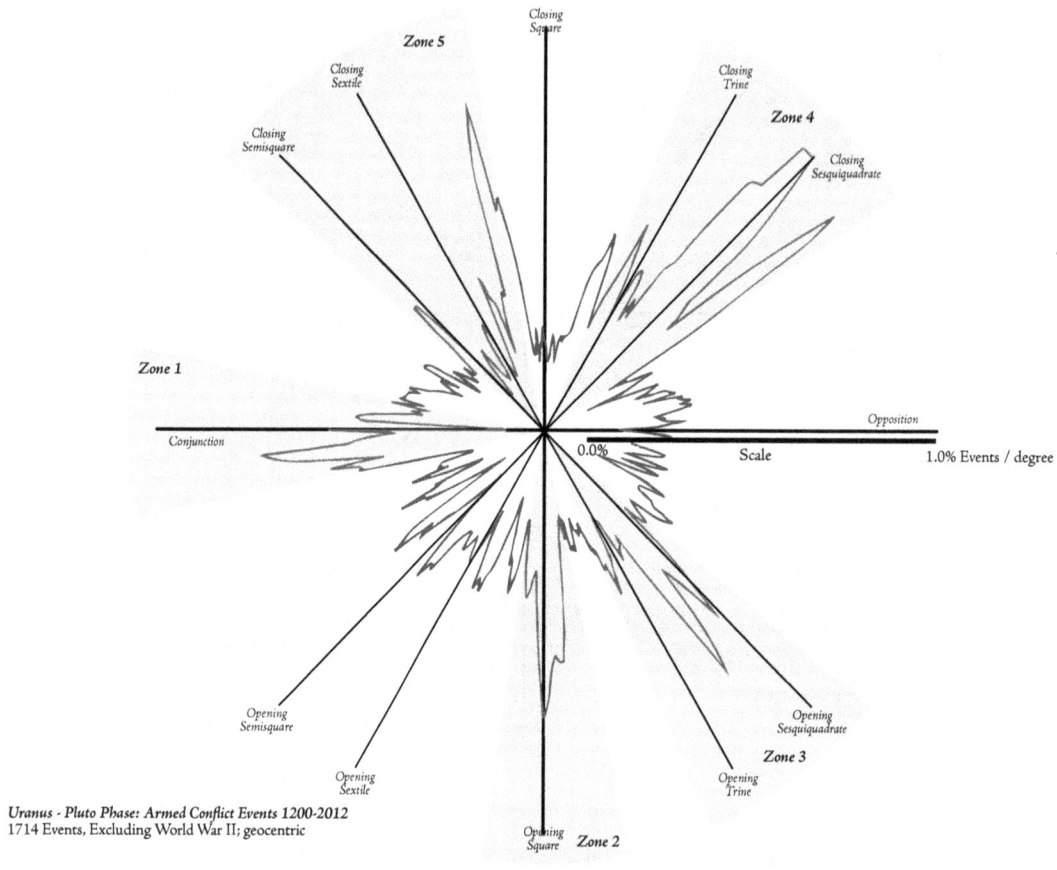

Figure 30. Uranus - Pluto: Armed conflict event distribution excluding World War II events, geocentric

Compare with the heliocentric view of the same data:

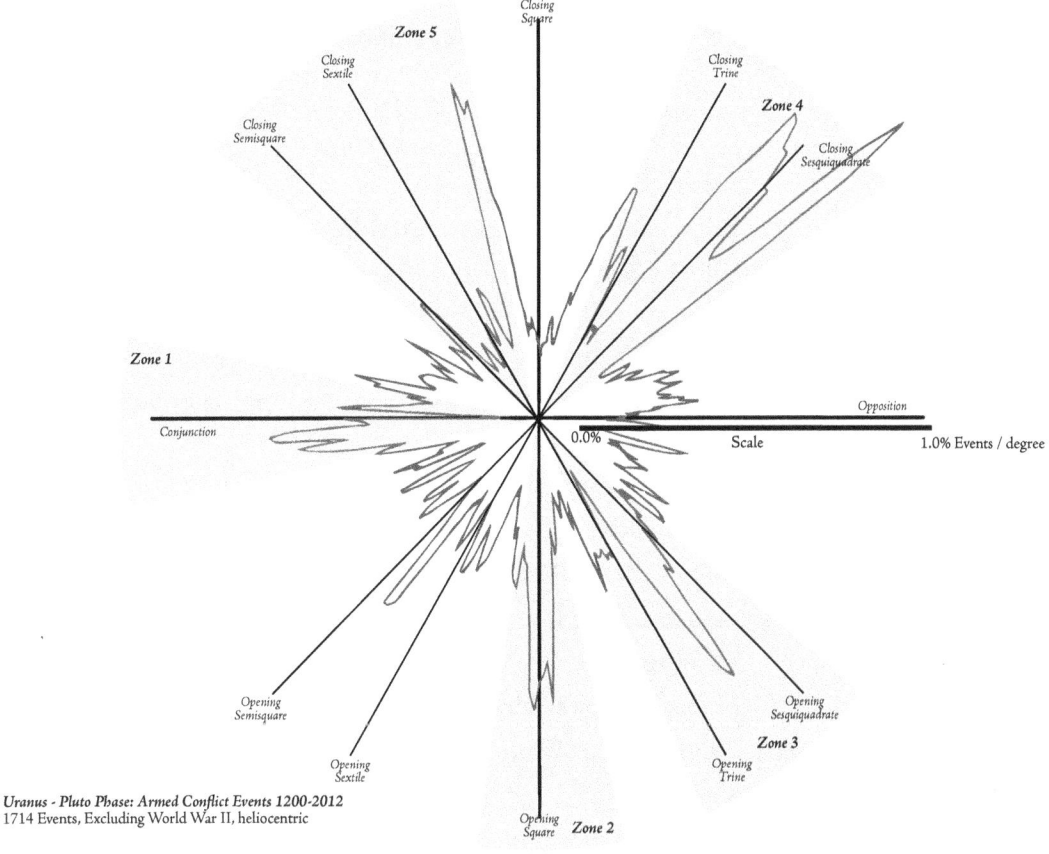

Figure 31. Uranus - Pluto: Armed conflict event distribution excluding World War II events, heliocentric

Without the World War II events, the rescaled graph shows peaks aligning closely around the conjunction, the opening square and sesquiquadrate, and around the closing sesquiquadrate. Other peaks appear, including the one at around 290°, just after the closing square.

Why are the heliocentric graphs so similar to the geocentric ones? One might expect the two to appear very different. As all the planets in these studies are so distant from the Sun and Earth, the difference between the geocentric and heliocentric distributions is low when measured over many events that occur over many years.

Because the heliocentric controls are so much clearer than the geocentric ones, all subsequent studies use only heliocentric data.

Zone 1: 345° to 12° (Conjunction)

Zone 1 relates to the Uranus / Pluto conjunction, spanning from fifteen degrees before the conjunction (from 345° to 360° separation before the conjunction), and twelve degrees after the conjunction.

Period beginning	Event
1203	Fourth Crusade
1451	Britain and France at war; Hundred Years' War ends
1453	Fall of Constantinople to Ottoman Empire; Byzantine Empire ends
1454	Thirteen Years' War
1594	European uprisings against Ottoman Empire; France defeats Spain; Siege of Amiens
1597	Japan and Korea at war
1707	Sweden attacks Russia; Peter the Great defeats Sweden
1706	War of the Spanish Succession
1709	France defeated
1846	Mexican-American War
1849	France occupies Rome; Danes defeat Prussians
1853	Crimean War; France declares war on Russia
1961	Vietnam War

Zone 2: 80°-100° (Opening Square)

Zone 2 are those events that occurred within a ten degree orb of the opening square.

Period beginning	Event
1236	Spanish battle Moors
1237	Mongols invade Rus
1241	Mongols defeat Poles and Knights Templar; Mongols withdraw
1493	Croatia battles Ottoman Empire
1499	Swiss defeat Holy Roman Empire; Ottoman Empire defeats Venice
1503	French-Spanish wars in Italy
1622	Thirty Years' War; Eighty Years' War; Dutch-Portuguese War
1624	Ottoman Empire driven from Baghdad

Period beginning	Event
1754	Seven Years' War; French and Indian War
1876	Ottoman Empire sacks Bulgaria; Serbia and Montenegro at war with Ottoman Empire; Second Russo-Turkish War

Zone 3: 110°-140° *(Opening Trine and Sesquiquadrate)*

Zones 3 lumps together historical events that occur within roughly a ten degree orb of the opening trine and sesquiquadrate: from 110° to 140° separation between Uranus and Pluto. I have grouped these aspects together into a single zone because most of these events here derive from long conflicts whose events span both aspects.

Period beginning	Event
1255	Cathar stronghold in southern France falls
1256	Mongols capture Anatolia
1261	Constantinople recaptured, re-establishing Byzantine Empire
1515	Ottoman Empire invades Persia and captures Cairo and Belgrade
1520	Battles between Aztec and Spanish forces
1521	War between France, Spain, and Holy Roman Empire
1522	Ottoman Empire conquers Rhodes; Knights Hospitaller resettle in Malta
1526	Mughal Emperor invades India
1633	Battles between Ming Dynasty in China and Dutch East India Company
1770	American Revolutionary War and events leading up to the war; First Russo-Turkish War
1885	Sino-French War ends; war between Britain and Russia
1887	Ethiopian forces defeat Italy

Zone 4: 215°-250° *(Closing Sesquiquadrate and Trine)*

Zone 4 combines historical events that occur within roughly a ten degree orb of the closing sesquiquadrate and trine: from 215° to 250° separation between Uranus and Pluto.

Period beginning	Event
1307	Knights Hospitaller conquer Rhodes
1805	First Barbary War between Tripoli and the United States; Napoleonic Wars

Period beginning	Event
1812	War of 1812
1914	World War I

Zone 5: 280°-320° (Closing Sextile and Semisquare)

Zone 5 combines historical events occurring within a twenty degree orb of the closing sextile and a five degree orb of the closing semisquare.

Period beginning	Event
1429	Joan of Arc active at Orléans
1683	Ottoman Empire siege of Vienna broken
1937	Sino-Japanese War; battle of Nanjing
1938	Germany occupies Czechoslovakia
1939	World War II
1951	Korean War

Analysis

Do the highlighted zones have a statistically greater number of armed conflict events than the non-highlighted areas when compared with the 34,000 event control cases? The following statistical distribution plot helps show the difference between the events in the shaded highlighted zones and the events outside the highlighted zones.

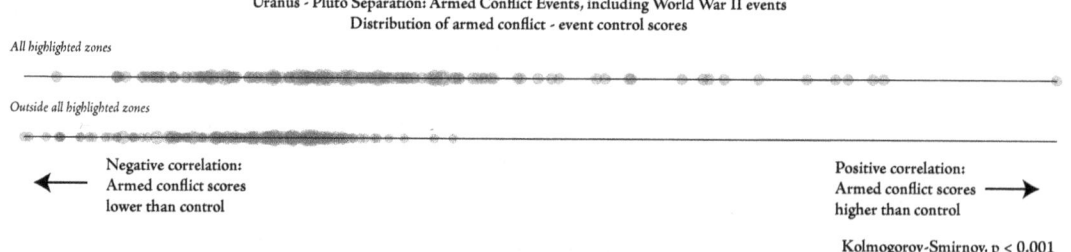

Figure 32. Distribution of Uranus - Pluto armed conflict with World War II events against event controls

Distribution plots like this appear frequently in these studies. A distribution plot has two or more groups of data: in the figure above, the top group represents data from the highlighted zones, while the bottom group represents data from all areas outside the highlighted zones. The distribution plot represents information from each degree in Figure 29 with a shaded circle. The circle's position indicates the strength of that degree's correlation with armed conflict events. For each degree the analysis takes the percentage of armed conflict events that occurred with the degree's separation between Uranus and Pluto and subtracts the percentage of event controls that have the same separation. When the number is larger, the degree's analysis indicates a stronger correlation with armed conflict events, and the circle appears to the right in the distribution plot. When the number is smaller, the analysis indicates a more negative correlation and the circle appears to the left.

To read the distribution plot, examine the proportion of circles that appear on the right and left sides for the two groups of data. For the top group representing the highlighted zones, more circles appear to the right of the plot, indicating a positive correlation. For the bottom group representing all other zones, all the circles appear to the left side of the plot, indicating a negative correlation. This means that there is a positive correlation for degrees in the highlighted zones and a negative one for degrees outside the highlighted zones. Simply stated, there is a significant correlation between the separation between Uranus and Pluto and armed conflict events.

Repeating the study with the day control cases gives a similar result:

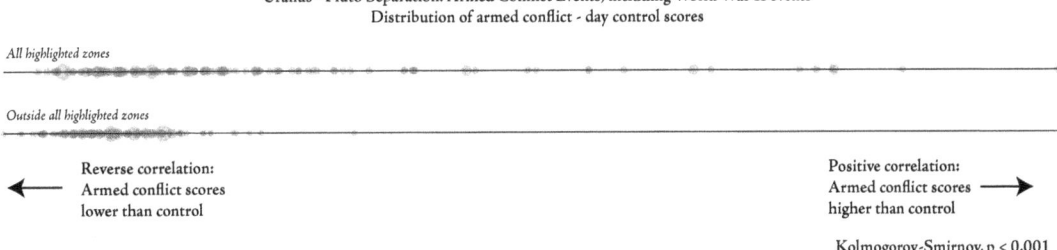

Figure 33. Distribution of Uranus - Pluto armed conflict with World War II events against day controls

Both groups of shaded circles shift to the left, but the highlighted zones still correlate more strongly with armed conflict events.

The highlighted zones are significantly more likely to have more armed conflict events than the areas outside the highlighted zones. The p-value for this test is less than 0.001, meaning statistically the result should occur randomly less than 0.1% of the time.

A key statistical test of significance is an analysis of variance (ANOVA) t-test. This test computes the average and the distribution of each group of scores:

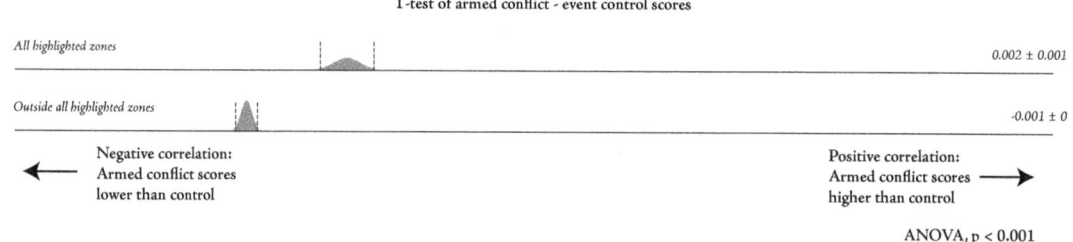

Figure 34. T-test of Uranus - Pluto armed conflict with World War II events against event controls

The top line shows the distribution of the highlighted zone scores, while the bottom line shows the distribution of the scores outside the highlighted zones. Each line has a shaded curve that represents the distribution of scores. The horizontal position of the shaded curve shows whether the events correlate positively or negatively with armed conflict events. The farther to the right the shaded curve appears, the stronger the positive correlation. Shifts farther to the left indicate a stronger negative correlation.

The short vertical lines represent the 95% confidence limits: 95% of expected scores occur within these vertical lines.

The figures that appear at the far right are the average values with the computed confidence range. In this case, the top line's value is 0.002±0.001. This means each degree in the highlighted zone on average has a 0.2%±0.1% greater armed conflict event score than expected. The bottom line's value is -0.001±0, meaning each degree has a 0.1% lower armed conflict event score than expected. These percentage values seem small, but when multiplied by 157° (the total number of degrees in the highlighted zones), overall there are 30% more armed conflict events in the highlighted zones than expected.

The highlighted zones shift to the right to show increasing positive correlation or to the left to show negative correlation. This test clearly shows that degrees in the highlighted zones have a higher correlation (top curve appears to the right) when compared with the degrees outside the highlighted zones (bottom curve appears to the left). The position of the curves is clearly separated with no overlap. This means the correlation is significant. Again, the correlation is significant with a p=0.001.

Repeating each study by omitting the World War II events gives similar results but show a less strong correlation. Here is the distribution computed without World War II events:

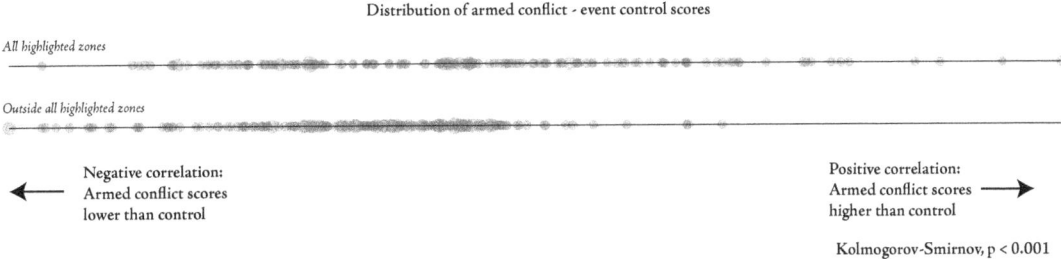

Figure 35. Distribution of Uranus - Pluto armed conflict without World War II events against event controls

Comparing this figure with Figure 32 shows that both groups of circles have shifted more to the center of the figure with a greater overlap. This indicates a reduced correlation. The same is true of the t-test:

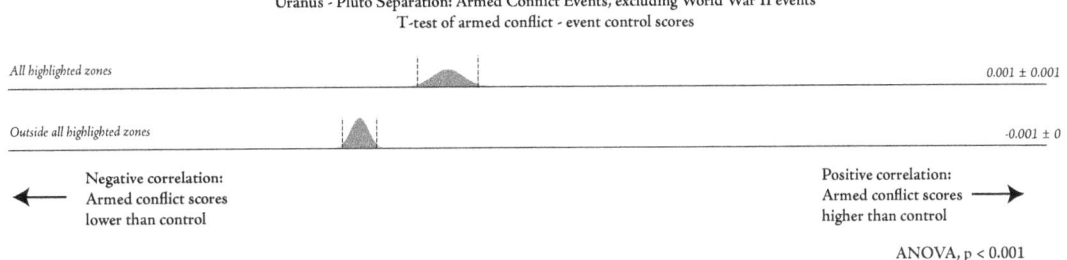

Figure 36. T-test of Uranus - Pluto armed conflict without World War II events against event controls

The results are similar, but the average score in the top line is now 0.001±0.001: half that of the previous case. Even though the correlation is reduced significantly by omitting the World War II events, it is still statistically significant.

The following table summarizes the results:

Including WWII	Armed conflict events	Event controls	Day controls
Highlighted zones	69.5%	44.4%	43.1%
Outside zones	30.5%	55.6%	56.7%
Excluding WWII	Armed conflict events	Event controls	Day controls
Highlighted zones	59.3%	44.4%	43.1%
Outside zones	40.7%	55.6%	56.9%

When including World War II events, the highlighted zones capture almost 70% of all armed conflict events, while the same zones in the control cases capture less than 45% of the control results.

Harmonic analysis

Chapter 2 opened with a discussion of the Moon's cycle and how dividing the circle by a fixed number gave significant angles that marked the major parts of the cycle. Recall that in the fourth harmonic the Moon's cycle divides into four parts of 90° each, and that the aspects associated with the fourth harmonic are the conjunction, square, and opposition. Astrologers often note aspects in a chart by lines connecting planets, and ignore any relationship between the planets other than these special angles.

Harmonic analysis is a different way to explore the connections between planets. Rather than draw lines signifying aspects, a harmonic analysis breaks the circle into multiple segments and overlays them to form a graph. The following figures show the process. In the first step, all the planetary data from the first ninety degrees of the planetary event distribution graph moves onto the line graph:

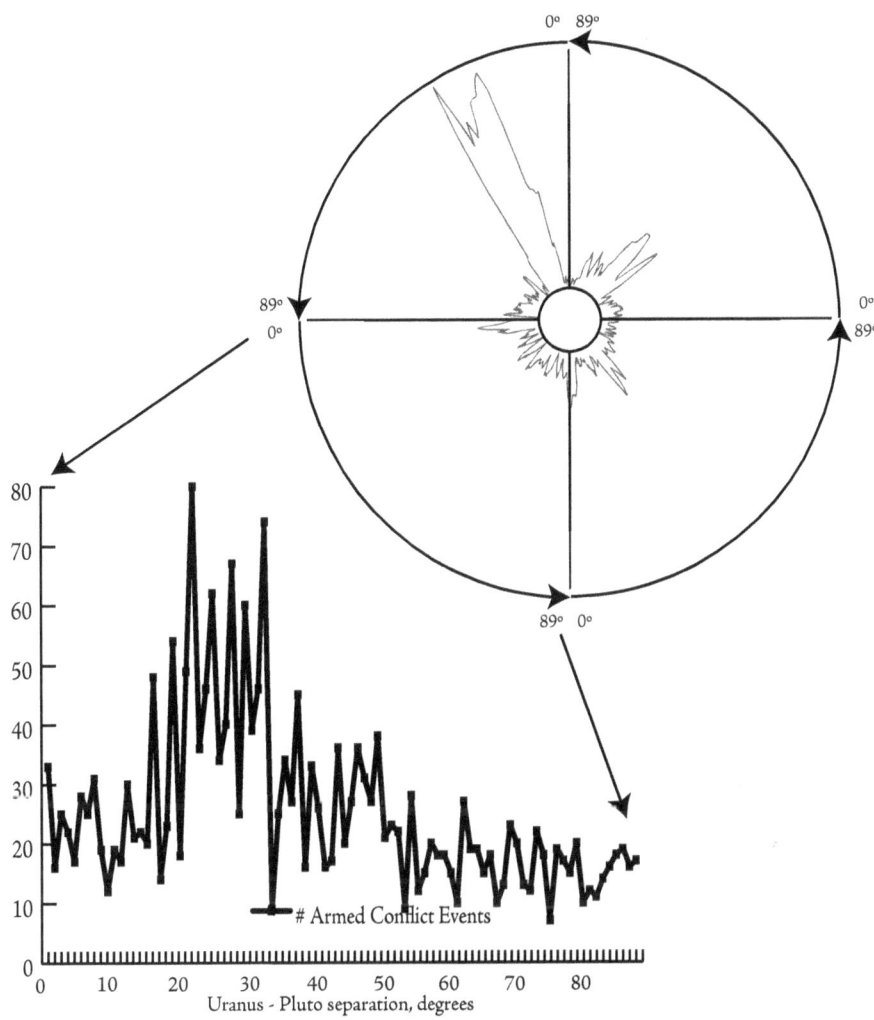

Figure 37. Harmonic analysis: mapping first quadrant onto graph

In the next step, all the planetary data from the second ninety degrees of arc goes onto the same degrees in the graph. This overlays the first and second ninety degree segments.

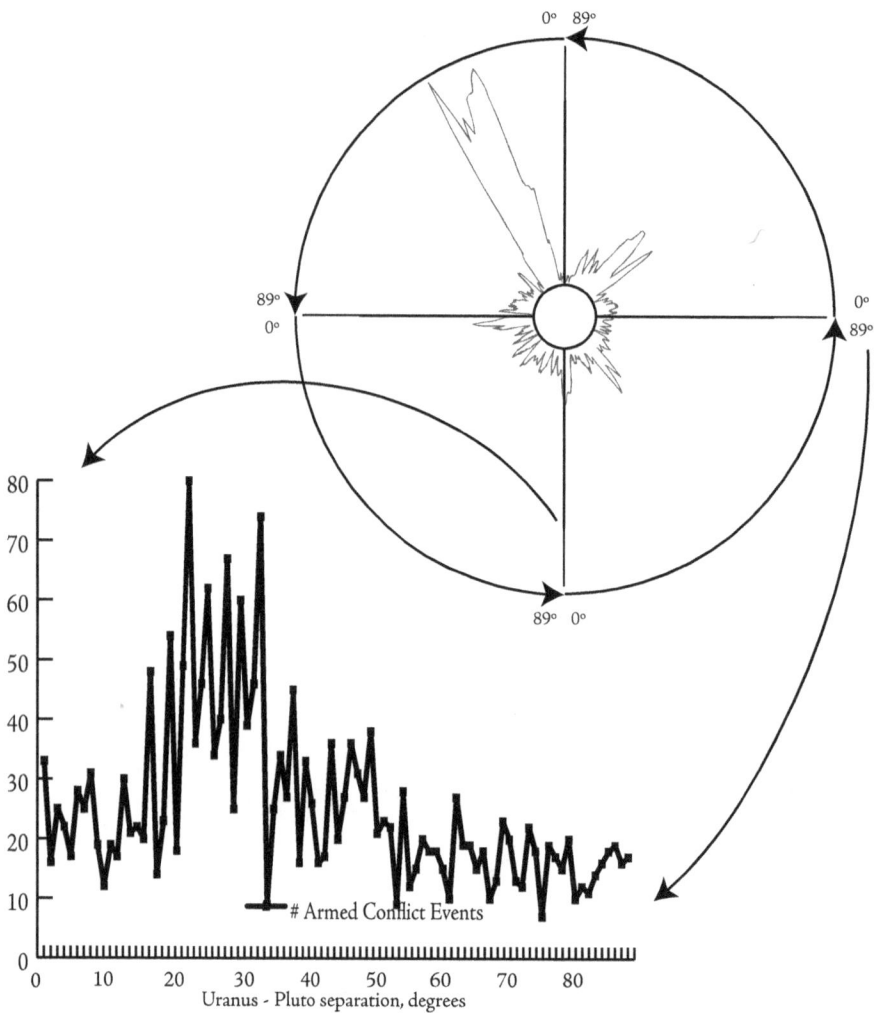

Figure 38. Harmonic analysis: mapping second quadrant onto graph

The process continues by mapping the third and fourth ninety degree segments from the original data onto the same graph. The resulting graph groups together around the zero degree and ninety degree marks all cases where the two planets are in conjunction, square, or opposition. Peaks that appear just after the zero mark result from the two planets being just after the conjunction, square, or opposition. Peaks that appear just before the ninety degree point result from the planets being just before the same aspects.

This process is well known to Uranian astrologers and to cosmobiologists, who map planetary positions onto circles marked in 90° (fourth harmonic) and 45° (eighth harmonic) divisions[27, 28, 56]. Planets appearing near each other on these 90° and 45° dials are in one of the fourth or eighth harmonic aspects. The precise aspect no longer matters: in a fourth harmonic plot conjunction, opposition, and square aspects appear alike.

This process works with any harmonic number. For the fifth harmonic, for example, one divides the circle in five segments of 72° each and overlays each 72° segment onto the same graph. For the ninth harmonic, the circle has nine overlaid segments of 40° each.

Recall the discussion of Figure 28 where a large peak appears roughly at 290° past the conjunction – about twenty degrees after the closing square. The preponderance of events at this zone stretches back hundreds of years to Joan of Arc's activity in 1429. The 290° figure is almost four times seventy-two: 288°. Seventy-two degrees is the basis of the fifth harmonic: dividing the circle by 5 yields seventy-two degrees. The fifth harmonic aspect series is 0°, 72°, 144°, 216°, and 288°. Recomputing the figures including World War II figures in the fifth harmonic yields the following striking result:

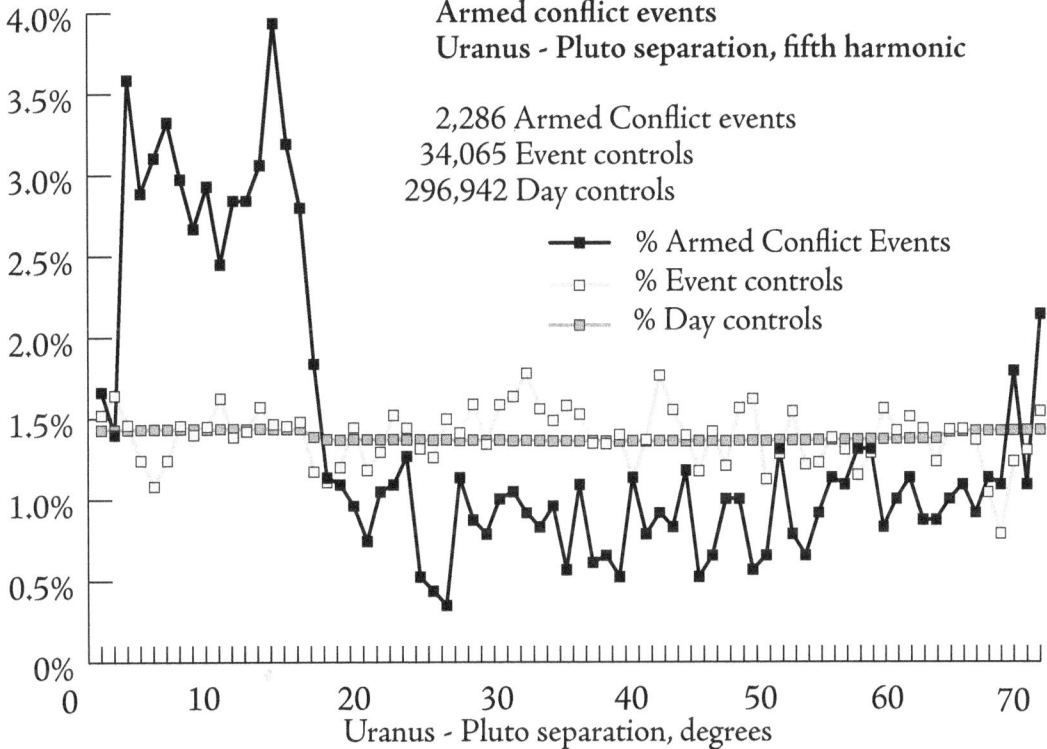

Figure 39. Armed conflict event frequency and Uranus - Pluto separation in the fifth harmonic, including World War II events

This graph plots the percentage number of events in the three groups against the separation of Uranus and Pluto. This is a fifth harmonic plot, meaning that the degrees run from 0° to 72° rather than from 0° to 360°. When the two planets are separated by a quintile-series aspect, the separation is near the 0° point. If the planets are just past the quintile, the separation is just a bit more than 0°. If the planets are just before the quintile aspect, the separation is near 72° – the bottom axis effectively wraps around so that 0° and 72° are the same.

The dark line represents the percentage of armed conflict events that occur with respect to the fifth harmonic Uranus - Pluto separation. The light grey line represents the percentage of the event controls, while the medium gray line shows the percent of all the observed Uranus - Pluto separations for each day between 1200 and 2012.

In this graph the dark line has a very sharp peak from 0° through about 20°, and then drops off. This means that there are many armed conflict events that occurred where Uranus and Pluto are just past a quintile aspect. The two control lines do not show this peak.

Performing a t-test gives these results:

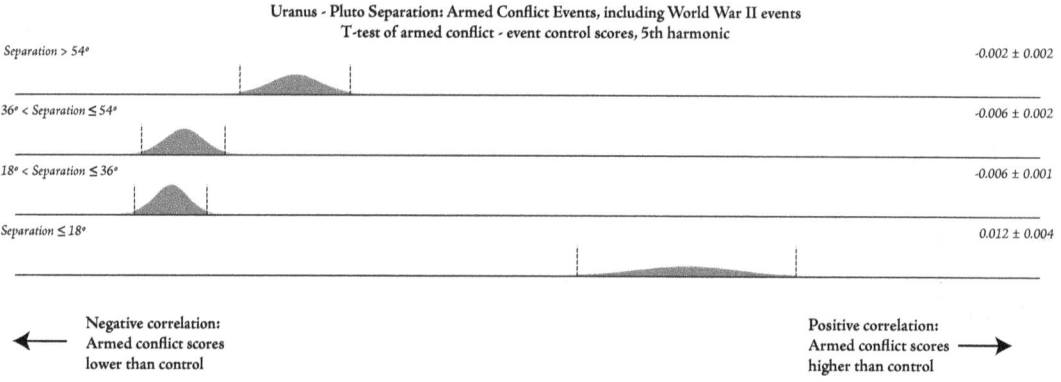

Figure 40. T-test of Uranus - Pluto armed conflict including World War II events against event controls, fifth harmonic

The analysis breaks the 72° in the fifth harmonic into four bands: zero to 18°, 18° to 36°, 36° to 54°, and 54° to 72°. The shaded curves display the distribution of the difference between the armed conflict events and the event controls. Shaded curves shifted to the right are positively correlated with armed conflict events scoring higher than the control; those shifted to the left are negatively correlated, so that armed conflict events score lower than the control. The numbers appearing to the upper right with each graph are the computed mean and standard deviation.

In the graph above, the curve for the band less than 18° is strongly positively correlated, with an average of 1.2% higher for the armed conflict events than the control events for each degree in the sample. The curves for the 18°-36° and 36°-54° segments are negatively correlated by 0.6% per degree; this means that having a Uranus - Pluto separation within these ranges is less likely for armed conflict events than for the control events. The curve for the 54°-72° zone is less negatively correlated. The p-value for this result is less than 0.001; this means that this result would occur randomly less in than 0.1% of the cases.

Repeating the analysis by omitting the World War II events shifts the separation curves:

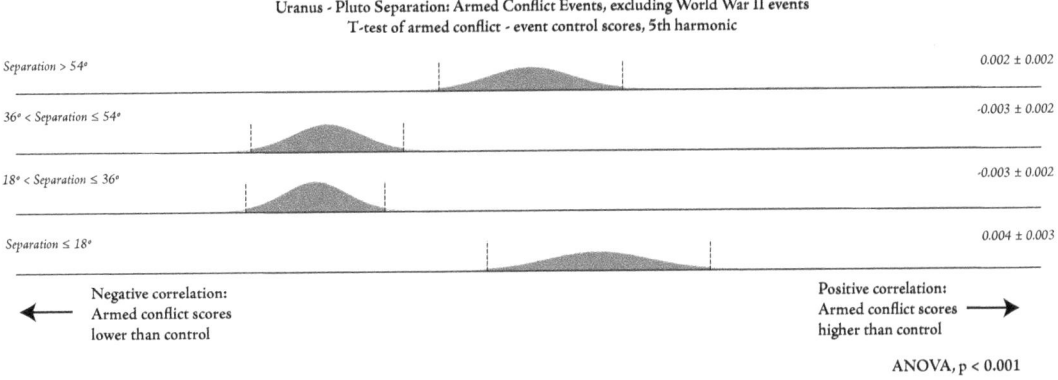

Figure 41. T-test of Uranus - Pluto armed conflict excluding World War II events against event controls, fifth harmonic

This result shows less strong correlation for degrees less than 18°, but a positive correlation for degrees greater than 54°. The other zones continue to show negative correlation.

The following t-test shows the result of combining these two intervals into a single band representing both 0°-18° and 65°-72°, and comparing this against all other separations. The result is highly significant:

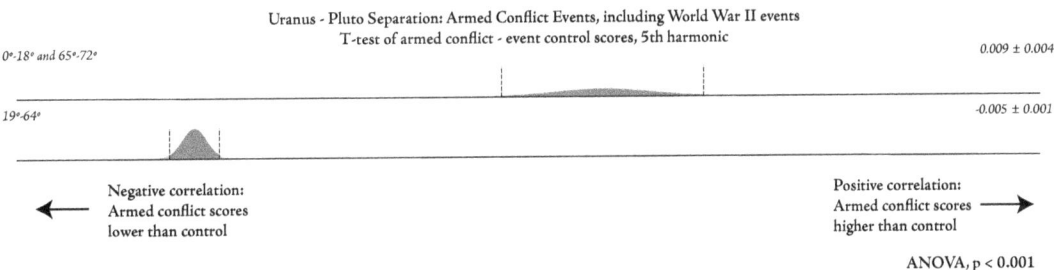

Figure 42. T-test of Uranus - Pluto armed conflict including World War II events against event controls, by fifth harmonic intervals

The zones between 0°-18° and 65°-72° show a strong positive correlation (roughly 0.9% higher per degree) with armed conflict events while the zone between 19°-64° has a negative correlation (roughly 0.5% lower per degree) with armed conflict events. Comparing this result with Figure 34, the harmonic analysis gives a much stronger correlation (greater separation between the two shaded curves) than the *ad hoc* zones do.

A distribution analysis of the two intervals confirms the result:

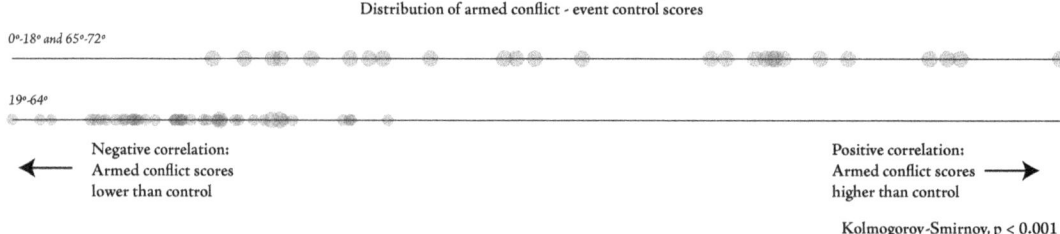

Figure 43. Distribution of Uranus - Pluto armed conflict including World War II events against event controls by fifth harmonic intervals

The circles in the top band representing the selected intervals appear largely to the right, indicating strong correlation. The bottom band representing all other degrees has circles at the left side, indicating a negative correlation of armed conflict events when Uranus and Pluto are outside the selected intervals. Comparing this result with Figure 32, the harmonic intervals clearly include the armed conflict events with higher positive correlation and exclude the controls with stronger negative correlation much more effectively than the *ad hoc* zones do.

This table summarizes the results:

Including WWII	Armed conflict events	Event controls	Day controls
0°-18° and 65°-72°	59.0%	35.1%	37.1%
19°-64°	41.0%	64.9%	62.9%

Excluding WWII	Armed conflict events	Event controls	Day controls
0°-18° and 65°-72°	47.6%	35.1%	37.1%
19°-64°	52.4%	64.9%	62.9%

In standard astrological language, armed conflict events are significantly more likely to occur when Uranus and Pluto are separated by one of the quintile series of aspects (0°, 72°, 144°, 216°, 288°) with an orb of 18° after the aspect and 7° before the aspect.

Drawing the results of the Uranus - Pluto fifth harmonic analysis onto the full circle looks like this:

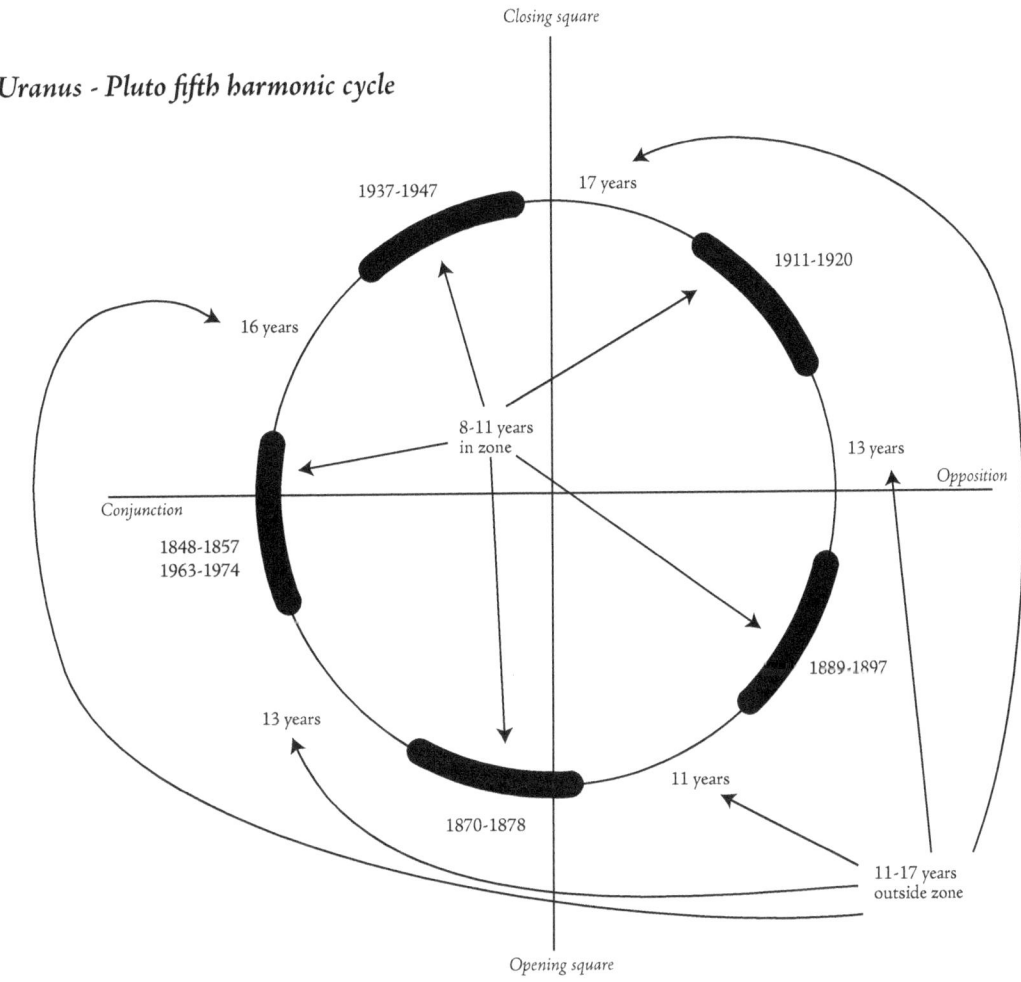

Figure 44. Uranus - Pluto fifth harmonic areas associated with armed conflict events

The bold arcs show the region seven degrees before the quintile aspect and eighteen degrees after the aspect. Ranges of years appear next to each arc.

While the cycle's geometry is regular, the overall time intervals are not uniform when the planets are in the bold arcs and when they are between the bold arcs. Pluto's orbit is highly eccentric and its rate of orbital motion changes at different points in its orbit. The time interval between the bold arcs varies from eleven to seventeen years, while the time interval within a bold arc varies from eight to eleven years.

95

Saturn / Uranus and Armed Conflict Events: 1200-2012

Plotting the Saturn - Uranus phase angle distribution for armed conflict events gives the following striking graph:

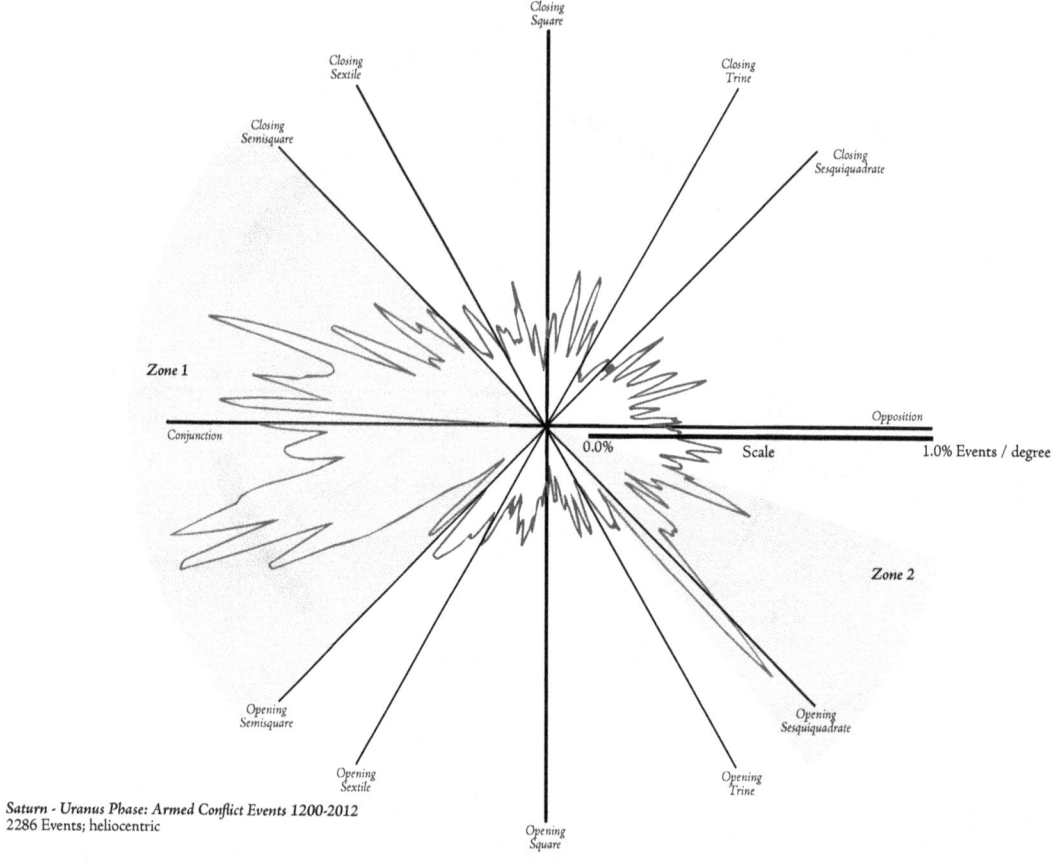

Saturn - Uranus Phase: Armed Conflict Events 1200-2012
2286 Events; heliocentric

Figure 45. Saturn - Uranus: armed conflict event distribution including World War II events, heliocentric

The very strong clustering of events 45° either side of the conjunction is a combination of World War II events along with many other conflicts.

Zone 1 (315° to 45°) Closing Semisquare to Opening Semisquare

This zone spans forty-five degrees before and after the conjunction. This ninety degree zone encompasses the Saturn - Uranus phase angle for the following armed conflicts:

Period beginning	Event
1347	Hundred Years' War
1576	Eighty Years' War
1618	Thirty Years' War
1667	War of Devolution
1756	Seven Years' War
1805	Napoleonic Wars
1812	War of 1812
1846	Mexican-American War
1853	Crimean War
1898	Spanish-American War
1899	Philippine-American War
1937	Sino-Japanese War
1939	World War II
1982	Falklands War; Soviet Union in Afghanistan
1983	Cold War: Soviets shoot down Korean Air plane
1991	Gulf War/Operation Desert Storm
1993	Bosnian War

Zone 2 (125° to 145°) Opening Sesquiquadrate

Zone two spans ten degrees around the opening sesquiquadrate, and contains the Saturn - Uranus phase angle for these two armed conflicts:

Period beginning	Event
1776	American Revolutionary War
1914	World War I

Analysis

All subsequent analyses following the same analysis approach as the previous Uranus - Pluto example. Plotting the difference between the armed conflict and event control values for each degree gives the following figure:

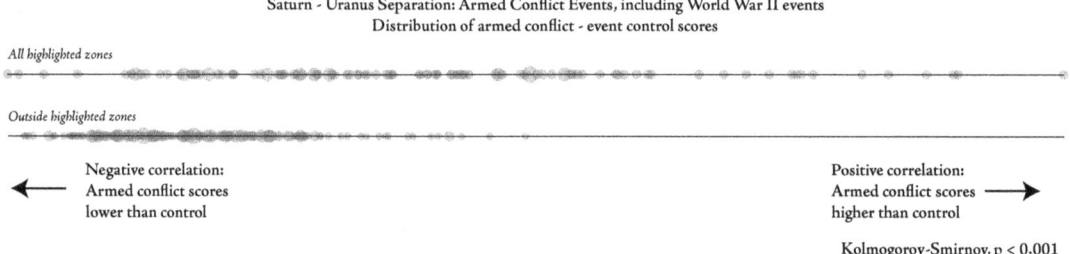

Figure 46. Distribution of Saturn - Uranus armed conflict with World War II events against event controls

As expected, the highlighted zones have more positively correlated events while the areas outside the highlighted zones have stronger negative correlation with armed conflict events. Excluding the World War II data, however, largely eliminates the correlation:

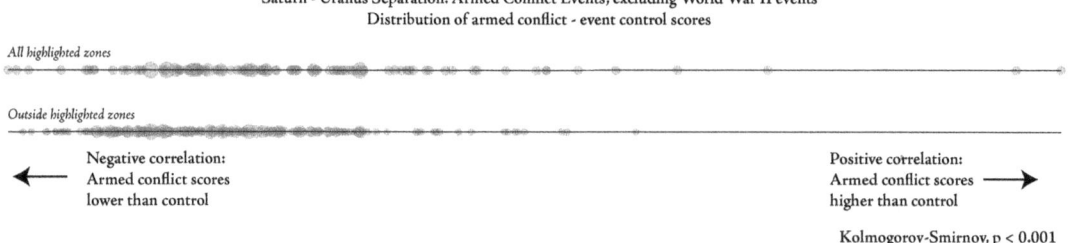

Figure 47. Distribution of Saturn - Uranus armed conflict without World War II events against event controls

The circles both inside and outside the highlighted zones now tend to overlap considerably. This means the correlation above is mostly due to World War II events and is not reproducible.

Harmonic analysis

Figure 35 shows a two-fold symmetry of peaks just before and after the conjunction and opposition. Analyzing the event distribution in the second harmonic yields this distribution:

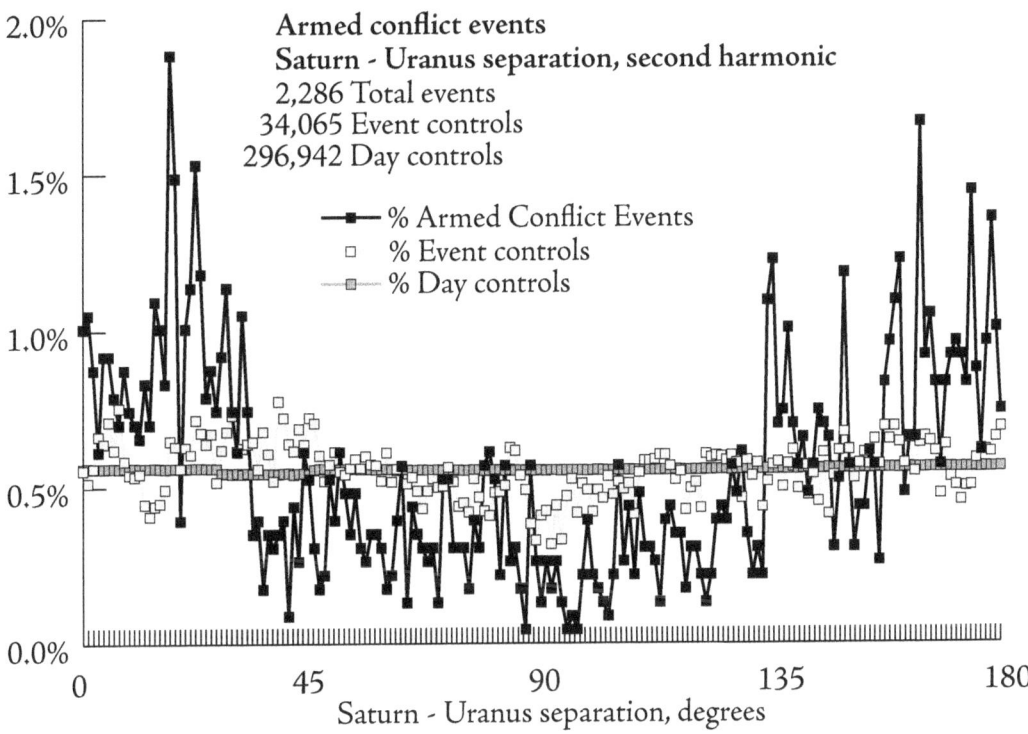

Figure 48. Armed conflict event frequency and Saturn - Uranus separation in the second harmonic, including World War II events

A t-test shows the strong correlation with intervals less than 45° and greater than 135°:

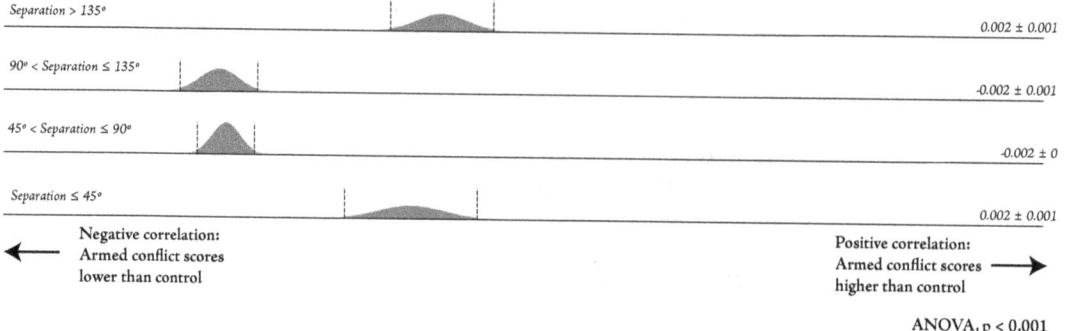

Figure 49. T-test of Saturn - Uranus armed conflict with World War II events against event controls, second harmonic

Excluding the World War II events gives this distribution plot:

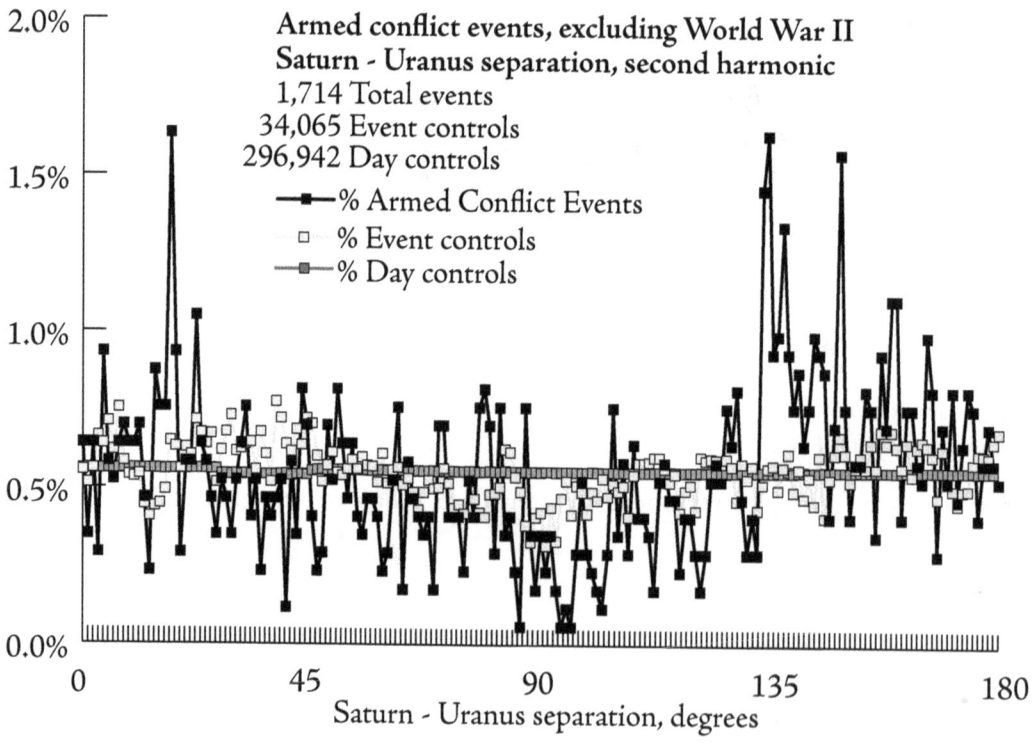

Figure 50. Armed conflict event frequency and Saturn - Uranus separation in the second harmonic, excluding World War II events

While not nearly as pronounced, the intervals near the 0° and 180° points show increased clustering of events.

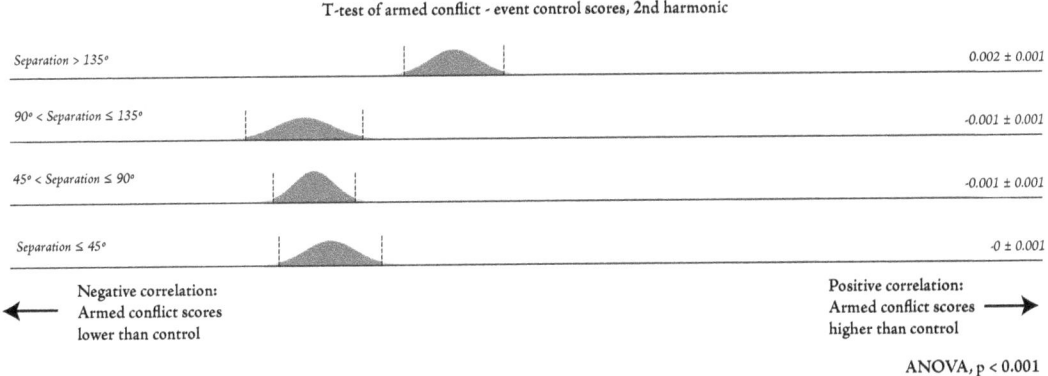

Figure 51. T-test of Saturn - Uranus armed conflict without World War II events against event controls, second harmonic

Refining the interval to be 45° or less before the conjunction or opposition and less than or equal to 28° after the conjunction or opposition gives a best fit for both the data sets with and without World War II data. Here are the distribution graphs with and without World War II events:

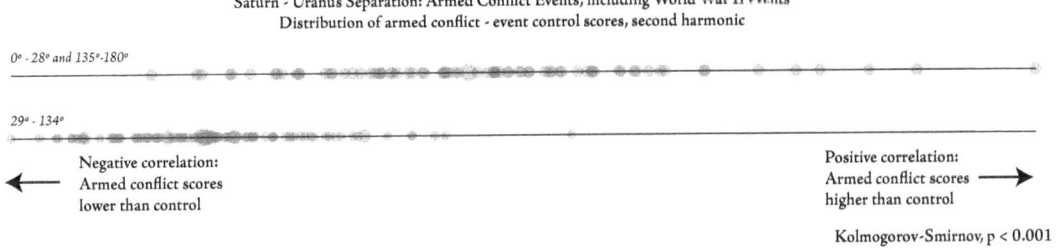

Figure 52. Distribution of Saturn - Uranus armed conflict with World War II events against event controls, second harmonic

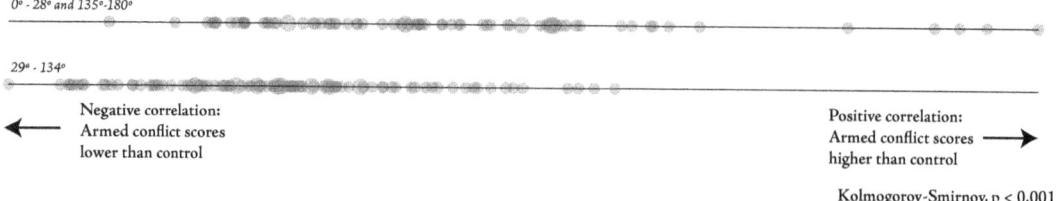

Figure 53. Distribution of Saturn - Uranus armed conflict without World War II events against event controls, second harmonic

Comparing these figures with Figure 46 and Figure 47, the second harmonic results show positive correlation within the 0°-28° and 135°-180° interval, and negative correlation outside those intervals. A t-test confirms the strong correlation, with a distinct separation between the two shaded curves for the selected intervals compared with all others:

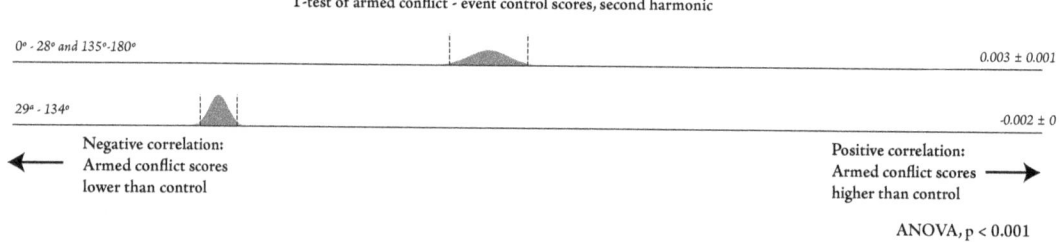

Figure 54. T-test of Saturn - Uranus armed conflict with World War II events against event controls, second harmonic

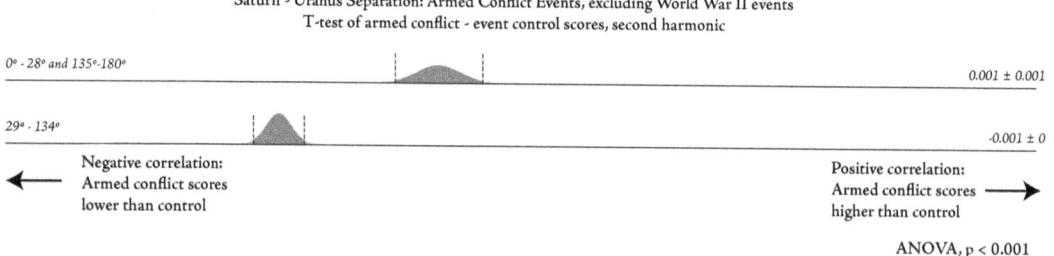

Figure 55. T-test of Saturn - Uranus armed conflict without World War II events against event controls, second harmonic

The results when excluding World War II events show a reduced correlation. Both tests are highly significant, with a p < 0.001 (chance of random occurrence less than 0.1%). This table summarizes the results:

Including WWII	Armed conflict events	Event controls	Day controls
0°-28° and 135°-180°	64.8%	44.2%	42.5%
29°-134°	35.2%	55.8%	57.5%
Excluding WWII	Armed conflict events	Event controls	Day controls
0°-28° and 135°-180°	55.1%	44.2%	42.5%
29°-134°	44.9%	55.8%	57.5%

In standard astrological language, armed conflict events are significantly more likely to occur when Saturn and Uranus are separated either by conjunction or opposition, with an orb of 45° before the aspect and 28° after the aspect.

Drawing the results onto the full circle looks as follows:

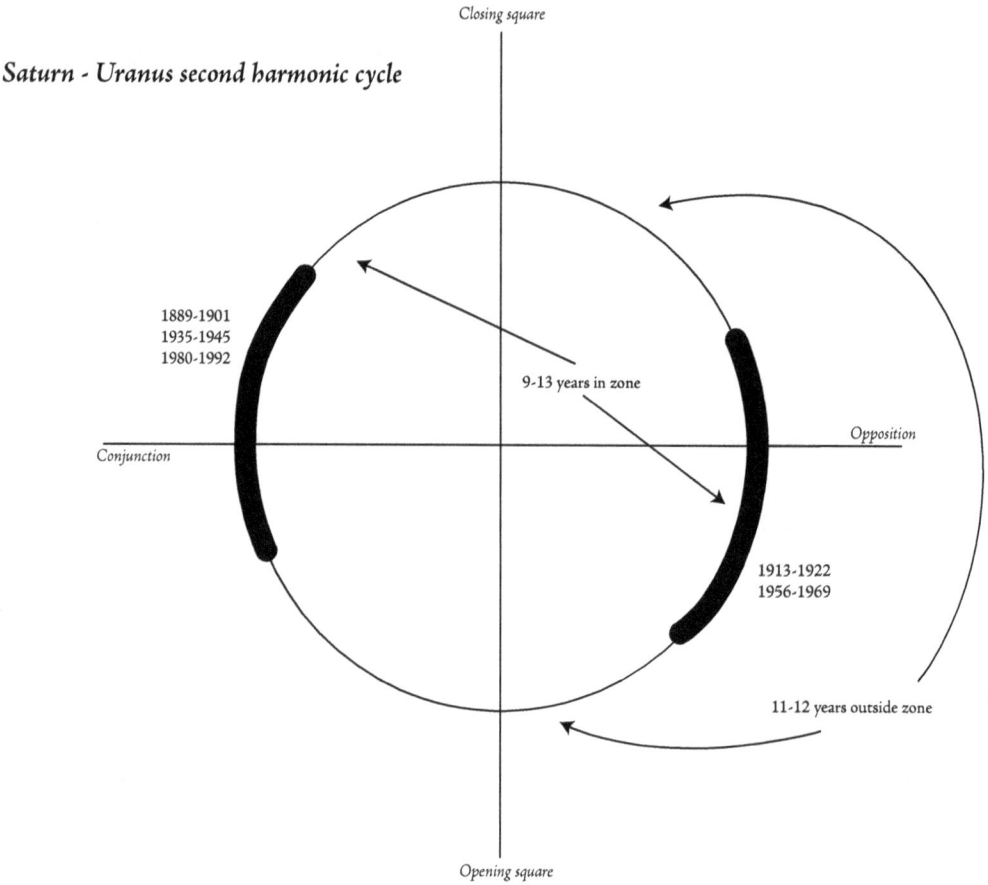

Figure 56. Saturn - Uranus second harmonic areas associated with armed conflict events

The bold arcs show the region roughly 45° degrees before the conjunction or opposition and 28° degrees after the aspect. Ranges of years appear next to each arc.

Combining cycles

While each cycle alone gives good results, combining the Uranus - Pluto and Saturn - Uranus cycles together selects for very significant armed conflicts. Just over half of armed conflict events take place when both the Saturn - Uranus and Uranus - Pluto cycles are within their respective critical intervals, including: Thirty Years' War, Eighty Years' War, Seven Years' War and French and Indian Wars, American Revolutionary War, Napoleonic Wars, Greek War of Independence, Russo-Persian War, Crimean War, World War I, Sino-Japanese War, World War II, and Vietnam War.

Saturn - Pluto and Armed Conflict events: 1200-2012

Analyzing the Saturn - Pluto phase angle distribution for armed conflict events yields the following result. The striking peaks in Zone 2 arise from a large number of conflicts, including World War II.

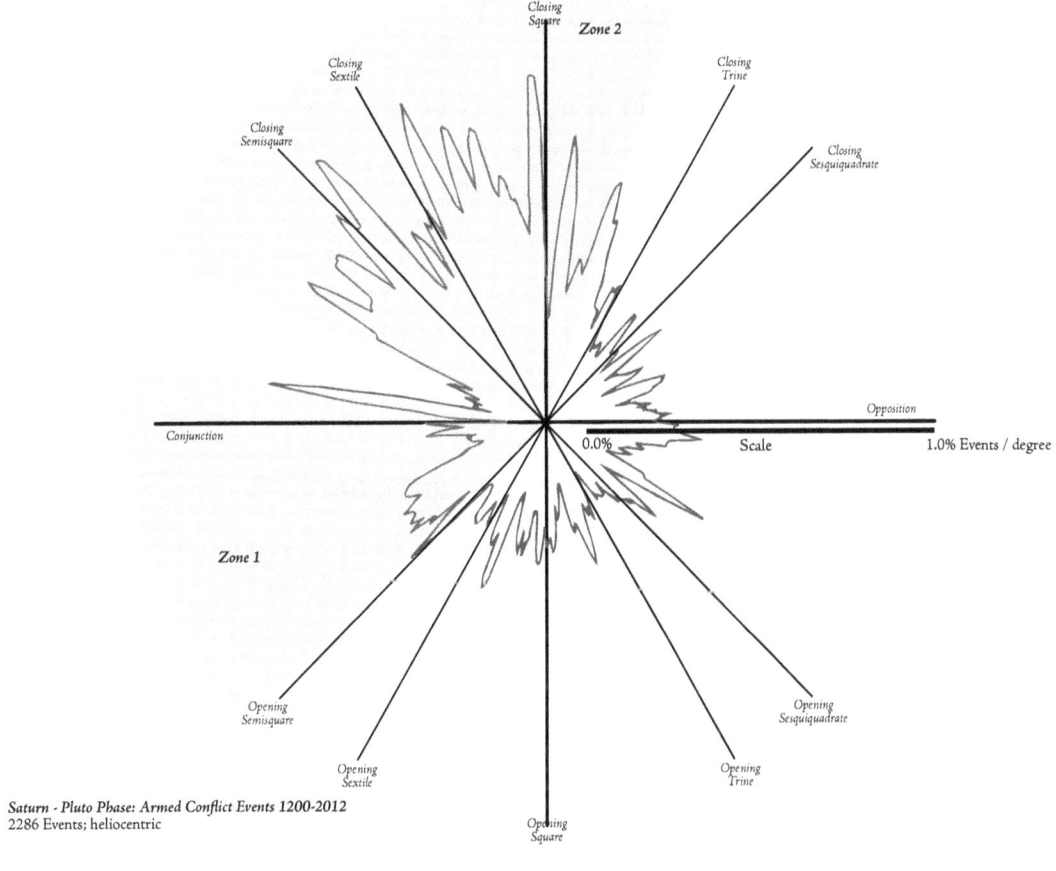

Figure 57. Saturn - Pluto: armed conflict event distribution including World War II events, heliocentric

The distribution of armed conflict events forms two broad zones taking up about a third of circle.

Zone 1 350°-40° (conjunction)

A fifty degree arc around the conjunction contains the Saturn - Pluto phase angle for the following armed conflict events.

Period beginning	Event
1446	Ottoman Empire defeated in Serbia
1520	Aztec and Spanish forces at war
1522	Ottoman Empire defeats Knights Hospitaller in Rhodes
1588	Spanish Armada defeated
1616	Tokugawa shogunate forces foreigners from Japan
1648	End of Thirty Years' War
1714	War of the Spanish Succession
1787	Russo-Turkish War
1822	Greek War of Independence
1854	Crimean War
1914	World War I
1947	War in Kashmir between India and Pakistan
1950	Korean War
1983	Soviet Union shoots down Korean Air jet

Zone 2: 250° to 330° (closing square, sextile, semisquare)

A broad arc, spanning the closing square, sextile, and semisquare, encompasses the phase angle for the following armed conflicts:

Period beginning	Event
1203	Fourth Crusade
1209	Albigensian Crusade against Cathars in southern France
1346	Edward III of England invades France
1512	War of the League of Cambrai between England and France
1745	War of the Austrian Succession
1775	American Revolutionary War
1809	Napoleonic Wars
1812	War of 1812
1846	Mexican-American War
1877	Greece declares war on Turkey; Russo-Turkish War
1939	World War II
1973	Yom Kippur War
1975	End of Vietnam War

Period beginning	Event
1978	Israel invades Lebanon; Ethiopian-Somali War; Vietnam invades Cambodia
1979	China invades Vietnam
2009	Israel invades Gaza

Analysis

Performing a t-test on armed conflict event data against event control data shows a strong effect when including World War II events:

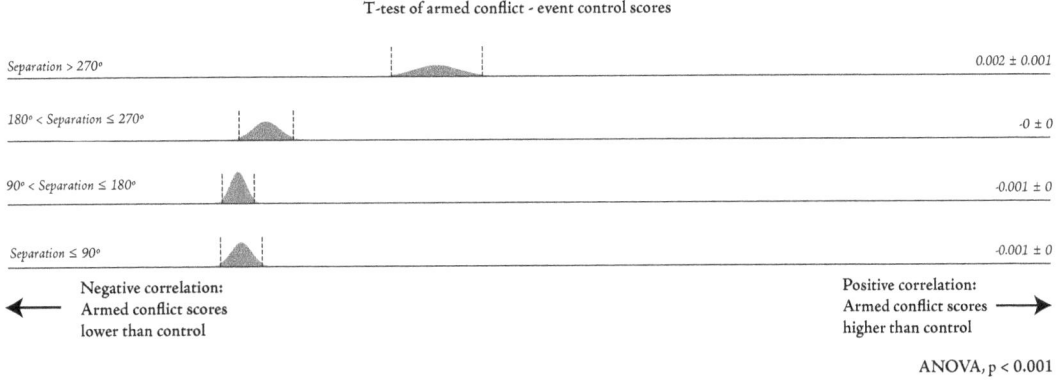

Figure 58. T-test of Saturn - Pluto armed conflict with World War II events against event controls

The distribution curve in the top band correlates positively with armed conflict events. However, the correlation disappears entirely without the World War II data:

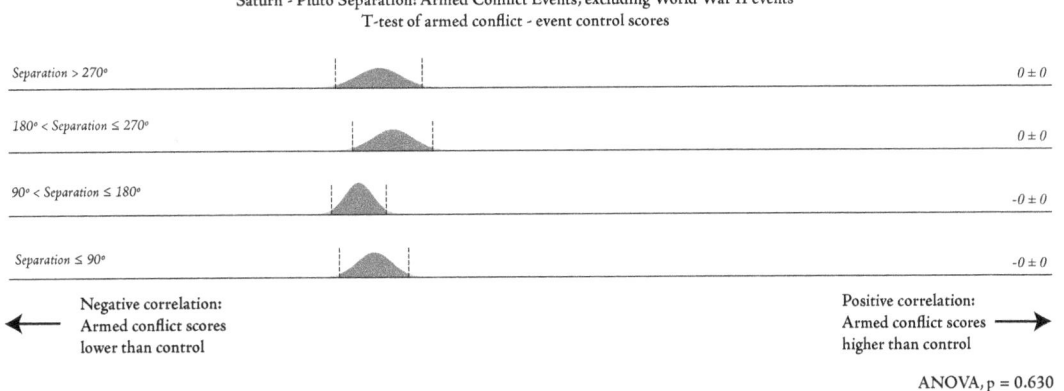

Figure 59. T-test of Saturn - Pluto armed conflict without World War II events against event controls

The distribution curves in the four bands overlap completely. The analysis shows no correlation at all, with a p-value of 0.630 (63% probability of no correlation).

Harmonic analysis applied to the Saturn - Pluto data is disappointing. No correlations exist when doing harmonic analyses up to harmonic sixteen. This is a surprising result considering the common view in astrological literature that Saturn and Pluto contacts are connected with events of mass violence.

9. Civil unrest events and planetary cycles

Uranus - Pluto and Civil Unrest Events

The graph below shows how the number of civil unrest events varies with the phase angle separating Uranus and Pluto at the time of the event. The graph is the result of analyzing 1918 events from 1200 to 2012.

Five highlighted zones appear on the graph where increased numbers of civil unrest events occur; these zones are numbered Zone 1 through Zone 5. Right below the plots are tables of the actual historical events that occurred within each zone.

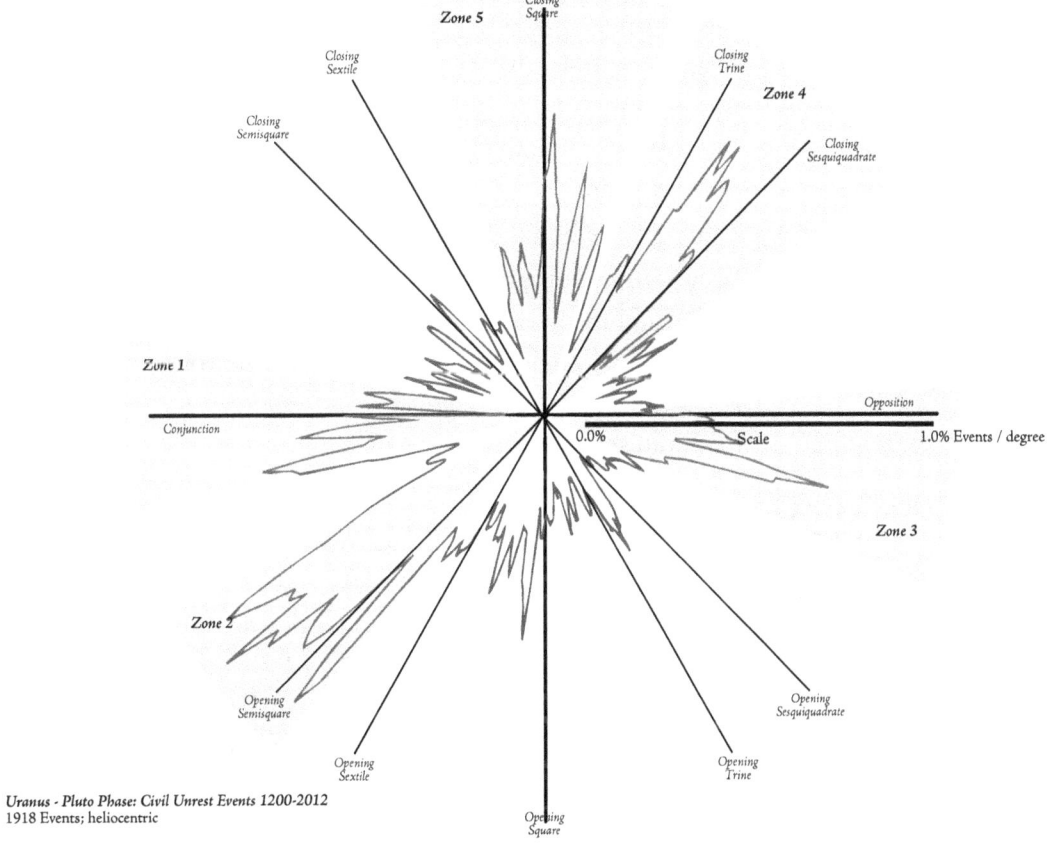

Figure 60. Uranus - Pluto: civil unrest event distribution, heliocentric

109

Zone 1: 345° to 15° (Conjunction)

Period beginning	Event
1455	War of the Roses in England
1594	Irish attempt to overthrow English domination
1705	Militiamen killed in Munich
1713	Defeat of Tuscarora Nation in North Carolina
1846	Border disputes between Mexico and Texas; US forces occupy California
1846	Sicilian revolution against House of Bourbon; Austrian army crushes working class revolt; French government dissolves national workshops; Rebellion in Sri Lanka against British rule; Young Irelander Rebellion
1849	Revolutions in German states; religious persecution in Madagascar; Second Cabalist War in Spain; Hungarian War of Independence
1850	Taiping Rebellion in China
1961	American Civil Rights Movement
1971	Unrest in Northern Ireland; conflict in former East Pakistan; founding of Bangladesh; Coup in Laos; Palestinian conflicts in Jordan
1972	Idi Amin seizes control in Uganda

Zone 2: 30° to 55° (Opening Semisquare)

Period beginning	Event
1358	Jacquerie peasant rebellion in France during the Hundred Years' War
1469	House of Lancaster defeats House of York in England; last battles in England between feudal magnates
1608	Massacre in Ethiopia
1722	Persian dynasty falls during Pashtun rebellion
1729	Natchez Indians slaughter French settlers
1861	American Civil War
1986	Unrest in South Africa; Perestroika in Soviet Union
1989	Fall of communist East European states; Tiananmen Square protests and violence in China

Zone 3: 160° to 190° (Opposition)

Period beginning	Event
1391	Anti-Jewish riots in Spain
1535	Anabaptists attempt coup in Amsterdam; Henry VIII orders Thomas More's execution; Anne Boleyn executed; Thomas Cromwell executed; Dissolution of the Monasteries in England
1536	Inquisition implemented in Portugal
1644	English Civil War; Manchu army captures Beijing, beginning the Qing Dynasty
1788	French Revolution
1897	British officers assassinated in India
1898	Dowager Empress Cixi engineers a coup d'état in China; Boxer Rebellion
1899	Second Boer War
1901	Filipino guerrillas kill US soldiers

Zone 4: 215° to 235° (Closing Sesquiquadrate)

Period beginning	Event
1297	Battles between Edward I of England and the Scottish army led by William Wallace
1407	Duke of Orléans assassinated leading to war with the Burgundians
1555	Religious persecution in England under Queen Mary I
1804	Serbian uprising; ethnic cleansing in Haiti
1913	Mexican Revolution
1914	Colorado National Guard attacks striking coal miners
1916	Irish Republican Brotherhood stages uprising; Armenian Genocide; last Chinese emperor abdicates
1918	Russian Revolution; Finnish Revolution
1919	Estonian Revolution; steel strike in US; Seattle general strike; Egyptian Revolution
1920	End of Ottoman Empire; Irish War of Independence

Zone 5: 260° to 290° (Closing Square)

Period beginning	Event
1312	Pope Clement V disbands Knights Templar; persecution follows
1566	Calvinists destroy religious art in the Low Countries
1567	Mary, Queen of Scots, forced to abdicate and is imprisoned; French Wars of Religion begin
1569	Coup attempt against Elizabeth I of England fails
1570	Huguenots promised religious and political freedom
1676	Battles between Indian tribes and settlers in New England
1678	Catholics banned from Parliament in England
1818	Seminole wars in Florida
1819	Bolivar victorious in Colombia
1821	Greek War of Independence
1929	Hebron massacre of Jews by Palestinians
1930	Mohandas Gandhi active in India; Salt March; massive riots between Hindus and Muslims; Turkish troops battle Kurdish insurgents
1931	Mao proclaims People's Republic of China; battles with Kuomintang begin; Long March begins
1932	Nazis claim power in Germany
1936	Stalin begins Great Purge; Arab revolt in Palestine
1937	Spanish Civil War

Harmonic analysis

In the Uranus - Pluto graph above there is clustering at around 40° and just before the opposition at around 160° degrees. These two phase angles belong to the ninth harmonic aspect series. Dividing the circle of 360° by nine gives 40° as the base aspect. The *novile*, or 40° aspect, is not widely used by astrologers because it is difficult to find without computer assistance. The novile series, however, contains one of the most important aspects in traditional astrology: three times 40° is 120° – the trine.

Analyzing the Uranus - Pluto cycle in the ninth harmonic gives the following results:

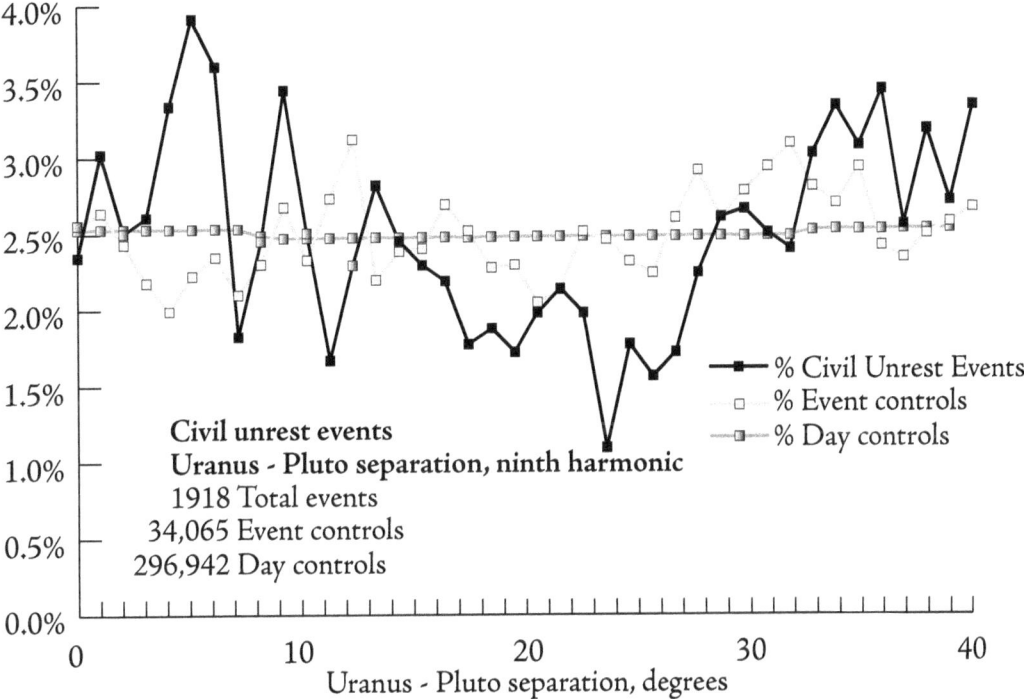

Figure 61. Civil unrest event frequency and Uranus - Pluto separation in the ninth harmonic

The peaks just after 0° and before 40° in the civil unrest event curve show the importance of the 40° novile aspect.

A t-test shows strong correlation:

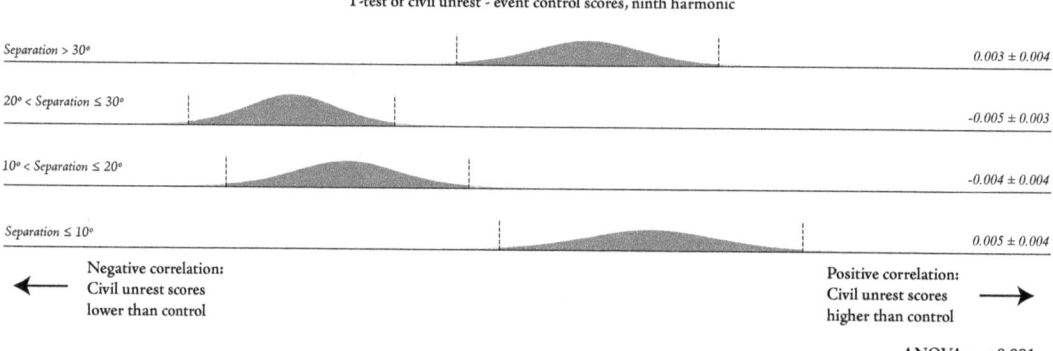

Figure 62. T-test of Uranus - Pluto civil unrest events against event controls, ninth harmonic

The intervals from 0°-10° and 30°-40° show strong positive correlation, while the other bands show significant negative correlation. Combining the 0°-10° and 30°-40 intervals gives the following t-test and distribution results:

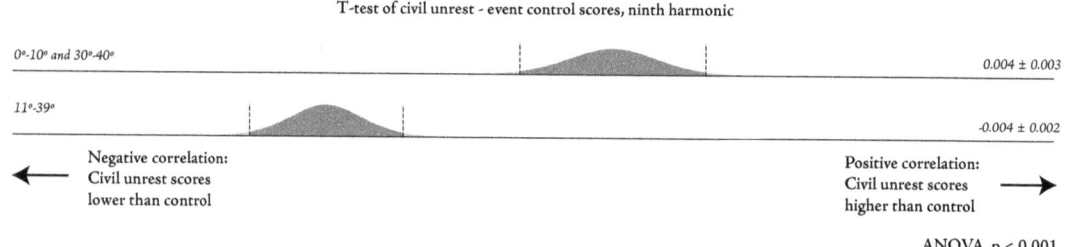

Figure 63. T-test of Uranus - Pluto civil unrest events against event controls, ninth harmonic, by interval

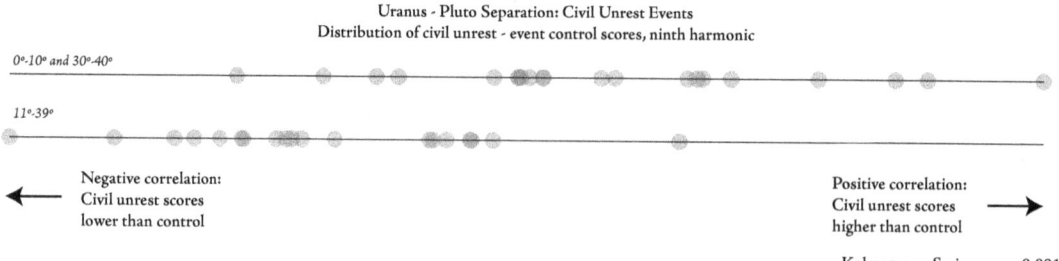

Figure 64. Distribution of Uranus - Pluto civil unrest events against event controls, ninth harmonic, by interval

The t-test shows clear separation between the positive correlation within the 0°-10° and 30°-40° intervals, and the negative correlation outside the intervals. The distribution study confirms this result. The correlations are significant, with a p-value < 0.001.

This table summarizes the results:

	Civil unrest events	Event controls	Day controls
0°-10° and 30°-40°	61.1%	52.8%	52.9%
11°-39°	38.9%	47.2%	47.1%

In standard astrological language, civil unrest events are significantly more likely to occur when Uranus and Pluto are separated a novile series aspect (0°, 40°, 80°, 120°, 160°, 200°, 240°, 280°, 320°) with an orb of 10° either side of the aspect.

Drawing the results of the Uranus - Pluto ninth harmonic analysis onto the full circle looks like this:

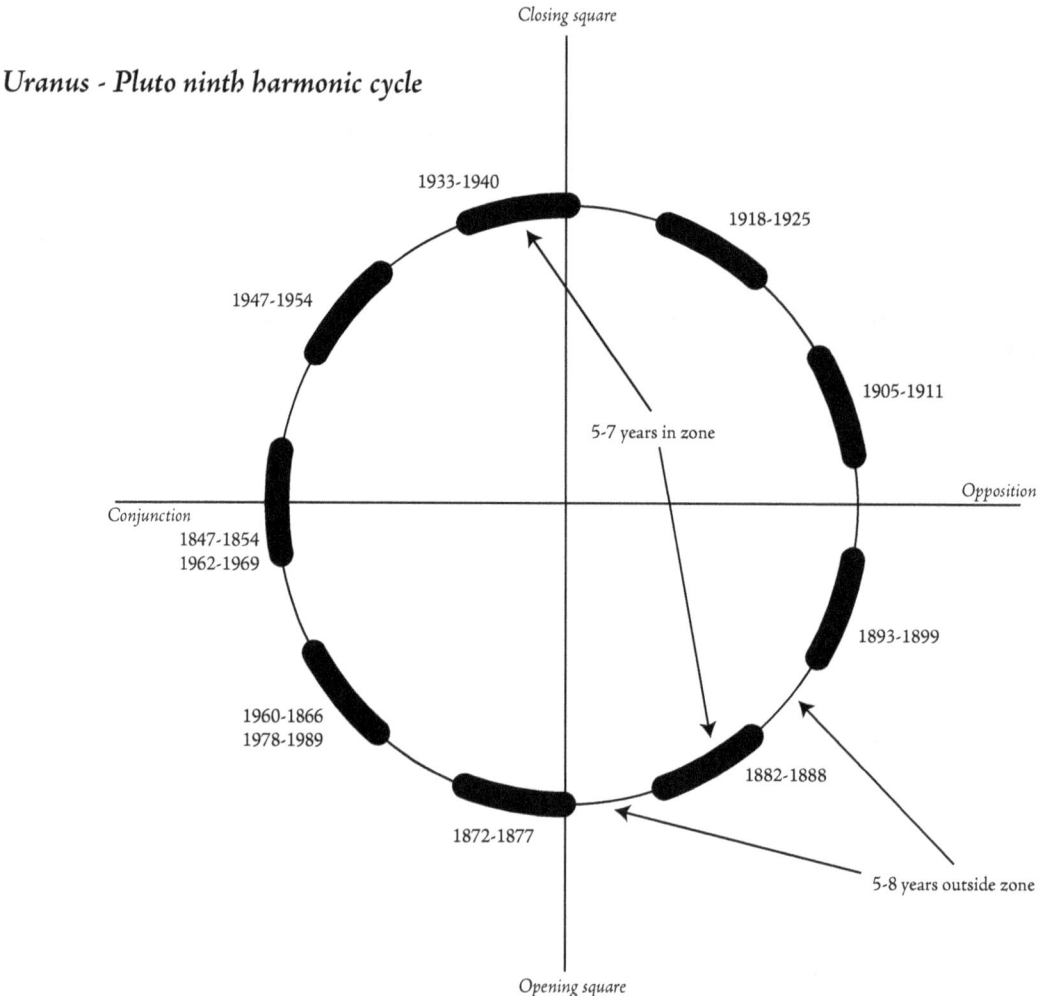

Figure 65. Uranus - Pluto ninth harmonic areas associated with civil unrest events

The bold arcs show the region ten degrees before and after the novile (40°) aspect series. Ranges of years appear next to each arc.

Saturn - Uranus and Civil Unrest Events: 1200-2012

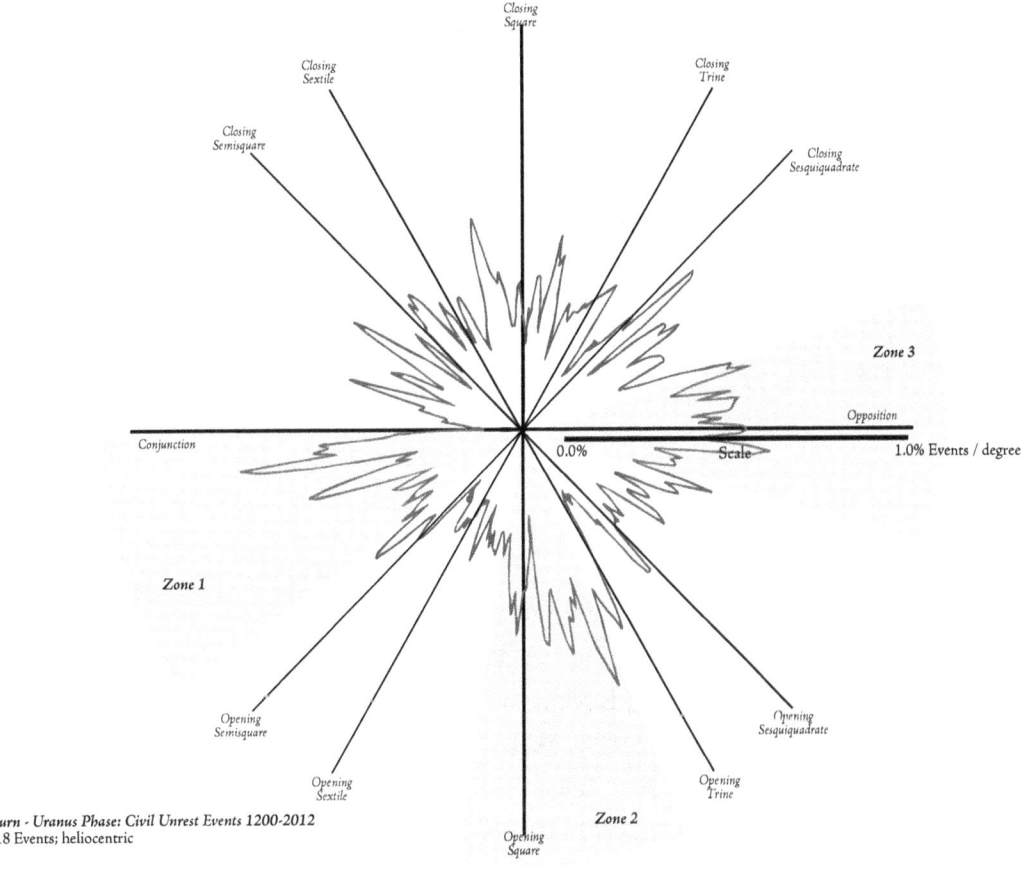

Figure 66. Saturn - Uranus: civil unrest event distribution, heliocentric

The Saturn - Uranus distribution plot shows three zones of strong emphasis at the conjunction, opening square, and opposition:

Zone 1: 0° to 40°

Period beginning	Event
1534	Henry VIII becomes head of Church of England; Anne Boleyn and Thomas More executed
1625	Huguenot rebellion in France
1762	Sikh genocide
1852	Second Burmese War; Taiping Rebellion

Period beginning	Event
1898	Boxer Rebellion
1899	Second Boer War
1945	Chinese Civil War
1989	Communist East European states fall; Tiananmen Square protests

Zone 2: 80° to 110° opening square

Period beginning	Event
1861	Taiping Rebellion; American Civil War
1911	Mexican Revolution

Zone 3: 160° to 190° opposition

Period beginning	Event
1645	English Civil War
1873	American Indian Wars
1917	Russian Revolution
1918	Finnish Civil War
1919	Egyptian Revolution
1920	Mexican Revolution; Polish-Soviet War; Irish War of Independence
1963	American Civil Rights Movement; Vietnam War protests
2008	Taliban insurgency
2011	Arab spring protests

Harmonic analysis

The Saturn - Uranus event distribution graph shows areas of emphasis that align with the fourth harmonic: conjunction, square, and opposition. A fourth harmonic study shows overall emphasis within the first twenty degrees of the harmonic:

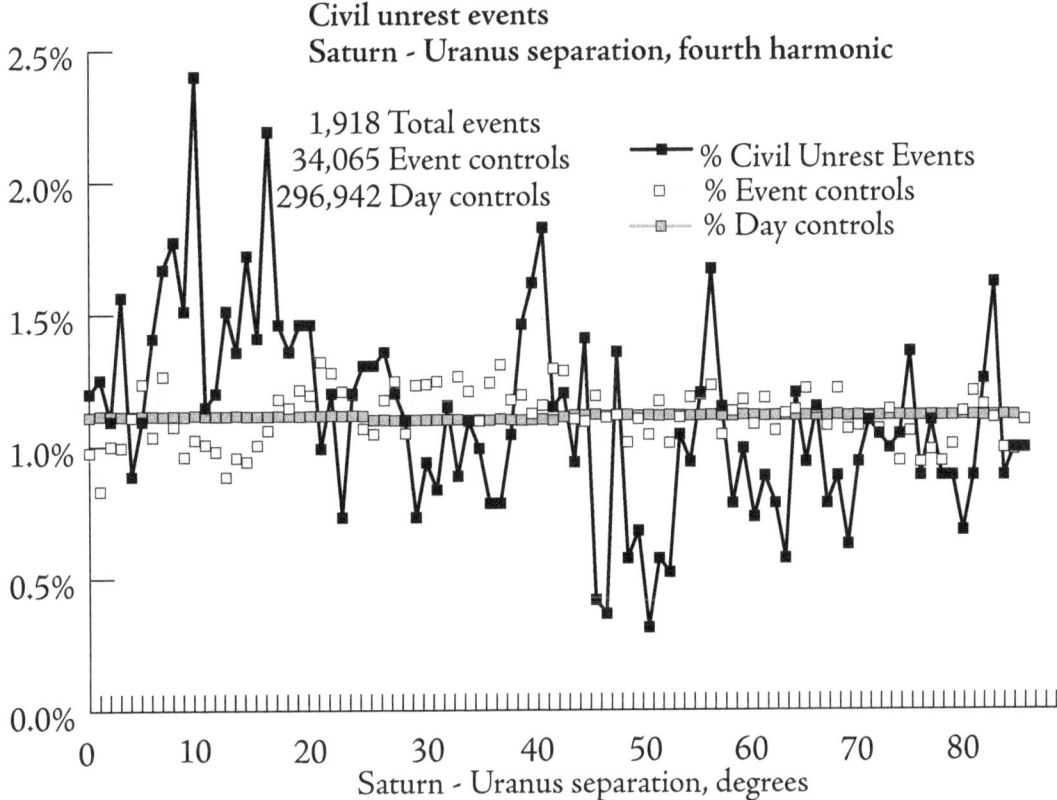

Figure 67. Civil unrest event frequency and Saturn - Uranus separation in the fourth harmonic

The control curves show no areas of strong emphasis.

A t-test clearly shows positive correlation for the interval between 0°-22°:

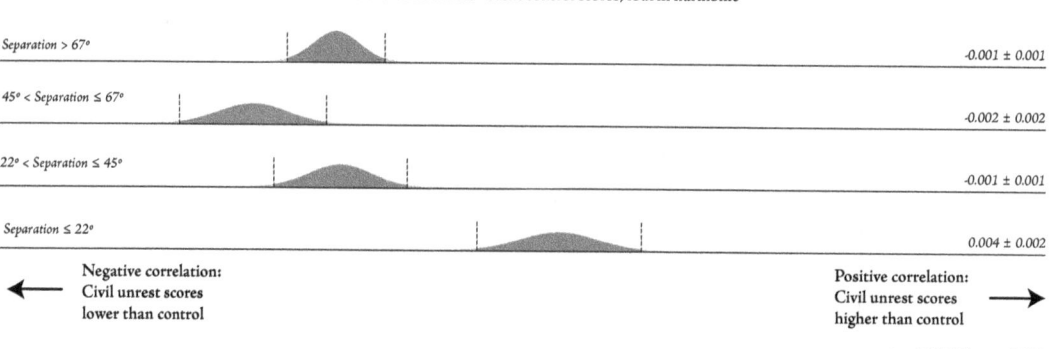

Figure 68. T-test of Saturn - Uranus civil unrest events against event controls, fourth harmonic

The correlation is significant, with a p-value of < 0.001. This table summarizes the results:

	Civil unrest events	Event controls	Day controls
0°-22° (inside interval)	33.1%	24.4%	25.6%
23°-90° (outside interval)	66.9%	75.6%	74.4%

In standard astrological language, civil unrest events are significantly more likely to occur when Saturn and Uranus are separated a fourth harmonic aspect (conjunction, square, opposition) with an orb of 22° after the aspect. Unfortunately this configuration only detects about a third of all civil unrest events, limiting its usefulness.

The Saturn - Uranus fourth harmonic results appear as follows when drawn onto the full circle:

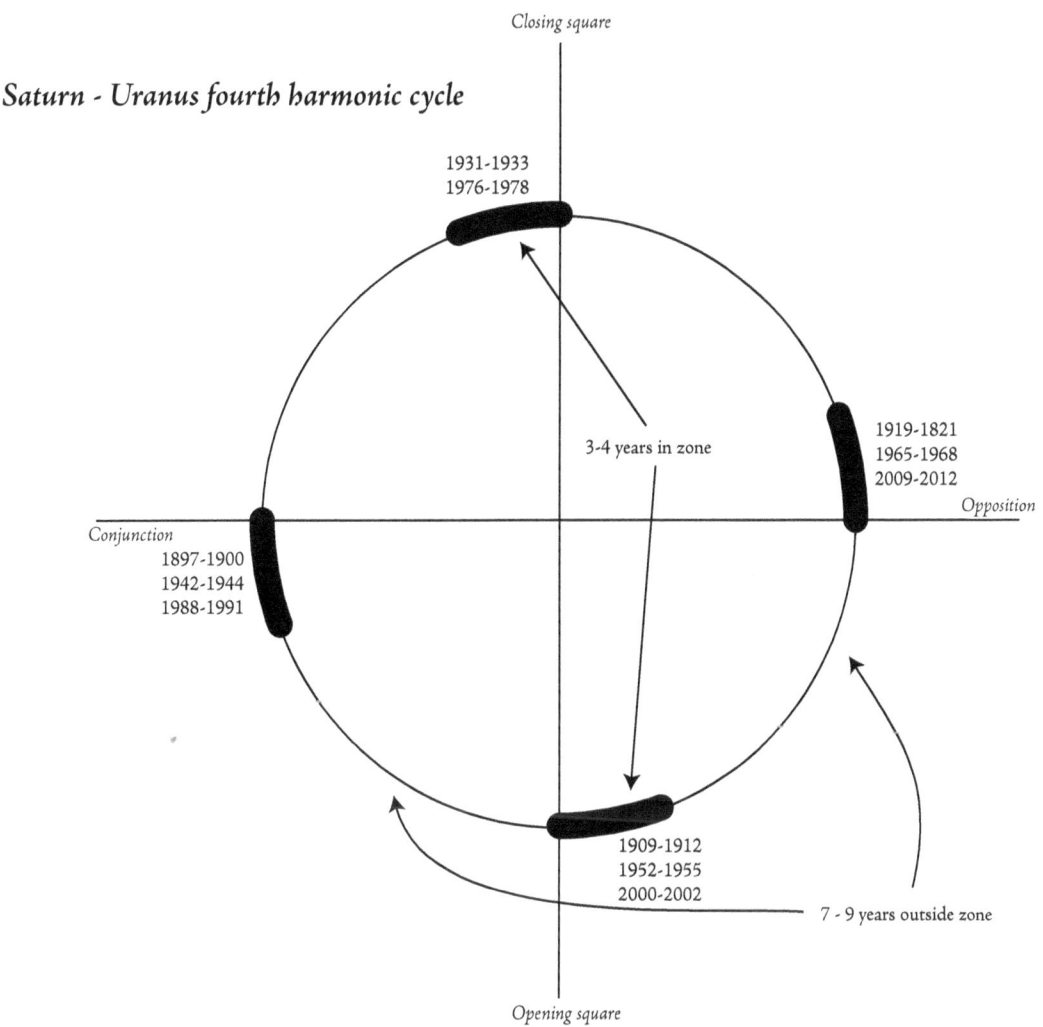

Figure 69. Saturn - Uranus fourth harmonic with civil unrest events

Saturn - Pluto and Civil Unrest events: 1200-2012

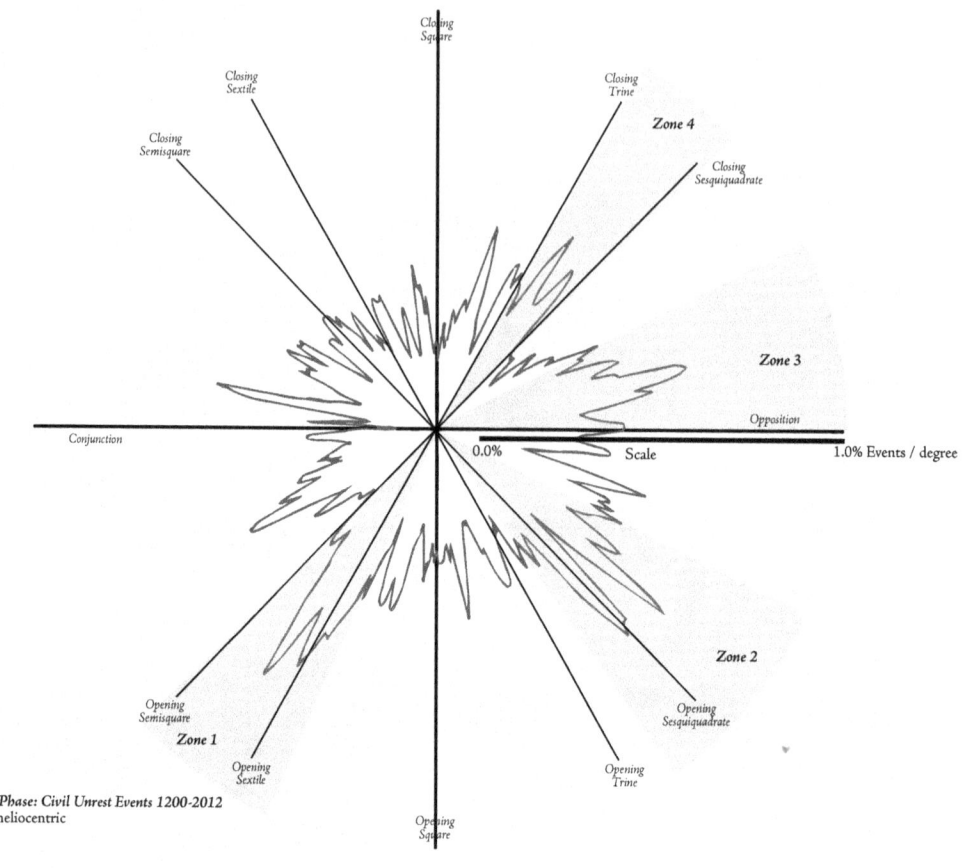

Figure 70. Saturn - Pluto: civil unrest event distribution, heliocentric

The Saturn - Pluto event distribution graph shows four emphasized zones:

Zone 1 50° to 70° (Opening sextile)

Period beginning	Event
1322	Wars between England and Scottish forces under Robert the Bruce
1621	Huguenot rebellions in France
1792	French Revolution
1856	Taiping Rebellion; civil unrest around slavery in US
1919	General strikes in US and Germany

Period beginning	Event
1920	Mexican Revolution
1989	Communist East European states fall; Tiananmen Square riots

Zone 2 (125° to 155°) Opening sesquiquadrate

Period beginning	Event
1629	Huguenot rebellions in France
1798	Irish Rebellion
1861	American Civil War; Russian Empire commits genocide against Circassians
1862	Dakota War between US and Sioux Nation
1894	US strikes; Coxey's Army arrives in Washington DC; Taiping Rebellion
1926	Chinese Civil War; Coup in Portugal; Trotsky pushed out of Soviet Union
1961	Riots in France over Algeria; US Civil Rights Movement

Zone 3 (170° to 210°) Opposition

Period beginning	Event
1464	Battles between Yorkists and Lancastrians
1534	Henry VIII becomes head of Church of England; Anne Boleyn, Thomas More executed
1932	Gandhi active in India; Nazis come to power in Germany
1965	US Civil Rights Movement
1966	Protests against Vietnam War

Zone 4 (225° to 240°) Closing sesquiquadrate and trine

Period beginning	Event
1572	Fourth War of Religion in France
1937	Spanish Civil War
1971	East Pakistan becomes Bangladesh
1972	Uprisings in Northern Ireland

Harmonic analysis

The emphasized zones align somewhat with the semisquare, opposition, and sesquiquadrate aspects. Analyzing the Saturn - Pluto results in the fourth harmonic yields these results:

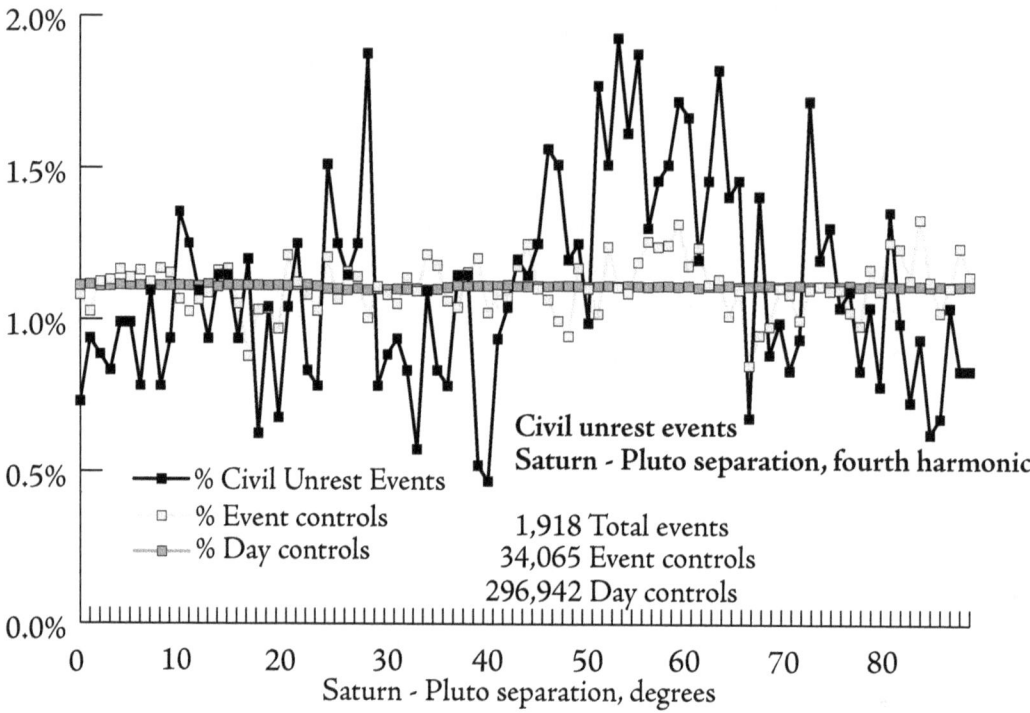

Figure 71. Civil unrest event frequency and Saturn - Pluto separation in the fourth harmonic

The peak in the civil unrest line and after the 45° mark means the semisquare (45°) and sesquiquadrate (135°) aspects are emphasized. The absence of any peaks at 0° and 90° means the conjunction, square, and opposition aspects are not emphasized.

A t-test shows correlation with civil unrest events between 45°-67° in the fourth harmonic:

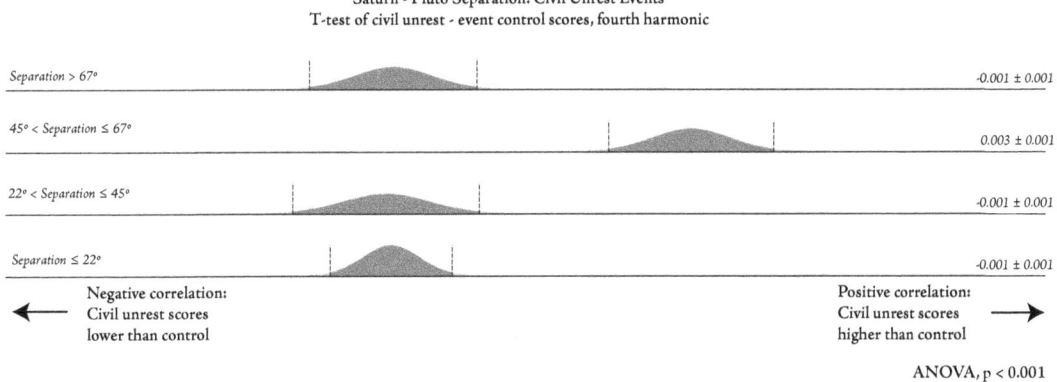

Figure 72. T-test of Saturn - Pluto civil unrest events against event controls, fourth harmonic

This correlation is significant, with a p-value < 0.001. This table summarizes the results:

	Civil unrest events	Event controls	Day controls
45°-67° (inside interval)	33.3%	26.0%	25.6%
0°-44° and 68°-90° (outside interval)	66.7%	74.0%	74.4%

In standard astrological language, civil unrest events are significantly more likely to occur when Saturn and Pluto are separated a semisquare or sesquiquadrate with an orb of 22° after the aspect. Unfortunately this configuration only detects about a third of all civil unrest events, limiting its usefulness. Interestingly, the conjunction, square, and opposition aspects correlate negatively with civil unrest events.

Redrawing the Saturn - Pluto fourth harmonic results onto the full circle looks like this:

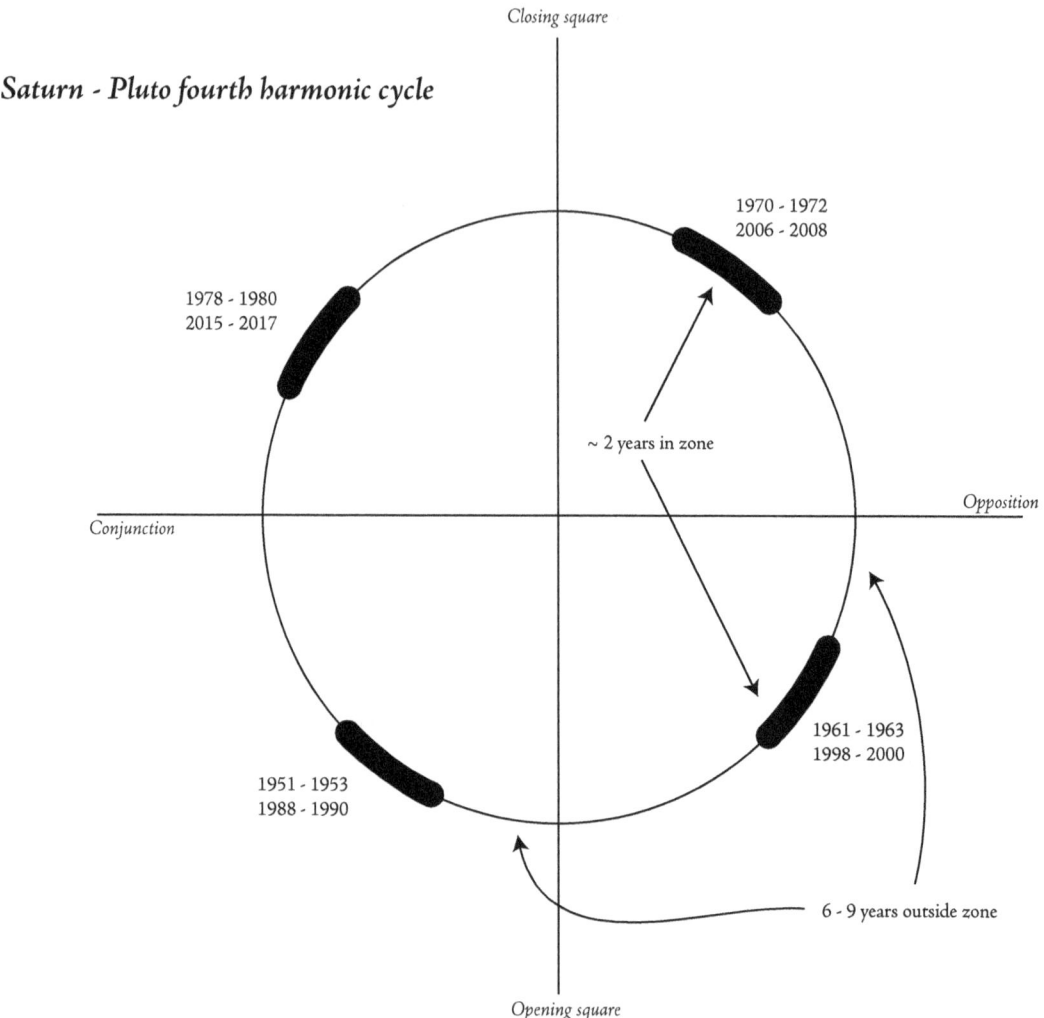

Figure 73. Saturn - Pluto fourth harmonic with civil unrest events

The bold zones are up to 20° after the semisquare and sesquiquadrate aspects. *The conjunction, square, and opposition aspects are not predominant in the results.* However, the large orb on the semisquare and sesquiquadrate aspects effectively includes the opening sextile, the opening quincunx, the closing trine, and the closing semisextile.

10. Regime change events and planetary cycles

There are fewer regime change events than armed conflict and civil unrest events. Most of these events date from 1800 to the present, giving a narrower historical coverage than the armed conflict and civil unrest studies.

Uranus / Pluto and Regime Change Events: 1200-2012

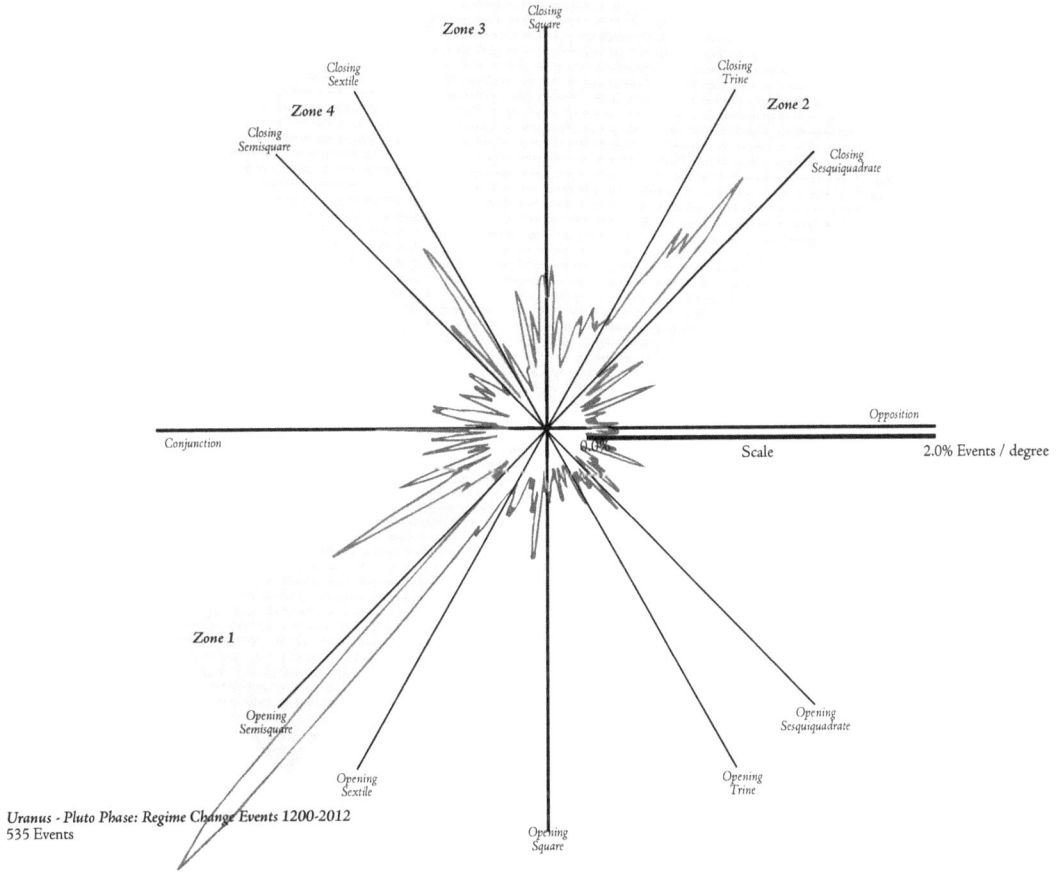

Figure 74. Uranus - Pluto: regime change event distribution, heliocentric

This graph's scale is twice that of other distribution graphs. Regime change events occur most often when Uranus and Pluto have a phase angle near the semisquare, sesquiquadrate, or square.

Zone 1 (30° to 55°) Opening Semisquare

Period beginning	Event
1985	Perestroika in Soviet Union; fall of communist East European states; fall of Soviet Union; Tiananmen Square unrest in China

Zone 2 (215° to 240°) Closing Sesquiquadrate and Trine

Period beginning	Event
1918	Fall of Ottoman Empire; creation of states at end of World War II

Zone 3 (260° to 280°) Closing Square

Period beginning	Event
1819	Bolivar revolution in Colombia
1820	Ecuador independent
1821	Greece independent; Dominican Republic independent
1931	Second Spanish Republic proclaimed
1933	Nazis gain control in Germany
1937	Irish Free State proclaimed

Zone 4 (305° to 320°) Closing Sextile and Semisquare

Period beginning	Event
1836	Mexico independent
1947	People's Republic of China proclaimed; East and West Germany proclaimed; Jordan proclaimed; Pakistan proclaimed; Israel proclaimed

Harmonic analysis

The emphasized zones in Figure 74 align with the semisquare, square, and sesquiquadrate aspects. Analyzing the data in the fourth harmonic gives the following results:

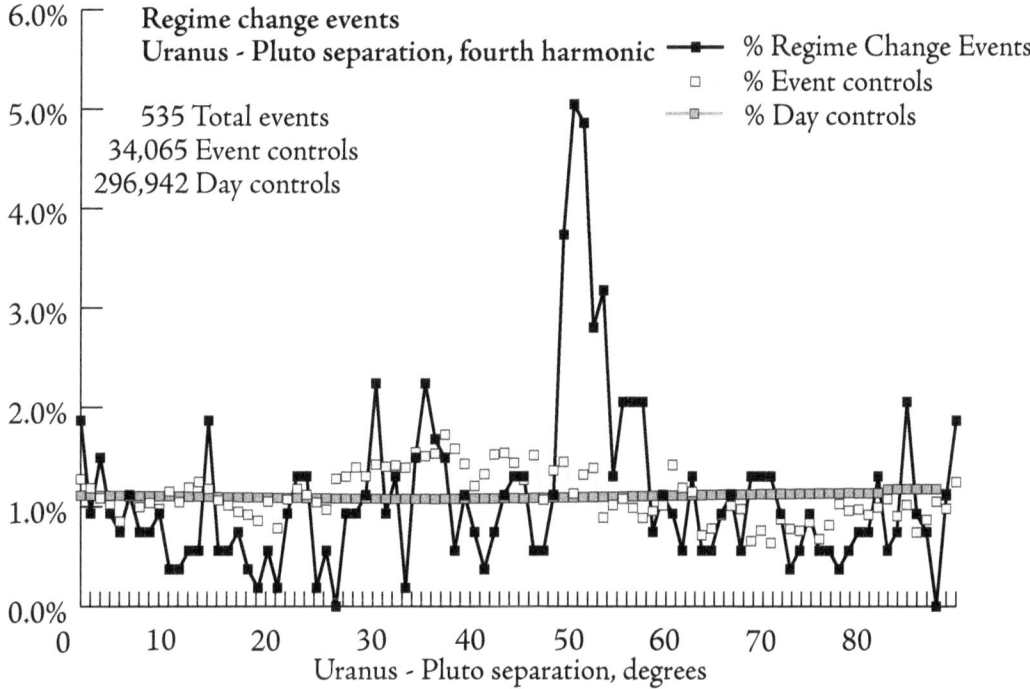

Figure 75. Regime change event frequency and Uranus - Pluto separation in the fourth harmonic

A t-test shows positive correlation in the 45°-67° interval, which matches the peaks near the semisquare and sesquiquadrate aspects in Figure 74. There is no statistical significance for correlation for conjunction, square, or opposition aspects.

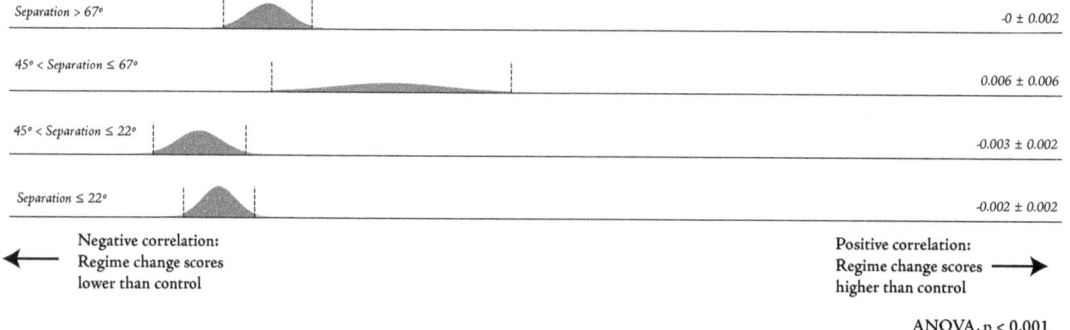

Figure 76. T-test of Uranus - Pluto regime change events against event controls, fourth harmonic

This correlation is significant, with a p-value < 0.001. The correlation improves slightly by using an interval of 45°-60° rather than 45°-67°. This table summarizes the results:

	Regime change events	Event controls	Day controls
45°-60° (inside interval)	32.5%	17.4%	16.5%
0°-44° and 61°-90° (outside interval)	67.5%	82.6%	83.5%

In standard astrological language, regime change events are significantly more likely to occur when Uranus and Pluto are separated a semisquare or sesquiquadrate with an orb of 15° after the aspect. Unfortunately this configuration only detects about a third of all regime change unrest events, limiting its usefulness. Interestingly, the conjunction, square, and opposition aspects correlate negatively with regime change events.

Drawing the results from the Uranus - Pluto fourth harmonic analysis onto the full circle looks like this:

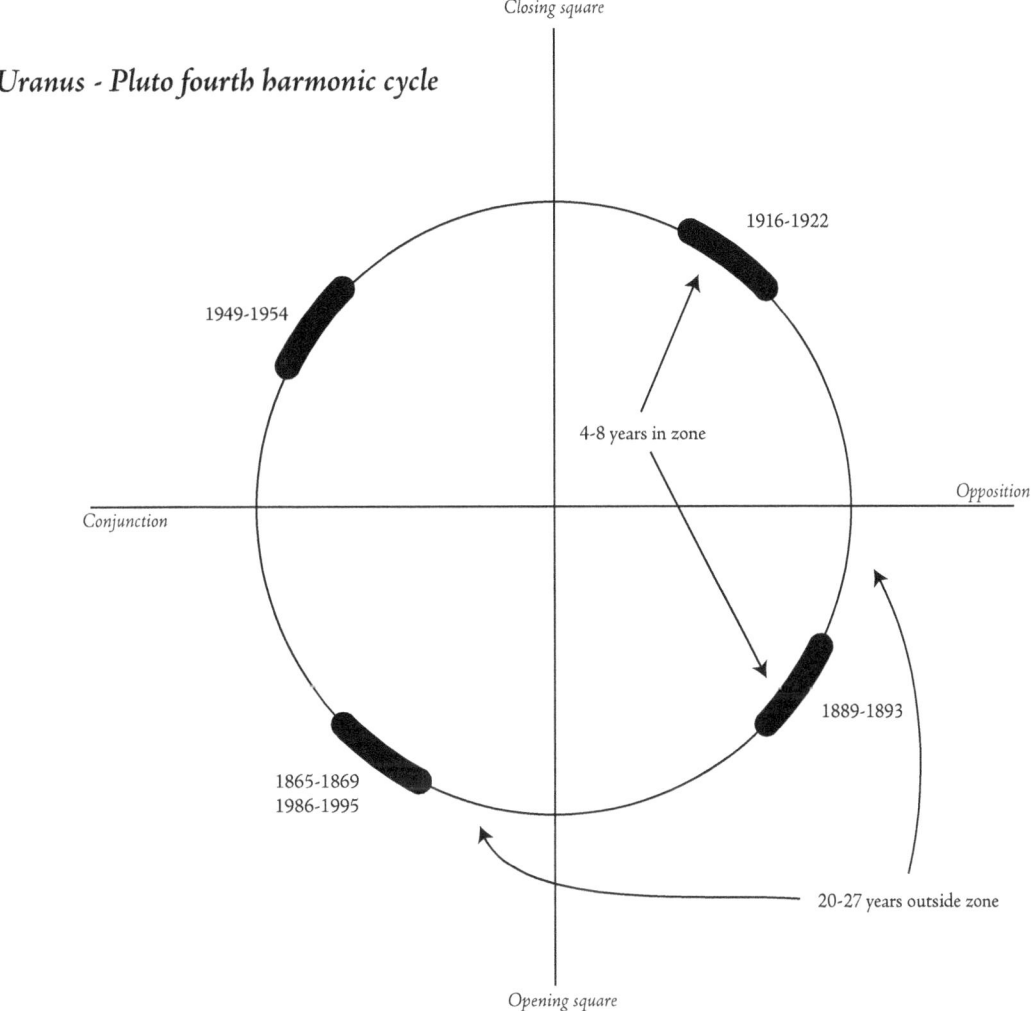

Figure 77. Uranus - Pluto fourth harmonic areas associated with regime change events

The bold arcs show the region up to fifteen degrees after the semisquare and sesquiquadrate. Ranges of years appear next to each arc.

Saturn - Uranus and Regime Change Events: 1200-2012

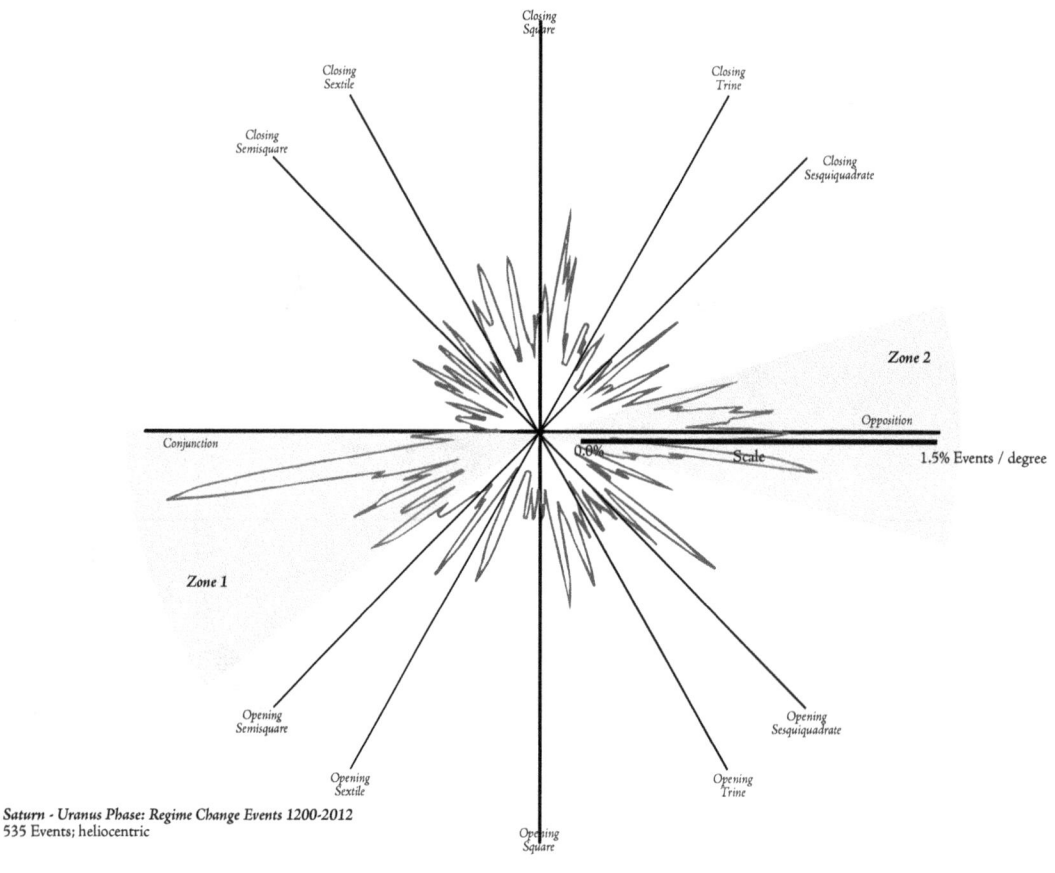

Figure 78. Saturn - Uranus: regime change event distribution, heliocentric

The distribution graph shows two strongly accented areas at the conjunction and the opposition:

Zone 1 0° to 30° (conjunction)

Period beginning	Event
1806	End of Holy Roman Empire
1809	Ecuador and Colombia independent
1854	Orange Free State independent
1901	Queen Victoria dies

Period beginning	Event
1989	Fall of communist East European states; German reunification; fall of Soviet Union
1991	End of apartheid in South Africa

Zone 2 170° to 190° (opposition)

Period beginning	Event
1558	Queen Elizabeth I crowned
1649	Death of Charles I of England; Commonwealth of England replaces monarchy
1829	Greece independent
1917	Russian Revolution; Weimar Constitution in Germany; Afghanistan independent; Poland, Czechoslovakia, Hungary, Latvia independent; End of Ottoman Empire; Turkey proclaimed
1965	Coup in Democratic Republic of the Congo; Coup in Nigeria; Ba'ath party takes control in Syria; Lesotho independent
2011	Arab Spring uprisings

Harmonic analysis

Both emphasized zones cluster along the second harmonic: the conjunction and opposition. There is some additional emphasis near the closing square. Analyzing the data in the fourth harmonic yields this result:

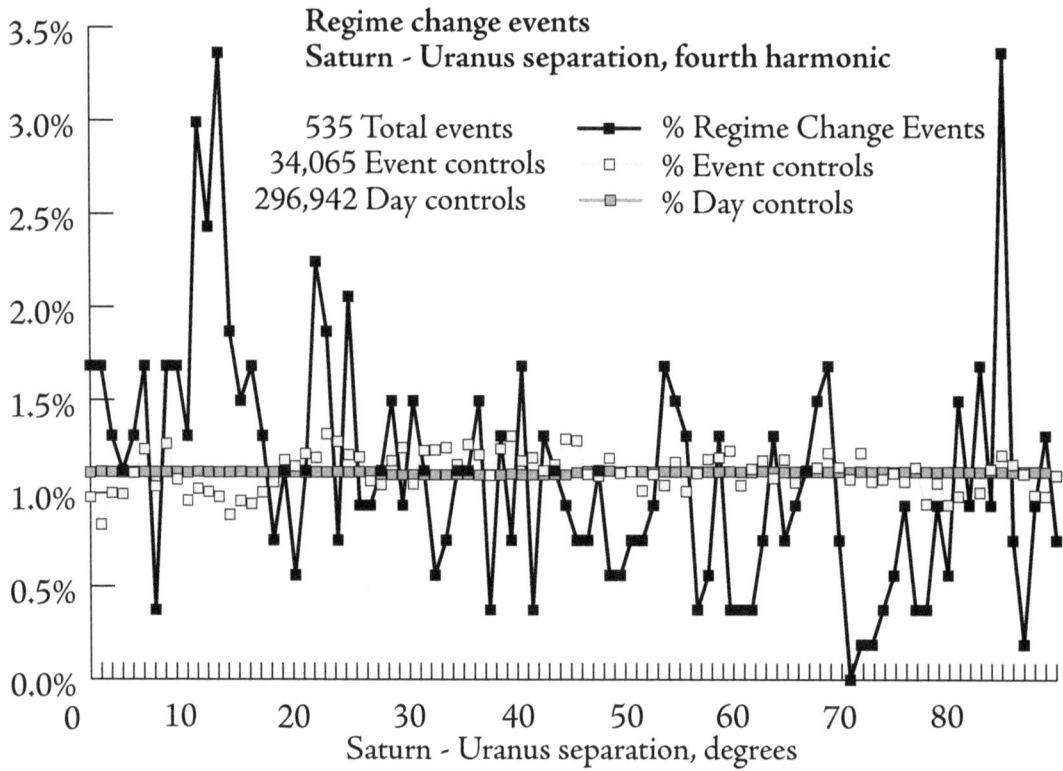

Figure 79. Regime change event frequency and Saturn - Uranus separation in the fourth harmonic

A t-test shows positive correlation in the 0°-22° interval:

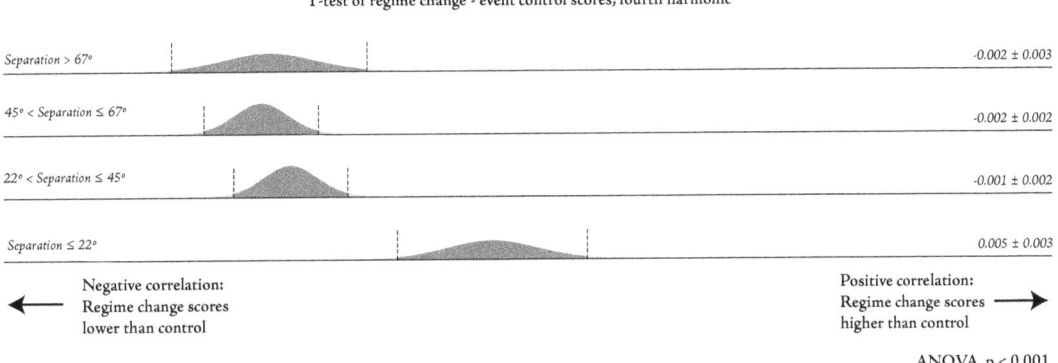

Figure 80. T-test of Saturn - Uranus regime change events against event controls, fourth harmonic

Adding the interval from 80°-90° improves correlation, with a p-value < 0.001. This table summarizes the results:

	Regime change events	Event controls	Day controls
0°-22° and 80°-90° (inside interval)	49.0%	35.0%	36.8%
23°-80° (outside interval)	51.0%	65.0%	63.2%

In standard astrological language, regime change events are significantly more likely to occur when Saturn and Uranus are separated a conjunction, square, or opposition with an orb of 22° after the aspect and 10° before the aspect.

Drawing the results of the Saturn - Uranus fourth harmonic analysis onto the full circle appears as follows:

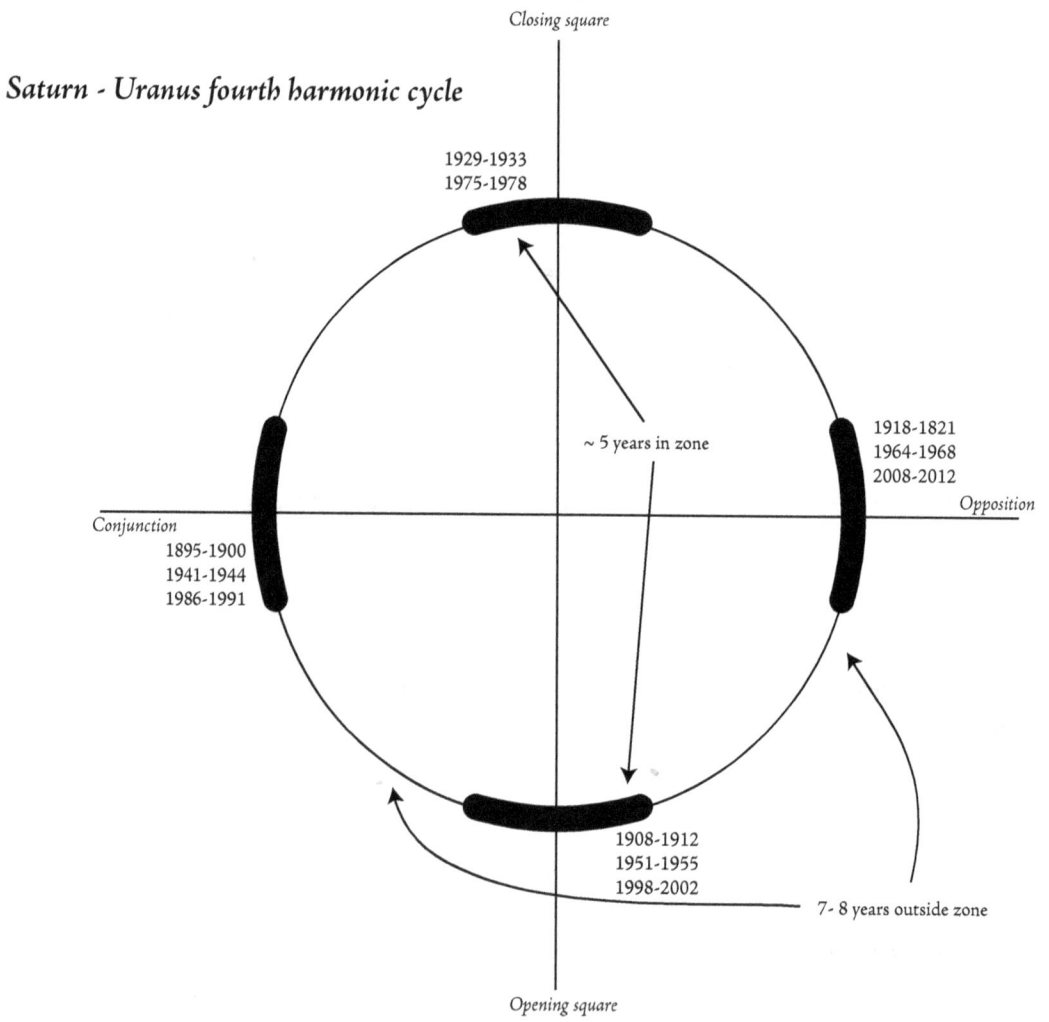

Figure 81. Saturn - Uranus fourth harmonic areas associated with regime change events

The bold arcs show the region roughly twenty degrees either side of the conjunction, square, and opposition. Ranges of years appear next to each arc.

Saturn - Pluto and Regime Change events: 1200-2012

Analyzing the Saturn - Pluto phase angle distribution for regime change events produces this graph:

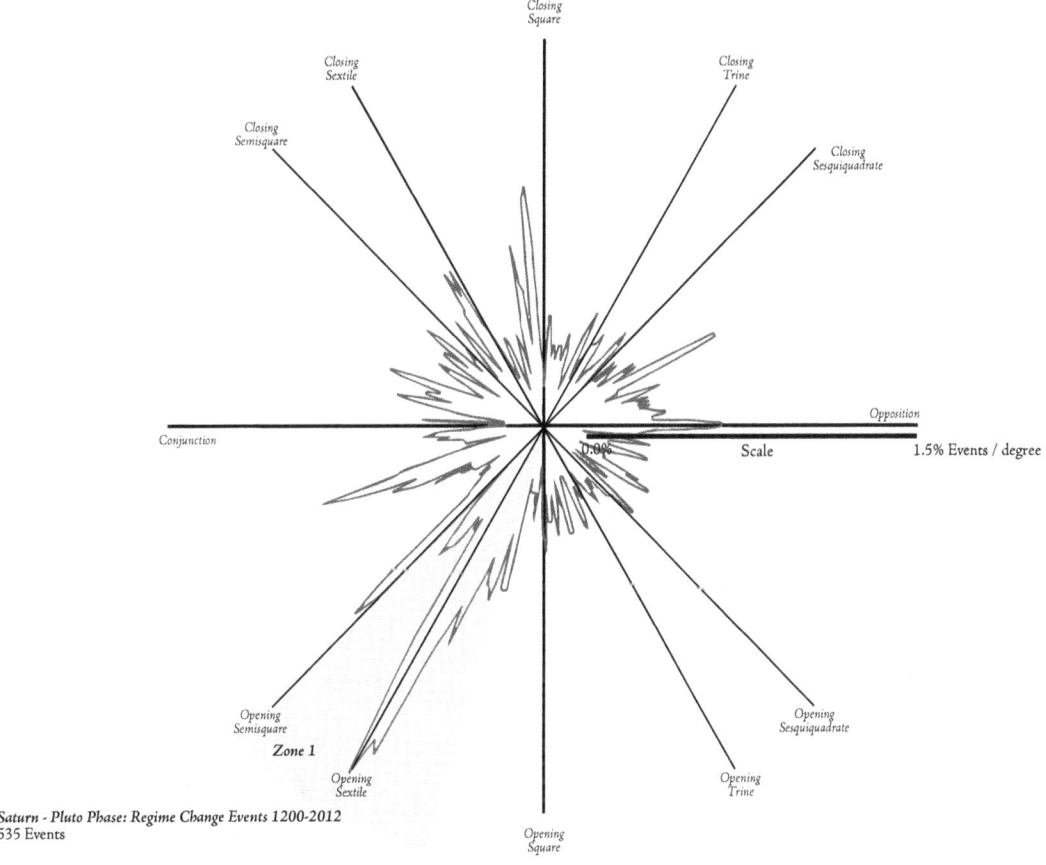

Figure 82. Saturn - Pluto: regime change event distribution, heliocentric

The event distribution graph shows an unusual single strongly emphasized zone around the opening semisquare and sextile aspects. This grouping encompasses two of the most significant periods of government reorganization in the Twentieth Century.

Zone 1 45° to 75° (Opening semisquare and sextile)

Period beginning	Event
1918	Ottoman Empire falls; European states proclaimed after World War II

Period beginning	Event
1989	Fall of communist Eastern European states; Fall of Soviet Union

Harmonic analysis

The emphasized zone aligns somewhat with the quintile (72°) aspect. Analyzing the data in the related fifth harmonic gives this result:

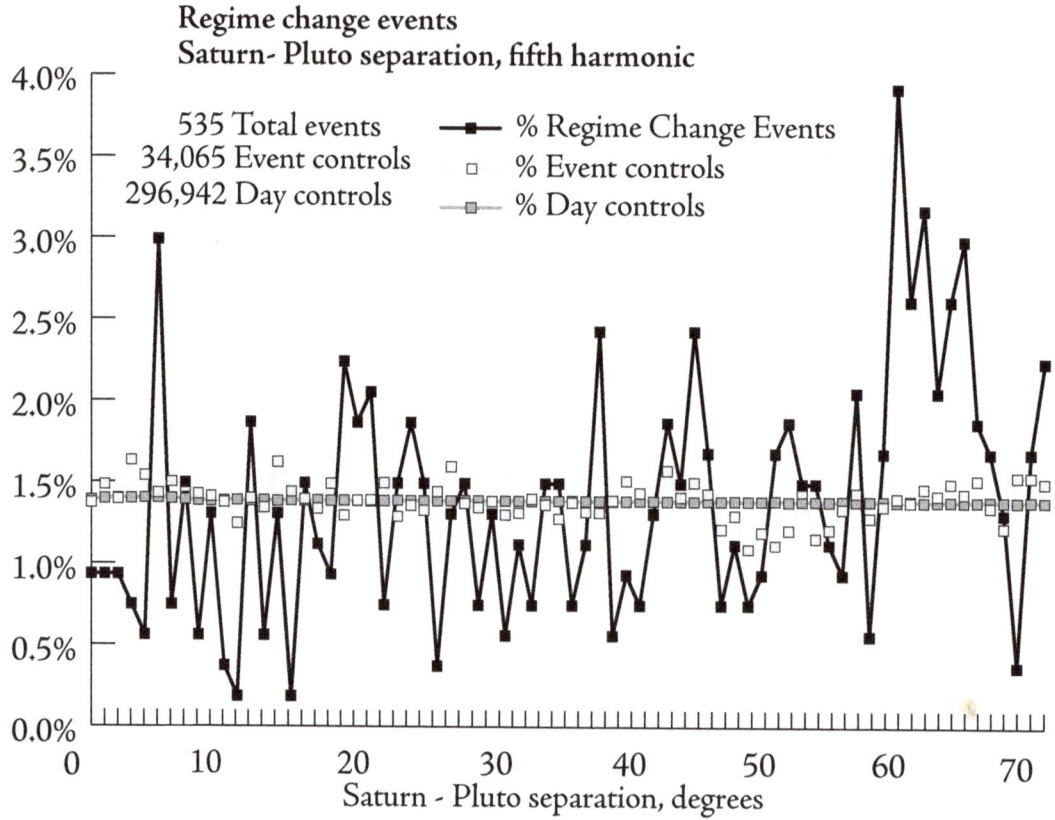

Figure 83. Regime change event frequency and Saturn - Pluto separation in the fifth harmonic

A t-test reveals a somewhat positive correlation:

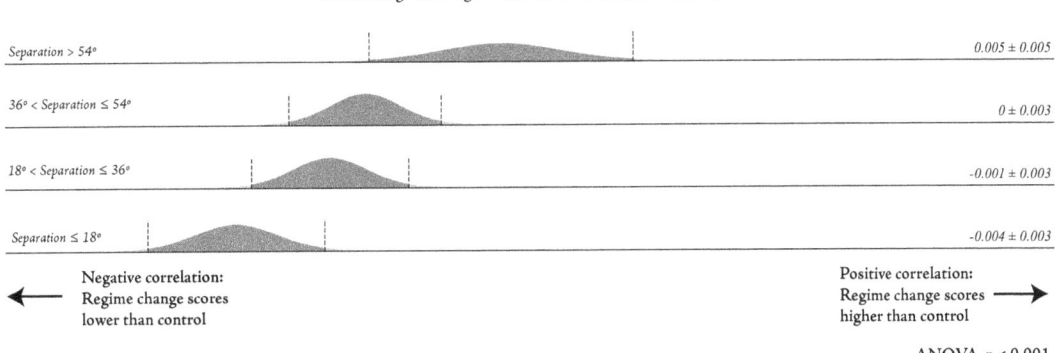

Figure 84. T-test of Saturn - Pluto regime change events against event controls, fifth harmonic

This correlation is significant, with a p-value < 0.001; adjusting the interval to 59°-72° improves the correlation. This table summarizes the results:

	Regime change events	Event controls	Day controls
59°-72° (inside interval)	28.0%	18.7%	18.1%
0°-58° (outside interval)	72.0%	81.3%	81.9%

In standard astrological language, regime change events are more likely to occur when Saturn and Pluto are separated a quintile series aspect (0°, 72°, 144°, 288°) with an orb of 12° before the aspect. Unfortunately this configuration detects less than 30% of all regime change events, limiting its usefulness.

11. US Economic downturns and planetary cycles

Deriving the data

The yearly summary event pages in Wikipedia contain mostly single events for major financial crashes. Usually these events began an economic downturn that may have lasted for many months. After unsuccessfully attempting to correlate planetary configurations with the sparse economic event data, I began to seek more comprehensive data about financial downturns, including information about the downturn's length.

The National Bureau of Economic Research (NBER) published a list of business cycle contractions in the US. A comprehensive article in Wikipedia enhances this list with more detailed dates for the downturns and provides a larger coverage period[61].

This section presents the results obtained by computing planetary positions for each day within a downturn cycle. A downturn cycle begins with date of the economic peak and ends with the date of the following economic trough. Unlike historical events, which always occur on a single day, each downturn cycle may last for months. Including results for each day during a downturn examines planetary cycles over the entire length of the downturn cycle. From the daily planetary positions the study computes the planetary phase information and creates graphs and statistics identical to those presented earlier for historical events.

There are issues with this approach:

- *The resulting planetary distribution graphs are 'blocky'*. This results from long runs of consecutive dates used in the analyses, rather than individual dates used in the prior historical studies.

- Unlike the historical data presented so far, *this study covers a relatively short period of time from 1793 to 2009*. This represents less than two complete Uranus / Pluto planetary cycles, making for poorer trend analysis for this very long cycle.

Controls

The economic studies use a different set of controls. Each downturn cycle consists of a consecutive number of days, from the economic peak to the subsequent trough. The control data consists of the remaining days from 1793 through 2012: these are the periods of an economic trough to a subsequent peak.

Uranus - Pluto US economic downturns: 1793-2009

Here is the graph of the heliocentric Uranus - Pluto phase angle distribution for the economic downturn days.

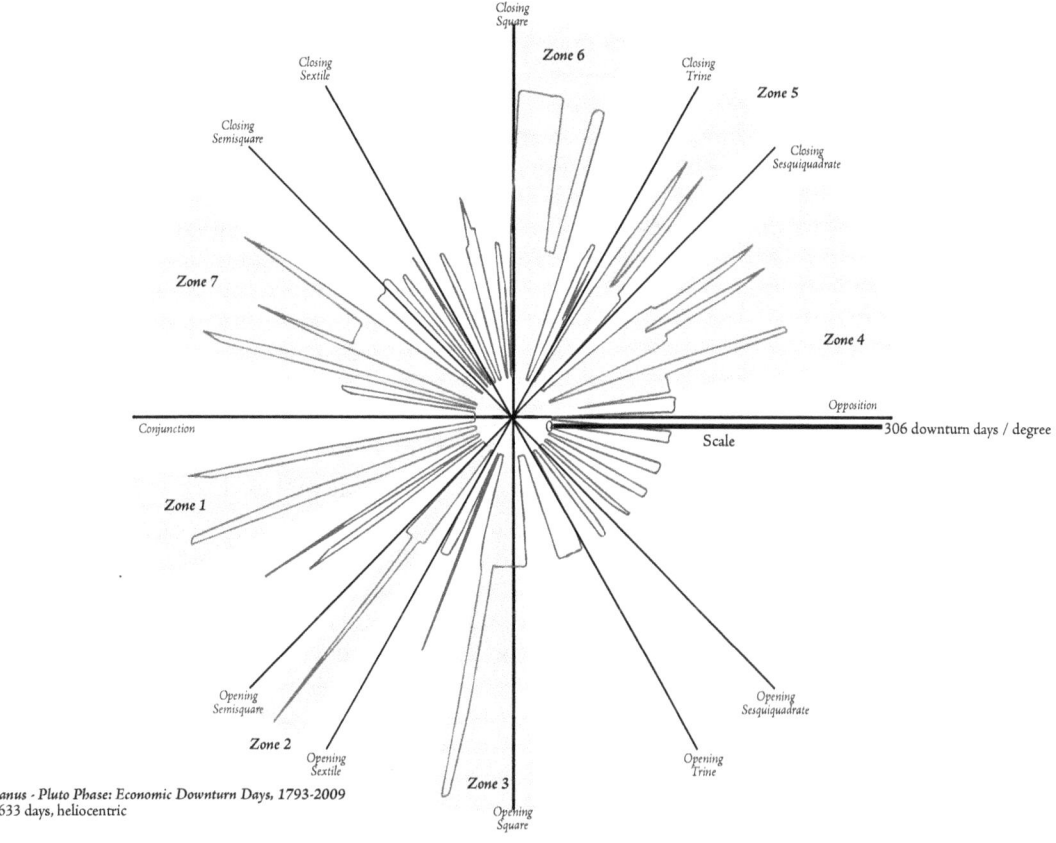

Figure 85. Uranus - Pluto: US economic downturn days distribution, heliocentric

Note the 'blocky' appearance of the heliocentric graph. The runs of consecutive days in each economic downturn cycle produce these zones of high event frequency. All these graphs depict raw, unsmoothed data.

The heliocentric figure has seven zones of emphasis:

Zone	Degree range	Description
1	8° - 24°	1853-54 Recession, Recession of 1969-70
2	45° - 55°	1865-67 Recession, Early 1990s Recession

Zone	Degree range	Description
3	75° - 95°	Panic of 1873 and Long Depression, Great Recession of 2008
4	180° - 200°	Panic of 1797, 1902-04 Recession, Panic of 1907
5	225° - 240°	Depression of 1807, Post World War I Recession, Depression of 1920-21
6	250° - 270°	1815-21 Depression, 1926-27 Recession, Great Depression
7	325° - 350°	Late 1839-43 Recession, Recession of 1953, Recession of 1958

Harmonic analysis

The planetary distribution graph is complex, with strong emphases between 0°-90° and 180°-270°. Analyzing the distribution in the second harmonic makes this emphasis clear:

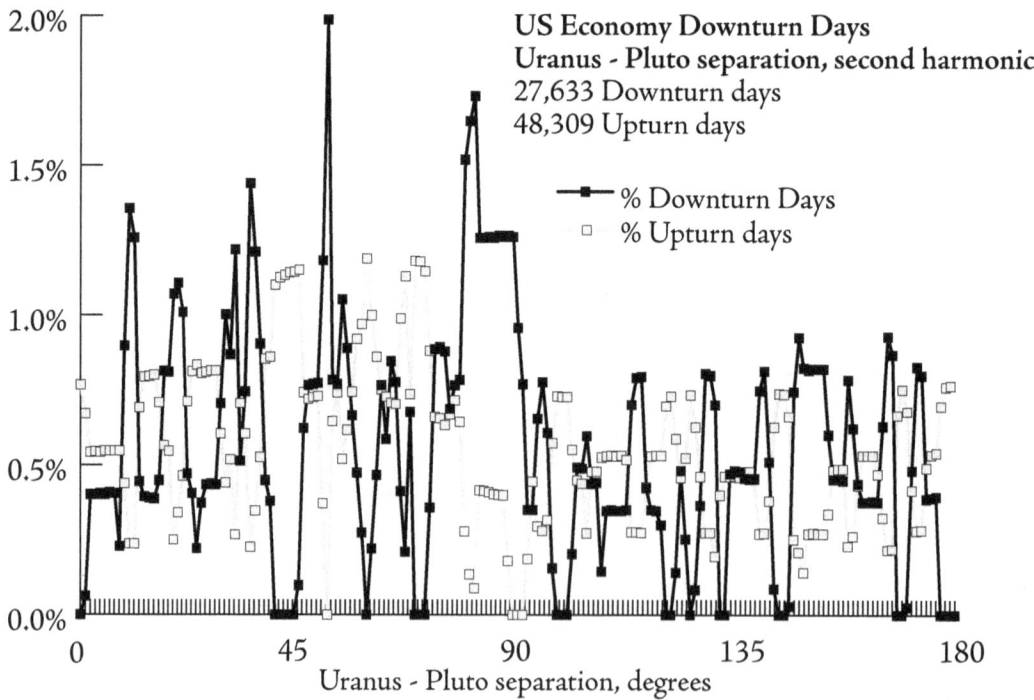

Figure 86. Economic downturn day frequency and Uranus - Pluto separation in the second harmonic

There are substantial repeating peaks throughout in the first half of the graph. The first half of the graph represents the emphasized zones of 0°-90° and 180°-270°.

Analyzing the distribution in the twelfth harmonic gives this striking result:

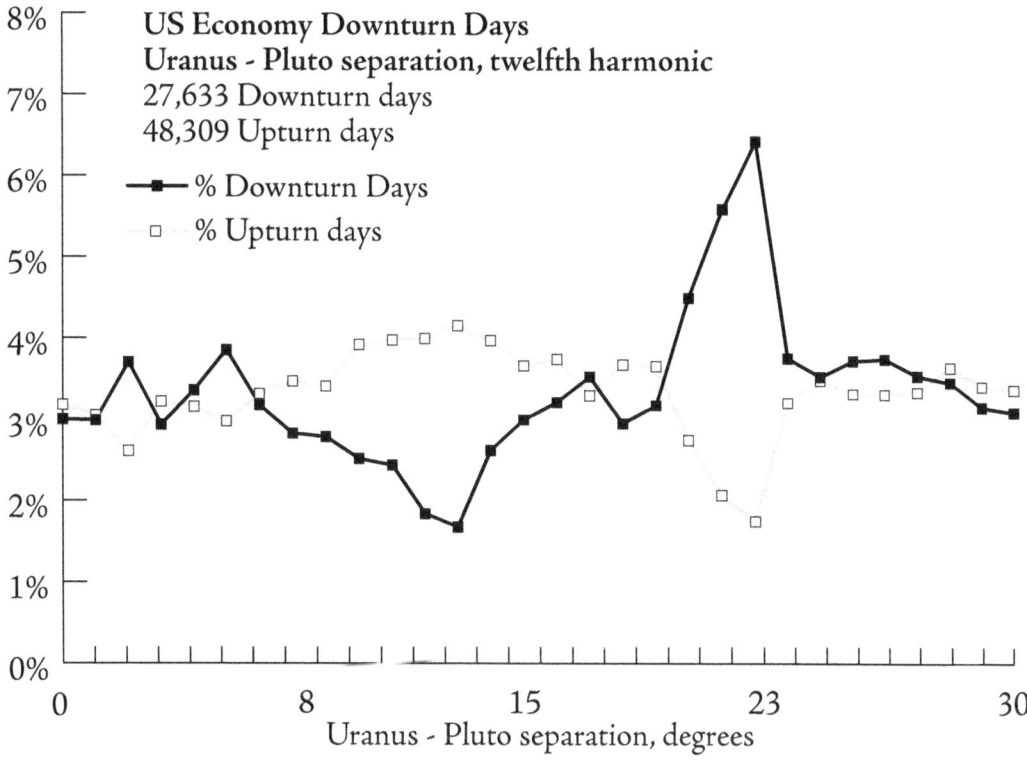

Figure 87. US economic downturn day frequency and Uranus - Pluto separation in the twelfth harmonic

The peak from 19°-26° corresponds to no known astrological aspect. This result is confirmed by a t-test:

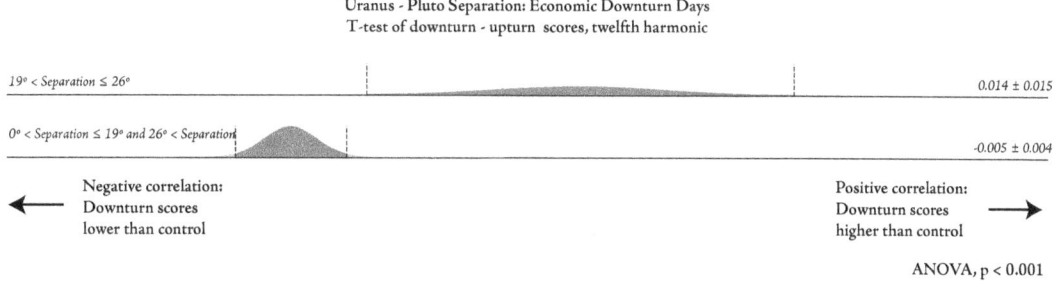

Figure 88. T-test of Uranus - Pluto downturn days against upturn days, twelfth harmonic by interval

This correlation is significant, with a p-value < 0.001.

This table summarizes the results of the twelfth harmonic analysis:

	Downturn days	Upturn days
19°-26° (inside interval)	54.1%	44.2%
0°-18° and 27°-30° (outside interval)	45.9%	55.8%

Combining the second and twelfth harmonics improves the correlation:

	Downturn days	Upturn days
19°-26° (from 0°-90° in 2nd harmonic, inside interval)	37.0%	23.9%
0°-18° and 27°-30° (outside interval)	63.0%	76.8%

While combining the second and twelfth harmonics reduces the number of downturn days selected (37% *versus* 54%), it also reduces the number of upturn days misidentified as potential downturn days (24% *versus* 44%).

In standard astrological language, US economic downturn days are more likely to occur when Uranus and Pluto are separated a twelfth harmonic aspect (conjunction, semisextile, sextile, square, trine, quincunx, opposition), where the angle is between 19° and 26° after the aspect. This corresponds to no traditional astrological aspect.

Drawing the results of the harmonic analysis onto the full circle looks like this:

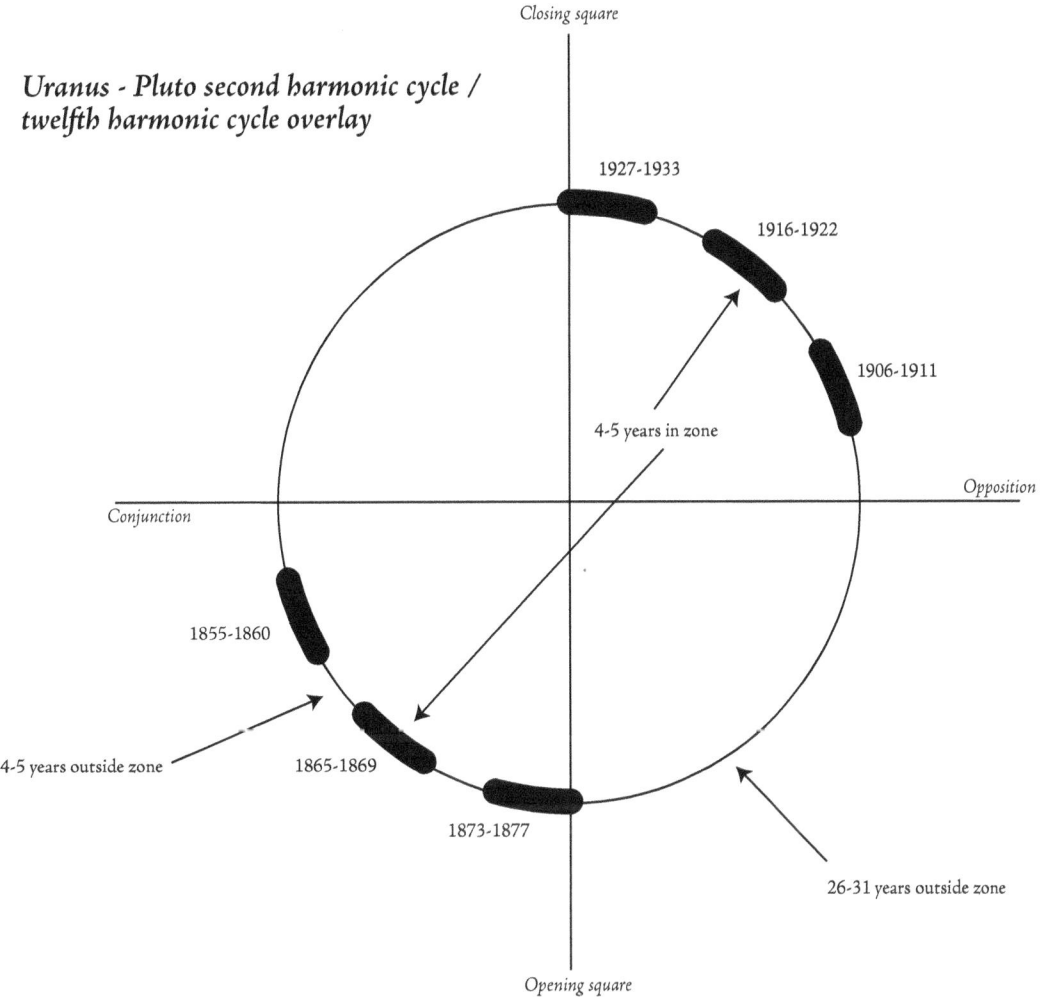

Figure 89. Uranus - Pluto second harmonic areas with twelfth harmonic overlay; areas associated with economic downturn days

The twelfth harmonic areas repeat every 30° for the areas between the conjunction and the opening square and between the opposition and the closing square. These areas correspond to 15° before the opening semisextile (30°), sextile (60°), and square (90°) aspects, and the closing quincunx (150°), trine (120°), and square (90°) aspects. There are periods of increased occurrence every four to five years beginning with the conjunction and repeating for three cycles. Then there is a lengthy quiescent period followed by another cycle of three increased periods. *Not all the twelfth harmonic aspects have equal strength.* The conjunction,

145

opposition, opening trine and quincunx, and the closing sextile and semisextile have reduced emphasis in the results.

Saturn - Uranus: US economic downturns 1793-2009

Examining the Saturn - Uranus heliocentric phase angle distribution for economic downturn days gives the following result:

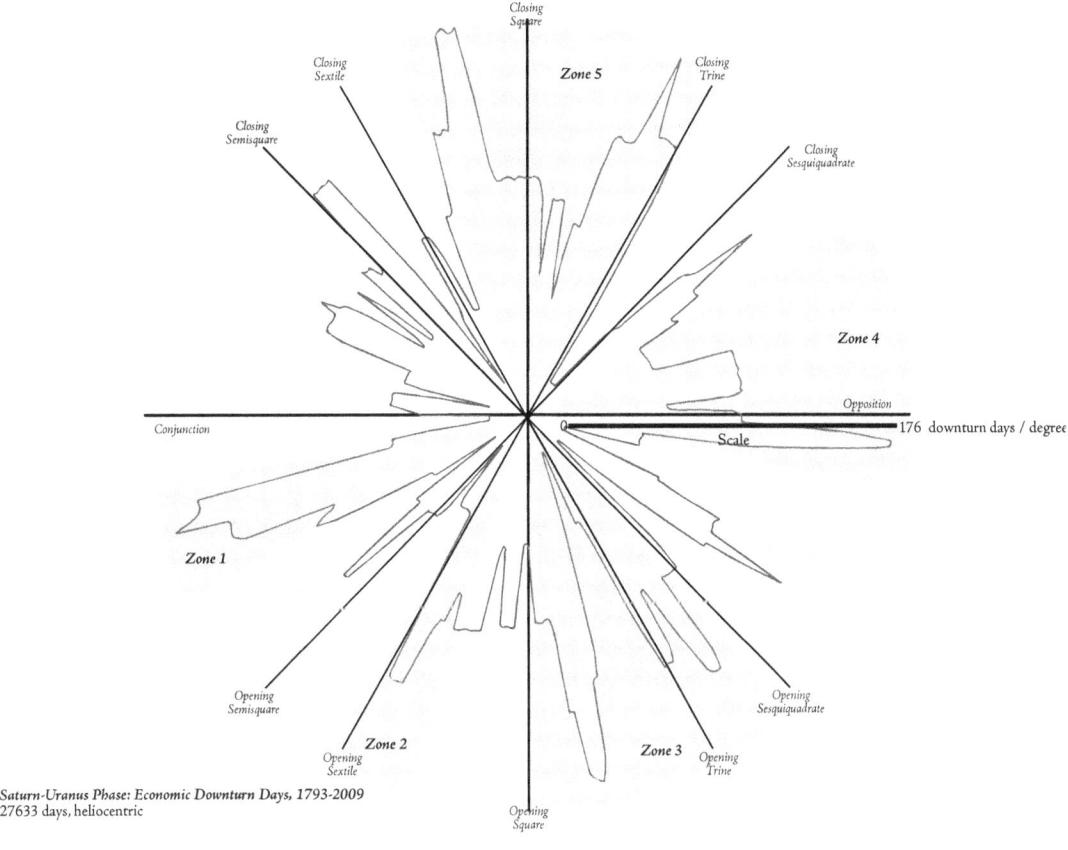

Figure 90. Saturn - Uranus: US economic downturn days distribution, heliocentric

Five zones of high emphasis appear on the diagram:

Zone	Degree range	Description
1	10° - 30°	Depression of 1807, 1853-54 recession, 1899-1900 recession, Recession of 1945, Recession of 1990-91
2	60° - 80°	1815-21 Depression, Panic of 1857, Panic of 1907, Recession of 1949

Zone	Degree range	Description
3	90° - 135°	1815-21 Depression, 1822-23 recession, 1865-67 recession, Panic of 1910-11, Recession of 1913-14, Recession of 1953, Recession of 1958, Dot-com crash of 2001
4	165° - 200°	1828-29 recession, Panic of 1873 and Long Depression, Post World War I-recession, Depression of 1920-21, Great Recession of 2008
5	235° - 295°	Panic of 1797, 1836-38 recession, late 1839-1843 recession, 1882-85 recession, 1926-27 recession, Great Depression, 1973-75 Recession

Harmonic analysis

The phase angle distribution graph has an interesting repetitive cycle that becomes much more obvious when computed in the eighth harmonic:

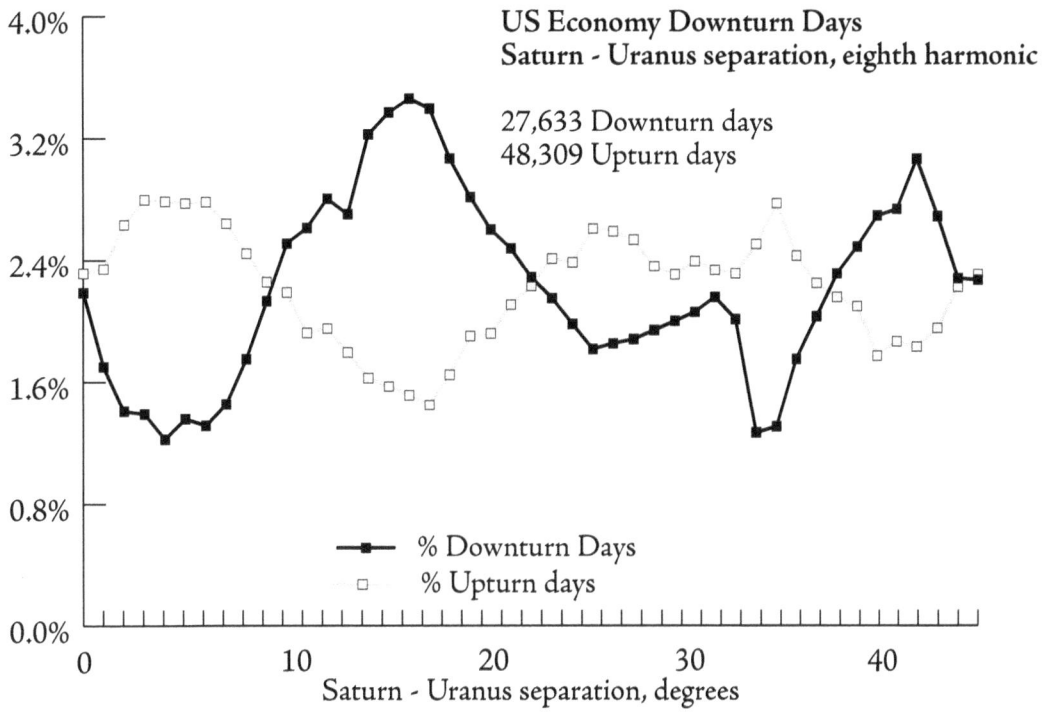

Figure 91. US economic downturn day frequency and Saturn - Uranus separation in the eighth harmonic

A t-test confirms the correlation:

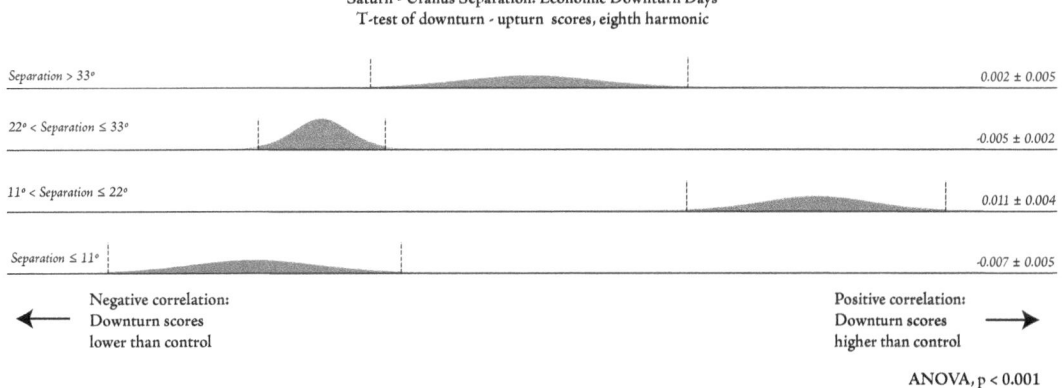

Figure 92. T-test of Saturn - Uranus downturn days against upturn days, eighth harmonic by interval

The test is significant, showing positive correlation for the 11°-22° and the 33°-45° bands. Refining these intervals slightly gives the following summary results:

	Downturn days	Upturn days
9°-25° and 35°-45° (inside interval)	69.7%	54.4%
0°-8° and 26°-34° (outside interval)	30.3%	45.6%

This finding is unlike any standard astrological aspect. While the pattern repeats every 45°, the waveform does not match that of any known aspect.

The Saturn - Uranus eighth harmonic cycle appears like this when drawn on the full circle:

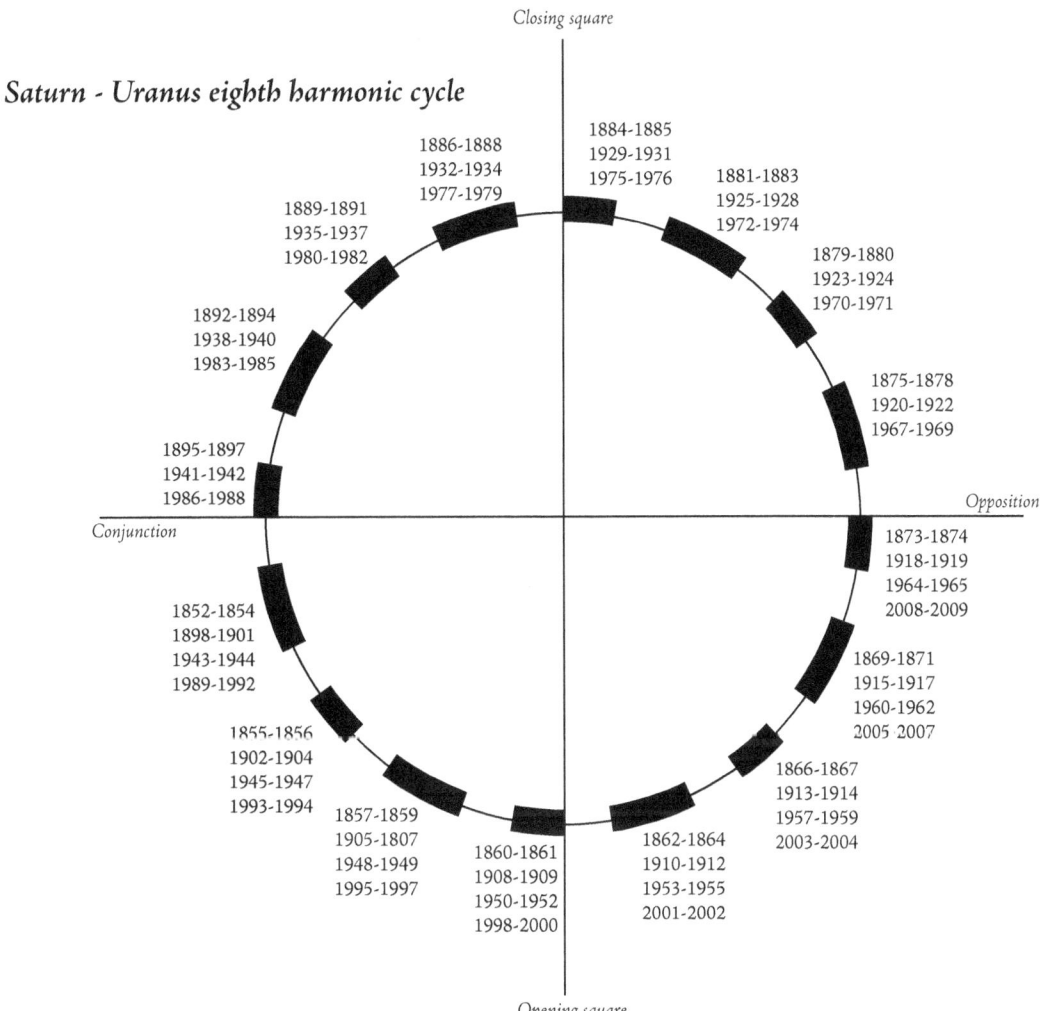

Figure 93. Saturn - Uranus eighth harmonic areas associated with economic downturn days

This unique pattern has eight repetitions of two highlighted intervals each. The figure above indicates the rough length of each interval in years; because these intervals are short, the actual length of the interval is less than the range of years indicated.

Saturn - Pluto US economic downturns: 1793-2009

Here is the distribution of Saturn - Pluto phase angles for economic downturn days:

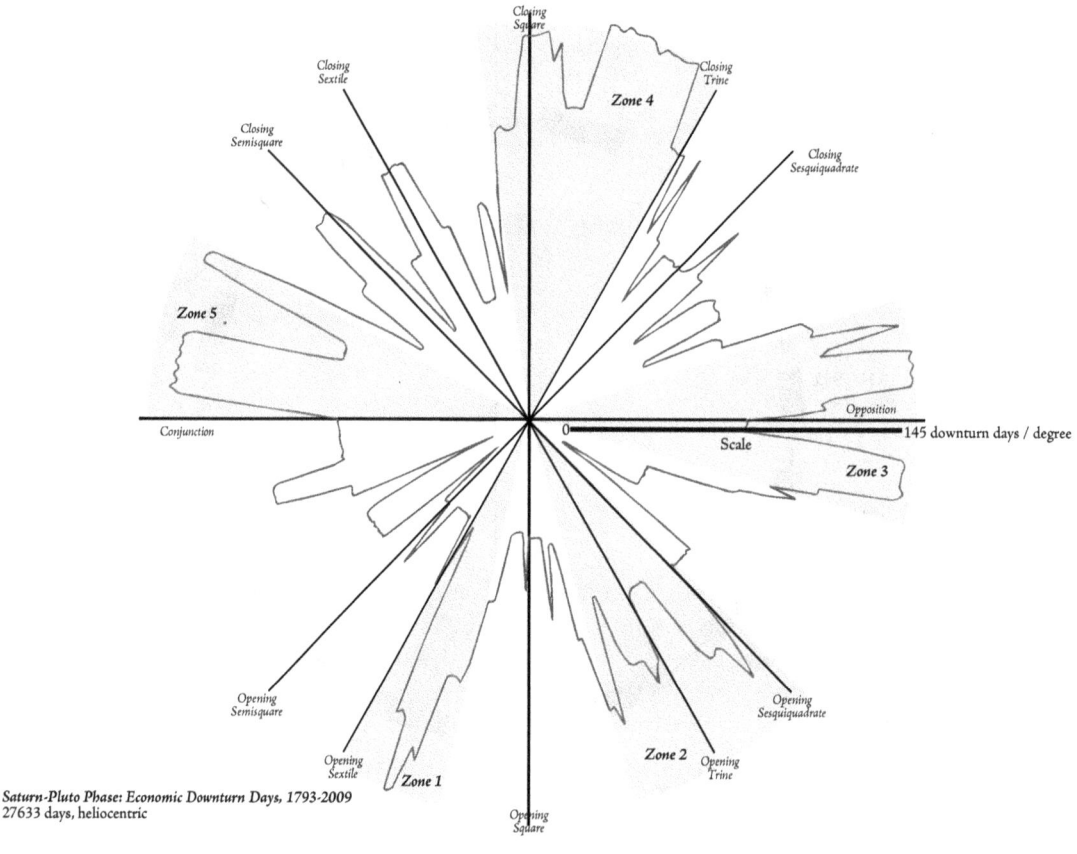

Figure 94. Saturn - Pluto: US economic downturn days distribution, heliocentric

The highlighted zones three, four, and five are mostly aligned with the major fourth harmonic aspects (conjunction, opposition, square).

Zone	Degree range	Description
1	60° - 80°	1825 Recession; Panic of 1857, 1887-88 recession, Depression of 1920-21, Recession of 1953-54, Early 1990s recession
2	105° - 135°	Panic of 1797, 1828-29 recession, 1860-61 recession, Panic of 1893, 1923-24 recession, 1926-27 recession, Recession of 1958, Recession of 1960-61

Zone	Degree range	Description
3	160° - 200°	1833-34 recession, 1865-67 recession, Panic of 1896, 1899-1900 recession, Great Depression, Dot-com recession of 2001
4	235° - 280°	Depression of 1807, late 1839-43 recession, 1873 and the Long Depression, Recession of 1937-38, 1973-75 recession, Great Recession of 2007-2009
5	345° - 360°	1815-21 depression, 1882-85 recession, Recession of 1913-14, Early 1980s recession

Harmonic analysis

Analyzing the fourth harmonic brings together zones three, four, and five (opposition, square, and conjunction):

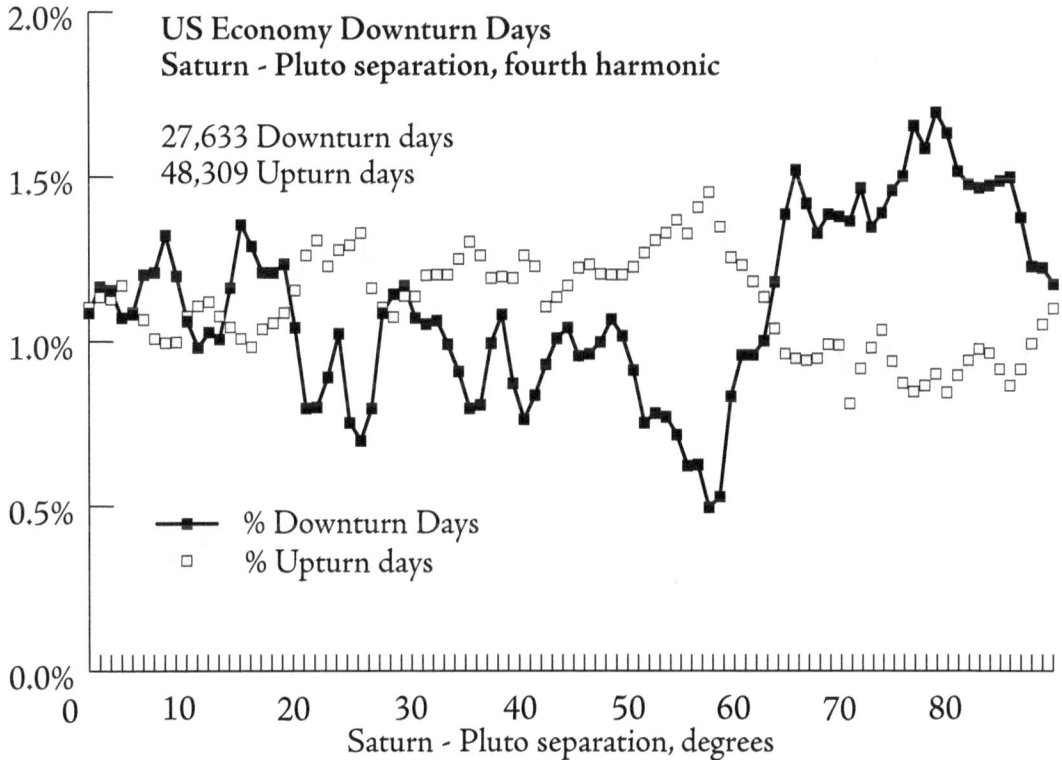

Figure 95. US economic downturn day frequency and Saturn - Pluto separation in the fourth harmonic

The peak from 60°-90° in the fourth harmonic is pronounced; a t-test confirms the result:

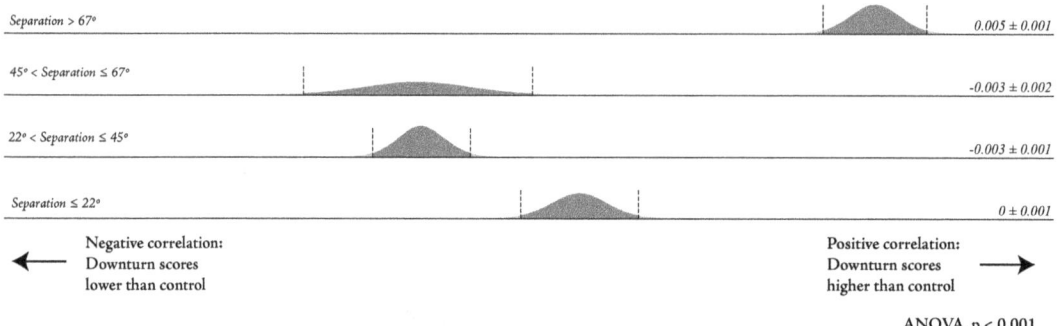

Figure 96. T-test of Saturn - Pluto economic downturn days against upturn days, fourth harmonic by interval

The strong correlation in the 67°-90° interval is significant. Adjusting this interval to 60°-90° improves the correlation, as shown in the summary table following:

	Downturn days	Upturn days
60°-90° (inside interval)	41.5%	29.0%
0°-59° (outside interval)	58.5%	71.0%

In standard astrological language, economic downturn events are more likely to occur when Saturn and Pluto are separated a fourth harmonic aspect (conjunction, square, opposition), where the orb is up to thirty degrees before the aspect.

The Saturn - Pluto fourth harmonic cycle has the following appearance:

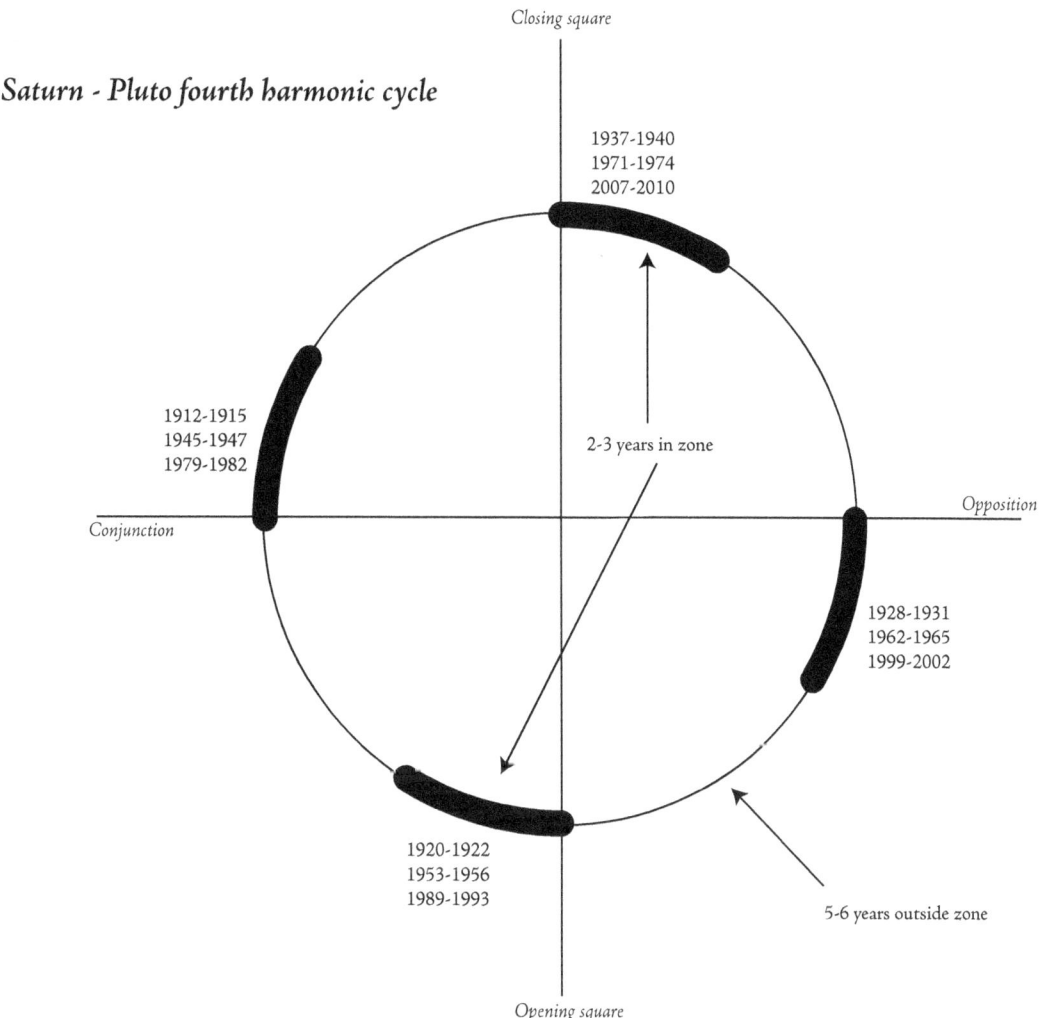

The highlighted areas correspond to the zone between the opening sextile and square, the opening quincunx and opposition, the closing trine and square, and the closing semisextile and conjunction.

Combining cycles

Combining all harmonic patterns (second and twelfth harmonics for Uranus - Pluto, eighth harmonic for Saturn - Uranus, and fourth harmonic for Saturn - Pluto) captures only 14% of the overall downturn days, but the days captured correspond to significant downturns: Depression of 1807, 1815-21 Depression, Panic of 1857, 1865-67 Recession, Long

Depression, Panic of 1907, Depression of 1920-21, Great Depression, and Great Recession of 2008.

12. Conclusions and implications

Here are the statistically significant correlations between armed conflict, civil unrest, regime change, and economic downturn events and the Uranus - Pluto, Saturn - Uranus, and Saturn - Pluto cycles. All are significant with a p-value < 0.001.

Armed Conflict

Planets	Aspects & Harmonics	% events detected	% controls detected	Ratio of events to controls
Uranus - Pluto	quintile series 5th harmonic	59.0%	35.1%	1.68
Saturn - Uranus	conjunction and opposition 2nd harmonic	64.8%	44.2%	1.47

Civil Unrest

Planets	Aspects & Harmonics	% events detected	% controls detected	Ratio of events to controls
Uranus - Pluto	novile series 9th harmonic	61.1%	52.8%	1.16
Saturn - Uranus	conjunction, square, opposition 4th harmonic	33.1%	24.4%	1.36
Saturn - Pluto	semisquare sesquiquadrate 8th harmonic	33.3%	26.0%	1.28

Regime change

Planets	Aspects & Harmonics	% events detected	% controls detected	Ratio of events to controls
Uranus - Pluto	semisquare sesquiquadrate 8th harmonic	32.5%	17.4%	1.87
Saturn - Uranus	conjunction square opposition 4th harmonic	49.0%	35.0%	1.40
Saturn - Pluto	quintile series 5th harmonic	28.0%	18.7%	1.50

US Economic downturns

Planets	Aspects & Harmonics	% events detected	% controls detected	Ratio of events to controls
Uranus - Pluto	mixed 2nd and 12th harmonics	37.0%	23.9%	1.55
Saturn - Uranus	mixed 8th harmonic	69.7%	54.4%	1.28
Saturn - Pluto	conjunction square opposition 4th harmonic	41.5%	29.0%	1.43

There is excellent evidence that these planetary cycles correlate with mundane events. Here are some implications for astrologers from this work:

- Most correlations correspond with traditional astrological aspects. The fourth harmonic ('hard', conjunction, square, and opposition) aspects and eighth harmonic (semisquare and sesquiquadrate) aspects correlate very well in many of these studies. These studies confirm the work of Witte[56] and Ebertin[28] about the importance of the semisquare and sesquiquadrate aspects. *Traditional astrologers should include the semisquare and sesquiquadrate in all work, treating them like conjunctions, squares, and oppositions.*

- Most sixth harmonic ('soft', sextile and trine) aspects do not correlate as strongly with world events. This result may be a side-effect of the type of events selected for study: armed conflict, civil unrest, regime change, and economic downturn events are symbolically more related to the traditional meanings for 'hard' fourth and eighth harmonic aspects.

- The quintile (72°) series of fifth harmonic aspects and the novile (40°) series of ninth harmonic aspects do correlate with world events. Traditional astrologers should consider adding these lesser known aspects as part of standard analyses.

- In some cases some but not all aspects correlate with world events. Figure 89 is an example of the significance of only some twelfth harmonic (30°) series of aspects. This example shows that *certain phases of a planetary cycle have stronger significance than other phases do.* Understanding which are the significant phases of planetary cycles is an area of great interest for future research.

- *The effective orbs for most of the study findings are much larger than astrologers typically use.* This may relate to the nature of the study. Armed conflict and economic downturn events tend to stretch out over an extended period of time. The results reflect these broad time spans. Based on future research astrologers might consider using fewer carefully selected aspects and employing wider orbs for these aspects.

Part IV. Projecting Forward

13. Completing the cycles

This section presents each of major harmonic cycles projected forward through the end their current cycle, annotated with critical phases for armed conflict, civil unrest, regime change, and economic downturn events.

Armed conflict

The current Uranus - Pluto began in the 1960's and lasts through the end of the Twenty-first century. Here is the completed current cycle including the dates when Uranus and Pluto are separated by an amount that is associated with a higher rate of armed conflict events:

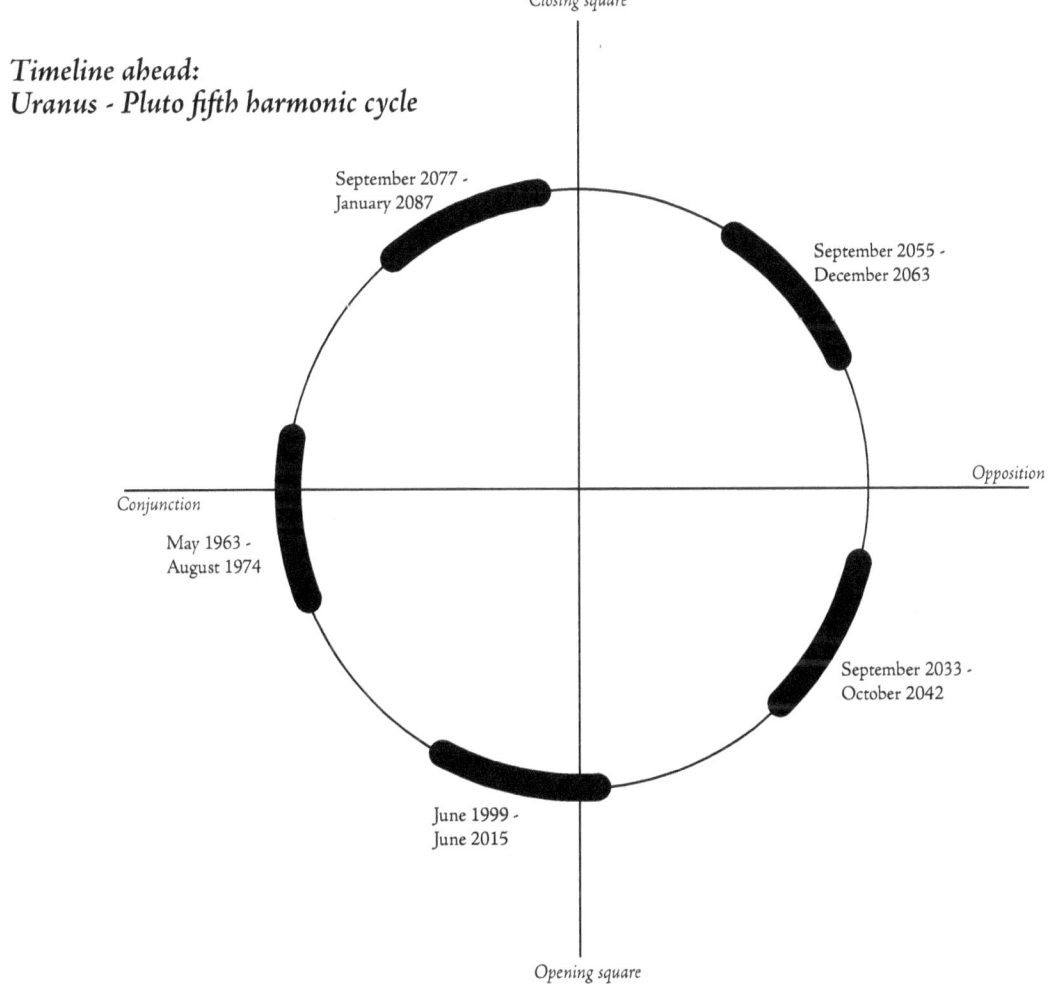

Figure 97. Uranus - Pluto armed conflict timeline

As of this writing Uranus and Pluto are concluding the first quintile aspect, lasting from late 1999 through mid-2015. This period saw the 2001 attack on the World Trade Center and the Pentagon, the second Iraq war, and the US incursion into Afghanistan. The following critical phase begins in late 2033.

The Saturn - Uranus cycle repeats much faster than the Uranus - Pluto cycle. The following figure shows dates when Saturn and Uranus in critical phase for armed conflict events:

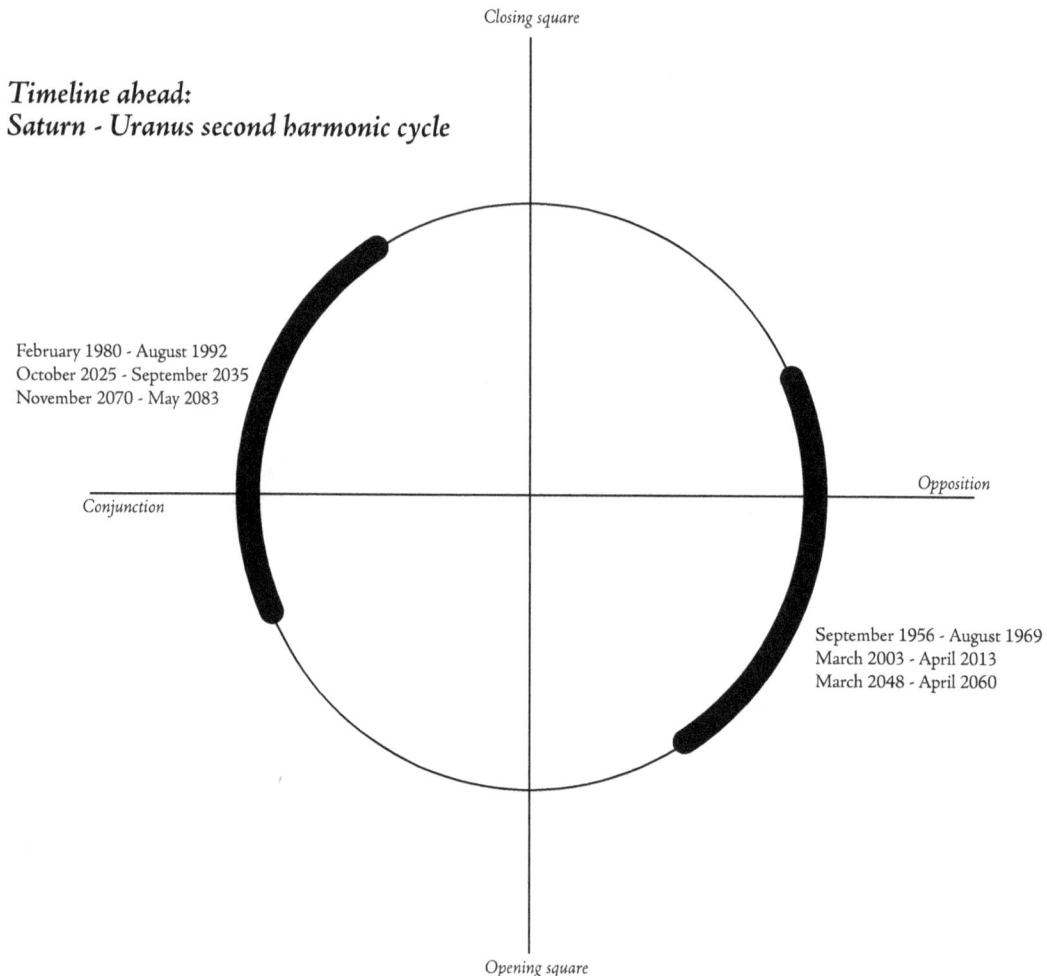

Figure 98. Saturn - Uranus armed conflict timeline

As of this book's writing Saturn and Uranus are concluding their critical phase in April 2013; the following critical phase begins in late 2025.

Civil unrest

For civil unrest events the Uranus - Pluto cycle has the following upcoming critical periods:

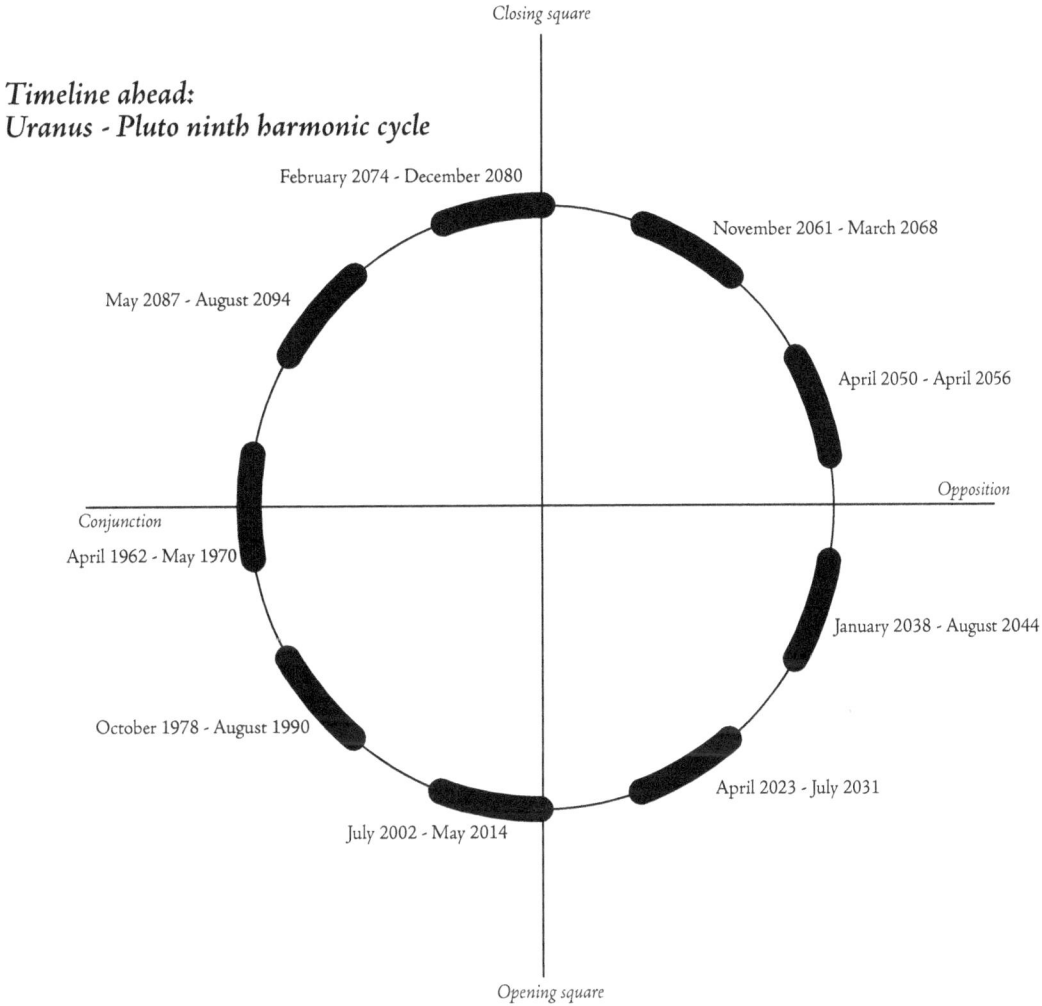

Figure 99. Uranus - Pluto civil unrest timeline

As of this book's writing Uranus and Pluto are still in a critical phase, ending in mid-2014. This current phase overlaps the zone of increased armed conflict events seen in Figure 97.

The upcoming critical phases in the Saturn - Uranus cycle for civil unrest events are as follows:

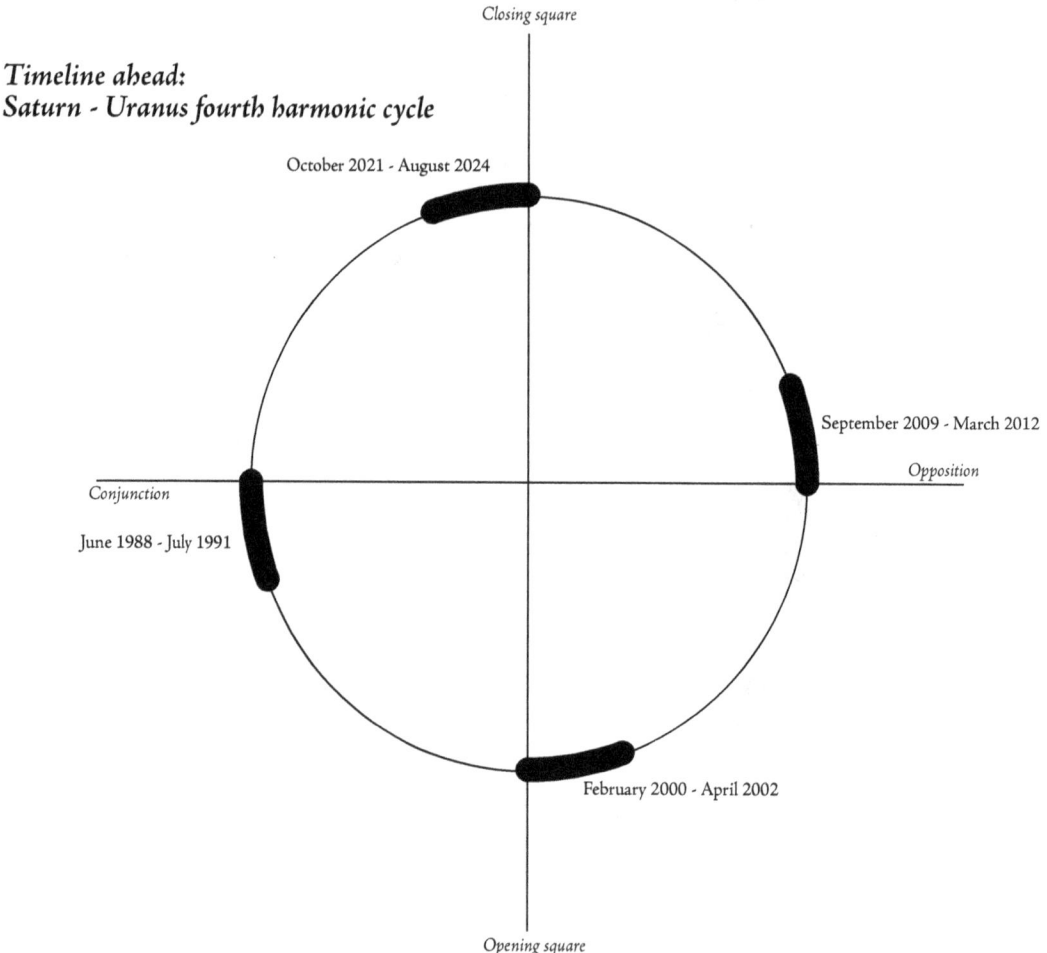

Figure 100. Saturn - Uranus civil unrest timeline

The most recent Saturn - Uranus critical phase coincided with the Arab Spring protests in 2011. This phase ended in March 2012, with the next phase beginning in October 2021.

The Saturn - Pluto critical phases for civil unrest events center around the semisquare and sesquiquadrate aspects:

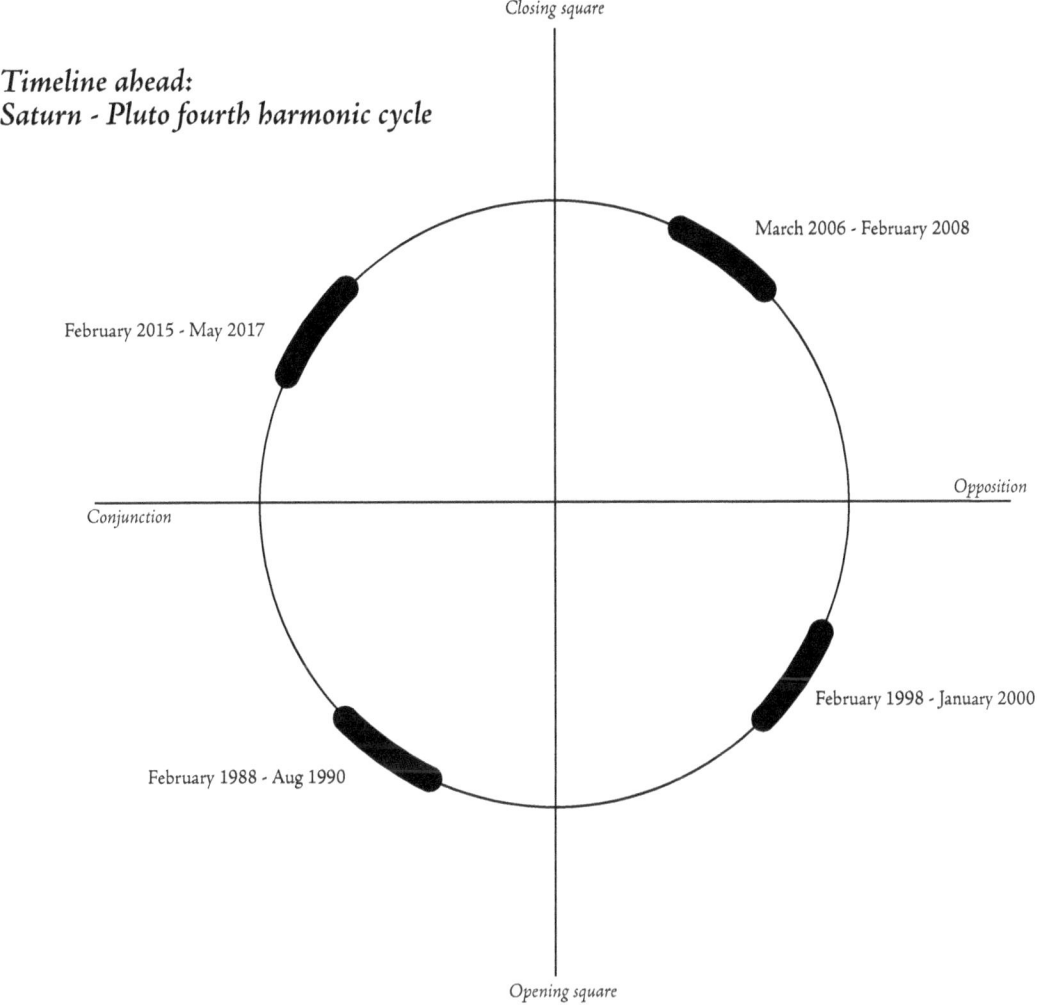

Figure 101. Saturn - Pluto civil unrest timeline

Saturn and Pluto were last in critical phase between 2006 and 2008. The next upcoming phase begins in early 2015 and lasts through mid-2017.

Regime change

For regime change events, the Uranus - Pluto eighth harmonic cycle looks as follows:

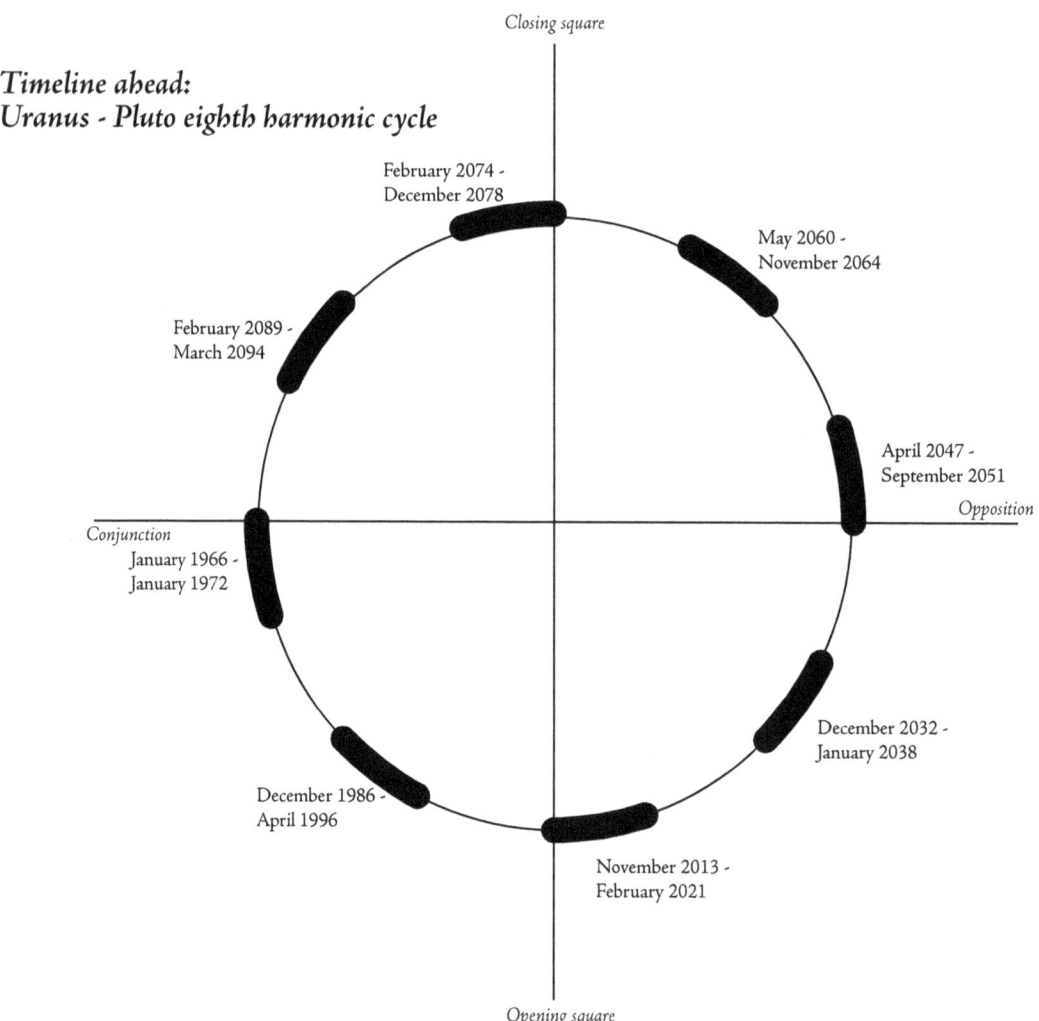

Figure 102. Uranus - Pluto regime change timeline

Uranus and Pluto next enter a critical phase for regime change events beginning in late 2013 and lasting through early 2021. The last time Uranus and Pluto were in a critical relationship was during the breakup of the Soviet Union and the downfall of communist regimes in eastern Europe.

The Saturn - Uranus fourth harmonic cycle for regime change events appears below:

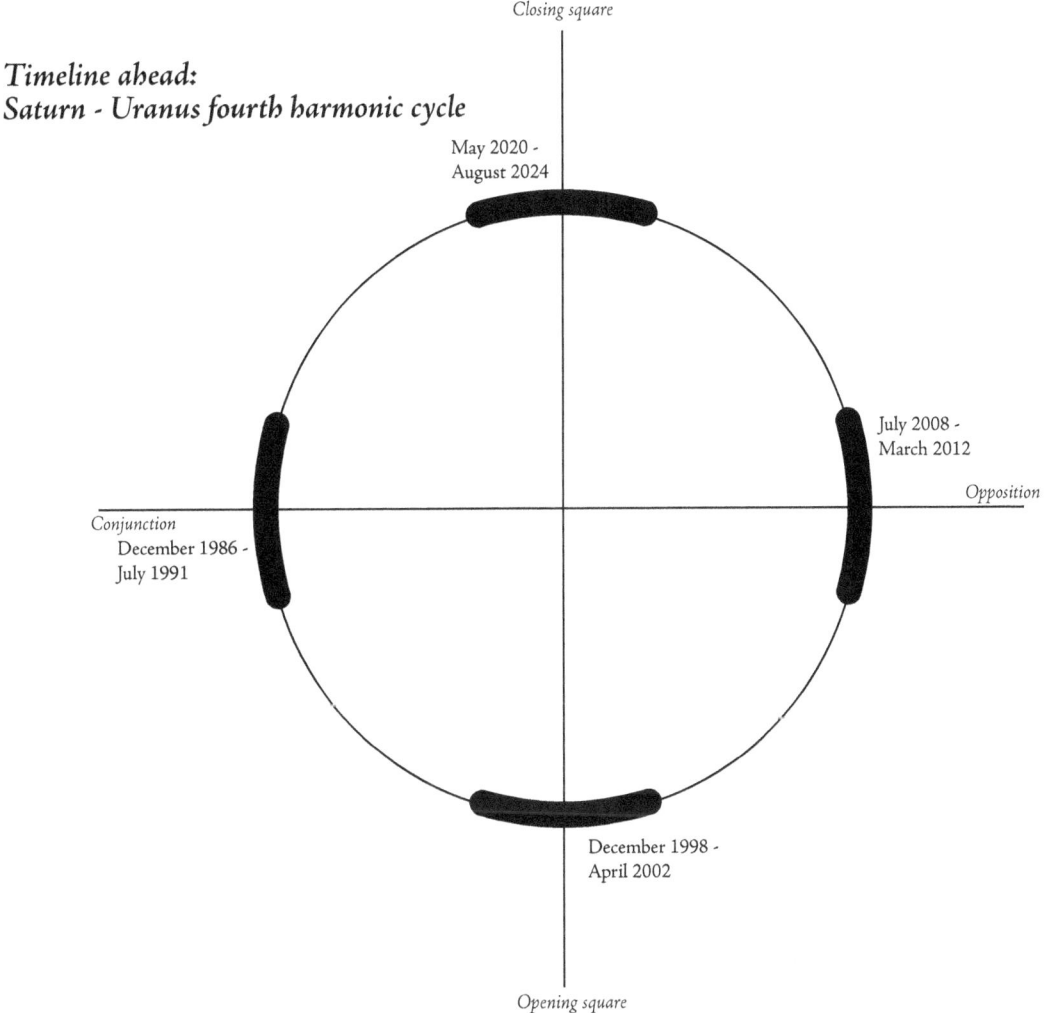

Figure 103. Saturn - Uranus regime change timeline

Between 1987 and 1991 this cycle overlapped the Uranus - Pluto cycle during the massive political shifts in eastern Europe and the former Soviet Union. The most recent phase ended in March 2012, with no subsequent critical phase until mid-2020.

Economic downturns

The unusual Uranus - Pluto combination second/twelfth harmonic cycle has the following upcoming critical dates.

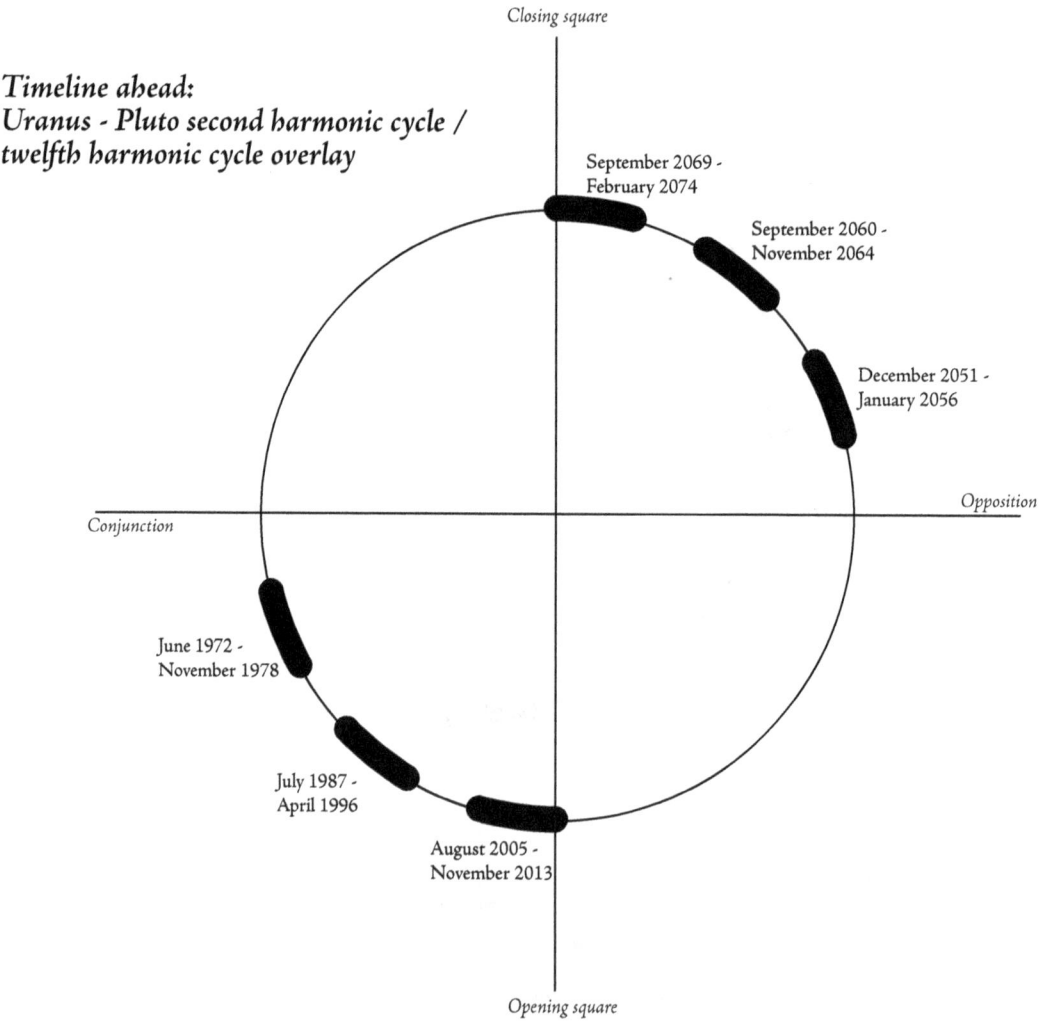

Figure 104. Uranus - Pluto economic downturn timeline

As of this book's writing Uranus and Pluto are still in a critical phase which began in mid-2005 and lasts through the end of 2013. The Great Recession of 2008 occurred during this phase. By 2014 this cycle enters a long quiescent phase with the next critical phase occurring in late 2051.

The Saturn - Uranus eighth harmonic cycle has a complex waveform (Figure 91) yielding the following graph:

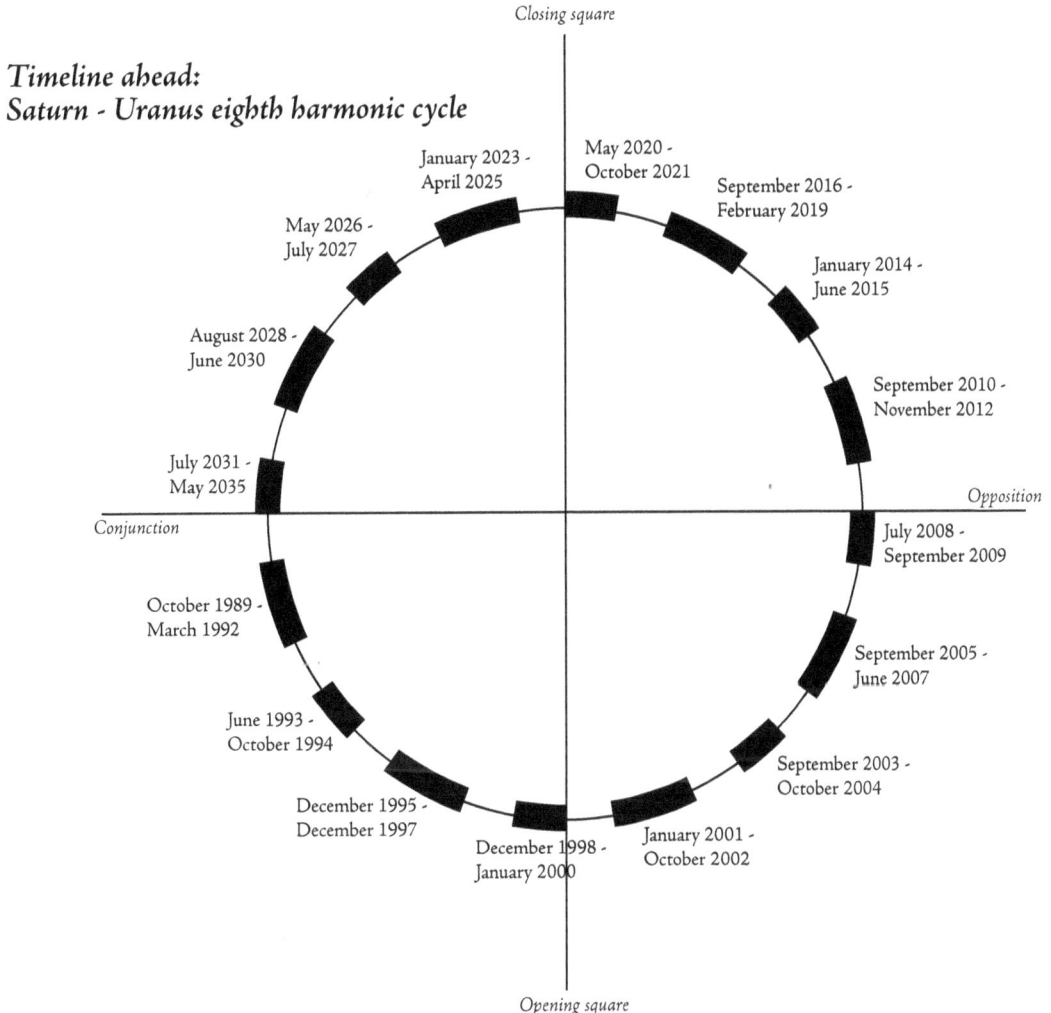

Figure 105. Saturn - Uranus economic downturn timeline

The Great Recession of 2008 coincided with this cycle entering a critical phase in July 2008. The planets left critical relationship in late 2012. The following critical phase begins in early 2014, with a subsequent phase beginning in late 2016.

The Saturn - Pluto fourth harmonic cycle has the following upcoming dates:

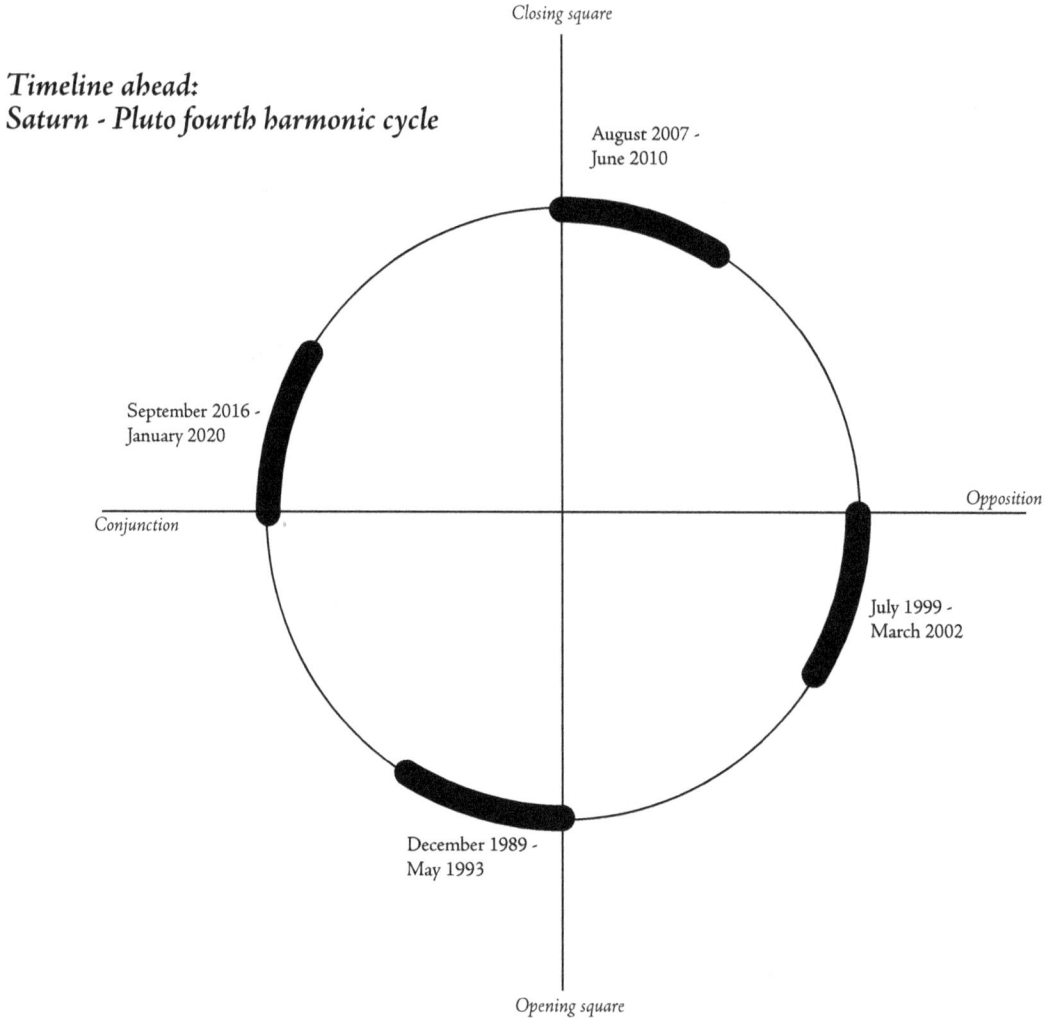

Figure 106. Saturn - Pluto economic downturn timeline

This cycle was last in a critical phase beginning in late 2007 through mid-2010: the Great Recession of 2008. The next critical phase begins in mid-2016, lasting through early 2020.

14. Consolidating the timelines

This chapter groups together all the cycles for a particular type of event and shows how the cycles overlap over time. These timelines make it easy to spot times where multiple cycles overlap, leading to a heightened tendency for events to occur.

The armed conflict timeline (Figure 107) shows the overlap between the Uranus - Pluto and Saturn - Uranus cycles. Uranus and Pluto entered into a critical phase for armed conflict events (quintile aspect) in 1999. This cycle continues through mid-2015. The Saturn - Uranus cycle entered critical phase in 2002, and runs through early 2013.

The figure shows a period of major overlap from 2002 through early 2013. This overlap included much of the second Iraq war and the US incursion into Afghanistan. Prior overlaps between these two cycles correlate with major armed conflicts: Eighty Years' War, Thirty Years' War, Seven Years' War, American Revolutionary War, Napoleonic Wars, Crimean War, World War I, Sino-Japanese War, World War II, and Vietnam War.

From early 2013 through mid-2015 only the Uranus - Pluto cycle is in a critical phase. Uranus - Pluto alone is associated with about 7% of all armed conflict events, including the Fourth, Sixth, and Eighth Crusades, Ottoman Empire incursions into Hungary and Austria (although many such conflicts occurred along with the Saturn - Uranus cycle as well), the War of the Austrian Succession, the Russo-Turkish War (1787-1792), and the Second Opium War. The period from early 2013 through mid-2015 should see a reduction in the level of armed conflicts, though the potential for significant conflicts – especially religiously-motivated ones – continues through mid-2015.

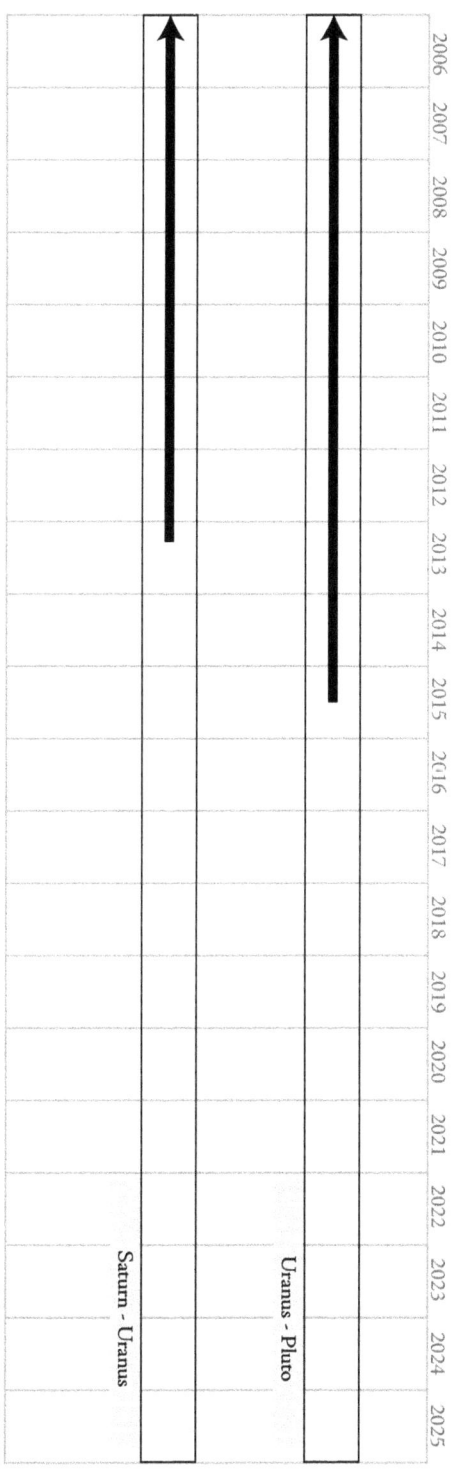

Figure 107. Armed conflict timeline

The civil unrest timeline (Figure 108) shows when the Uranus - Pluto, Saturn - Uranus, and Saturn - Pluto cycles are in critical phase. The Uranus - Pluto phase is critical from 2006 through mid-2014, while the other two cycles are intermittently critical through the years. From mid-2014 on, Uranus - Pluto is no longer critical, and the other two cycles do not overlap.

When all three cycles overlap, major internal revolutions have taken place. Historically these include the American Civil War, the Irish War of Independence, the Mexican Revolution, aftermath of the Russian Revolution in 1919 and 1920, the Tiananmen Square protests in China, and the civil unrest around the fall of eastern European communist states and the Soviet Union in 1989 and 1990. All three cycles do not occur simultaneously until the next Uranus - Pluto critical period which begins in 2023.

The period in 2009-2011 when both Uranus - Pluto and Saturn - Uranus were critical coincided with the Arab Spring protests and revolutions. Prior events under similar configurations include the Reichstag fire in Germany and subsequent unrest in 1933 and Vietnam War protests and multiple coups in Africa during 1966.

The period in 2006-2007 when both Uranus - Pluto and Saturn - Pluto were critical had no significant civil unrest events. Prior configurations include the 1937 Spanish Civil War and the 1979 unrest in Tehran around the invasion of the US Embassy.

From early 2012 through mid-2014 only Uranus - Pluto is critical. Historically roughly 30% of civil unrest events occur when only Uranus - Pluto is critical, including the American Civil Rights movement during the early 1960's, unrest in South Africa during the early 1980's, and the insurgency in Chechnya during 2004. This period until mid-2014 could continue to produce considerable worldwide civil unrest.

Only around 5% of civil unrest events occur when only Saturn - Uranus is critical. The period between late 2021 and mid-2024 is unlikely to have significantly increased civil unrest events.

Similarly few civil unrest events (roughly 5%) occur when only Saturn - Pluto is critical. Some of these events have been significant, including Leon Trotsky's ejection from the Communist Party in 1927, the 1961 coup in South Korea, the 1970 foundation of the Khmer Republic in Cambodia and subsequent civil war, and the 1971 unrest in East Pakistan and the creation of Bangladesh. The period from early 2015 through early 2017 bears watching for significant civil unrest events.

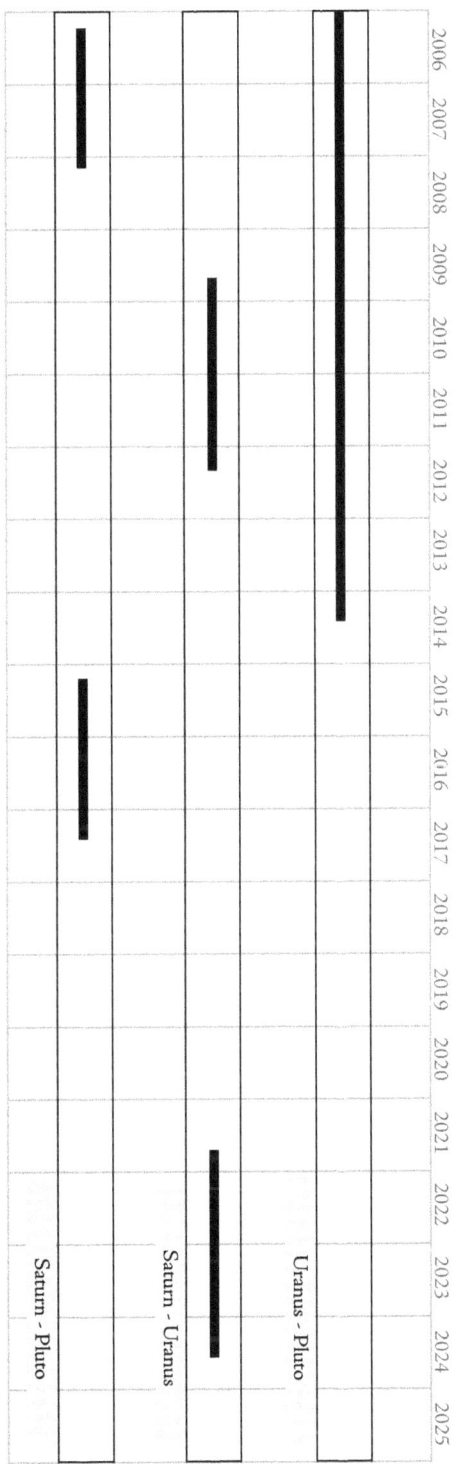

Figure 108. Civil unrest timeline

The regime change timeline (Figure 109) indicates when the Uranus - Pluto and Saturn - Uranus cycles are critical. Only during a brief period in 2020 are both cycles simultaneously critical; during such periods significant regime change events have occurred, including the proclamation of European republics after World War I, the proclamation of republics in Africa in 1966, and fall of some eastern European republics in 1989.

When Uranus - Pluto alone is critical, significant numbers of regime change events have occurred, including the proclamation of the People's Republic of China and the Deutsche Demokratische Republik in 1949, the fall of eastern European republics and the dissolution of the Soviet Union in 1990, and the freely democratic republic of South Africa in 1994. The period from late 2013 through 2021 is prime for the creation of new republics or significant shifts in governments.

When only Saturn - Uranus is critical, few regime change events have occurred. These include the Spanish democracy after Franco in 1977, and shifts in Arab republics after the 2011 Arab Spring protests.

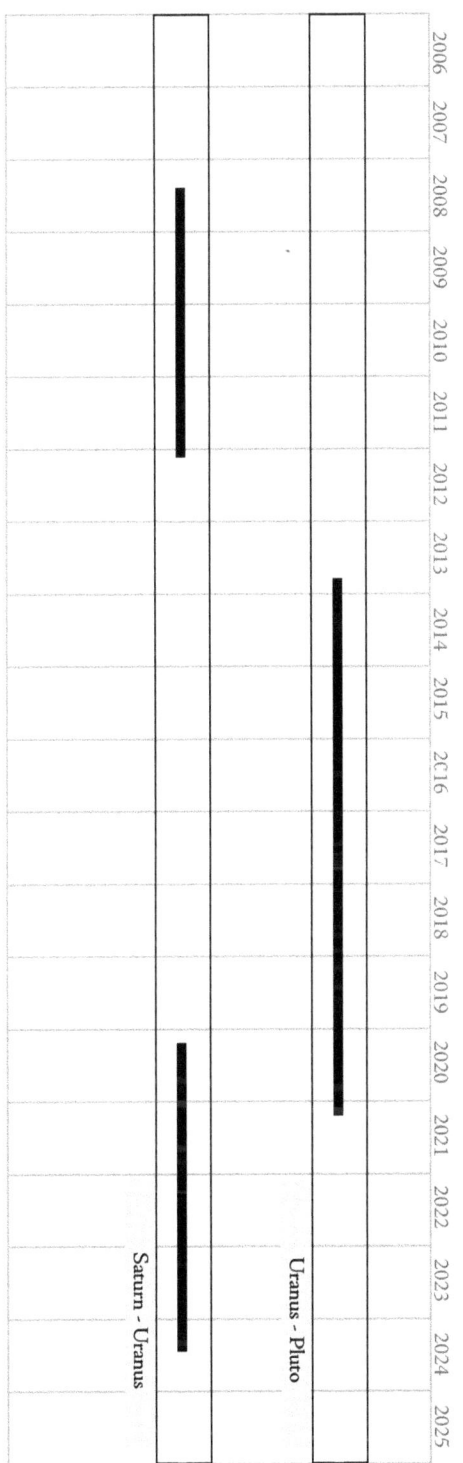

Figure 109. Regime change timeline

The US economic downturn timeline (Figure 110) shows the interplay of the three planetary cycles. During late 2008 - early 2009 all three cycles were critical; this was the beginning of the Great Recession. Having all three cycles simultaneously critical occurred during the Depression of 1807, portions of the 1815-21 Depression, the Panic of 1857, parts of the 1865-67 Recession, the Panic of 1873 and the Long Depression, the Panic of 1907, the Depression of 1920-21, the Great Depression, the 1973-75 Recession, and the Early 1990s Recession. 2008-2009 is the last time all three cycles are simultaneously critical until the Uranus - Pluto cycle becomes critical again in 2051.

Uranus - Pluto continues to be critical until late 2013. Because of the number of downturns with this cycle, it is again worth watching for signs of economic downturn until late 2013.

Combinations of the Saturn - Uranus and the Saturn - Pluto cycle occurred during a number of other important economic downturns: the Panic of 1797, the 1802-04 Recession, the depression of 1807, the 1865-67 Recession, the Panic of 1910-11, and the Post-World War I Recession. The period between 2016 and 2019 is worth watching for signs of economic downturn.

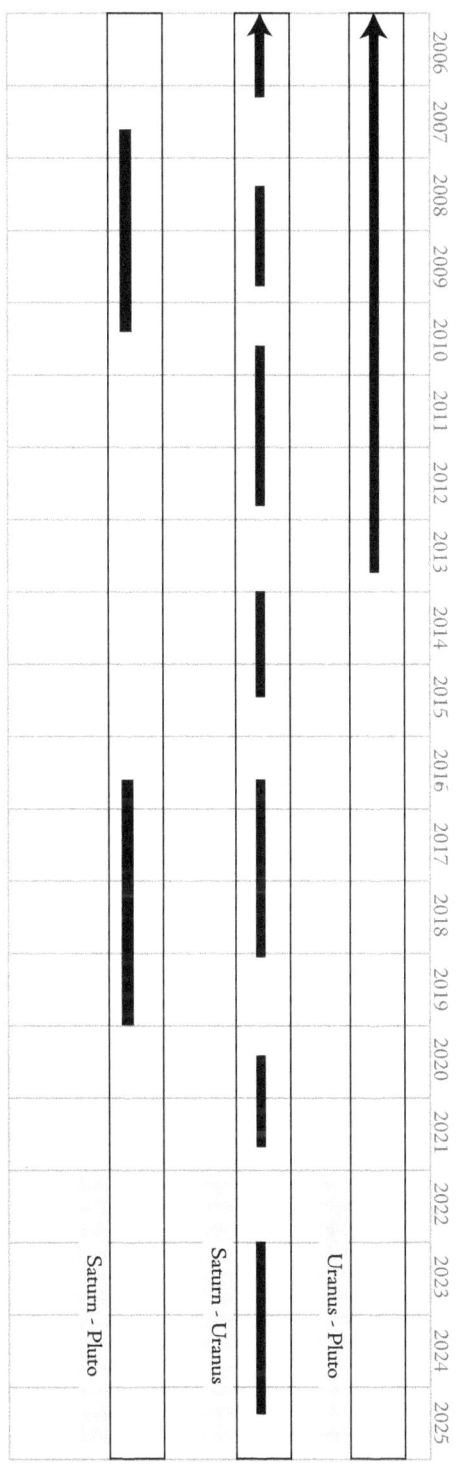

Figure 110. US Economic downturn timeline

15. A look farther out

These timelines provide a detailed view of potential changes over the next few years. But what does the current Uranus - Pluto cycle mean over its long run? Chapter 3 opened with two questions to ask when a Uranus - Pluto cycle begins:

- Who is the incumbent in power?
- What are the structures of power and the assumptions that underlie the execution of power?

At the beginning of the Uranus - Pluto cycle in 1710, Louis XIV ruled France and the French monarchy was completely secure in its power. At the beginning of the cycle in 1850, the British Empire was at the peak of its power, while China was in civil war and the United States struggled with slavery and control of most of North America.

During each of these cycles the structure of power completely changed. During the 1710 cycle the French abandoned the monarchy, created a republic only to explore imperial power in Napoléon I's reign, and eventually returned to a republic. During the 1850 cycle the British empire reached its zenith in power only to decolonialize with significantly decreased power and influence at the cycle's end.

In 1965 China began the Cultural Revolution while the United States addressed civil rights and welfare society programs. The Soviet Union and United States escalated in Cold War tensions, involving developing countries. And war broke out between India and Pakistan over Kashmir.

So what is the focus of this current cycle? Only historians in the Twenty-Second century can tell us, but here are some possible themes.

While the Soviet Union has already dissolved, the United States continues as a global superpower and hegemon, though chastened by the problematic adventures in Iraq and Afghanistan that began as Uranus and Pluto came to the first quintile in the early 2000's. China has completely transformed: a new economic titan replaced the fragmentation and civil disruption of the Cultural Revolution. This Uranus - Pluto cycle clearly concerns the relative trajectories of the United States and China.

This cycle also opened with military conflict between India and Pakistan. Tensions between these countries persist to the present day, except that both nations are now armed with weapons of mass destruction.

But there is a more fundamental question that this cycle poses: *Will large, centralized welfare states continue as the primary mode of geopolitical governance? If not, what might replace them? Could non-state actors, like multinational corporations, take on many of the roles of governance?*

In the mid-1960's Jacques Ellul, the French sociologist and thinker, wrote extensively[29, 30] about his views that large, centralized nation-states were increasingly practicing technique to control the masses and to standardize behavior and government. For Ellul, technique is not simply what one thinks of as technological means. Rather, *technique is purposeful means and the ensemble of means to attain ends.* While technology is a physical manifestation of technique, technique is equally present in organizational approaches that attempt to standardize and to control aspects of social life. For example, business students learn management techniques taught independently of a specific application domain, and then attempt to apply these approaches to optimize business results across various aspects of an enterprise without regard for the unique characteristics of each part of the business.

From Ellul's perspective in the 1960's, technique and technology would inevitably lead to an increasingly mechanized and standardized future. While the first years of this Uranus - Pluto cycle appeared to head in this direction, there has been a significant Uranian mutation. Information technology has changed in unimaginable ways since Ellul wrote *The Technological Society*. He foresaw large controlling industrial and governmental interests manipulating individuals, businesses, and societies through centralized command and control. What no one could have imagined in the 1960's is the dramatic increase in computing and communications power and a simultaneous dramatic decrease in costs. Rather than huge monolithic systems, decentralized independent service entities like Twitter were used in the Arab Spring uprisings of 2011. No governmental service facilitated the rapid exchange of social information, and no large corporate service forced individuals to use it. Rather, the rise of decentralized networks has fostered the rise of emergent information structures[58]. No one could have foreseen these systems prior to the commercialization of the Internet in the mid-1990's. Millions of people voluntarily make unimaginably large numbers of daily content contributions to networks such as Twitter and Facebook. These services provide open interfaces that anyone, from individuals to large government entities, can use to consolidate information about individuals, to understand broader social trends, and to foster both social change and societal control. Ellul's charges that technology inherently leads to mass depersonalization and conformity are no longer clear. On the contrary, some aspects of technology allow for increasingly individualized expression[59].

Radical transparency can transform these systems[7] – a Uranus - Pluto idea. Formerly people consumed media – and propaganda – as content arriving from large and static players like corporations and governments who created it with particular ends in mind. Increasingly now there is a blur between consuming and creating content. Formerly the 'they' controlled content. Now 'they' increasingly share control with those who consume the information. User-generated reviews and comments frequently become the most important part of commercial websites, and the boundary between content creators and consumers has softened.

Another theme for this Uranus - Pluto cycle: *Will technology continue to break new ground to achieve continued prosperity and growth?* Most projections assume continued technological advance to fuel the future. Peter Thiel, the founder of PayPal and prominent venture capitalist, calls this into question[97]. He charges that science and technology have slowed down in recent years particularly in transportation and energy generation. While information and communications technologies have leapt ahead, comparatively little progress has happened in other fields. He points to much slower than expected progress in biotechnology and medicine. The War on Cancer, for example, has yielded much less progress than expected when first launched in the 1970s. The Human Genome Project was to have led to a vast number of potential therapeutic targets for diseases. Instead, sequencing the human genome revealed a much more complex and subtly regulated system than anyone had anticipated – with correspondingly much slower progress at fostering major medical advances.

Resilience

The best response to the continual uncertainty that Uranus - Pluto poses is resilience. Nassim Nicholas Taleb coins the term *antifragile*[94] to describe ways of being that benefit from uncertainty and change. This is no different from the real meaning of Charles Darwin's phrase 'survival of the fittest'. While Social Darwinists mistook the phrase to construe that strength and power always win, Darwin actually meant that it is not always the strongest but rather *the most adaptable, the most transformable and responsive, the most flexible, that survives and thrives*. The question is not how to hunker down and attempt to maintain a valued *status quo*, but rather to respond to Uranus - Pluto's evolutionary pressure and to change in effective ways: to prosper from change.

Thus far in this book I have avoided much discussion of astrological symbolism, the archetypal meaning of the planets that makes astrology lively. To close this book and to point to astrological resources for personal resilience, consider these archetypal meanings of our three change agents: Saturn, Uranus, and Pluto.

Saturn

In ancient times Saturn's path marked the bounds of the known universe. Beyond this final wanderer were the eternally burning fixed stars, distant and radiant. Now Saturn marks the border between the known and the stable and the transformation – the mutation – taking us beyond the known. The dance between the known and the just ahead is the key to the unfolding age.

Saturn represents the stability of the known. He is the old devil, as Liz Greene says, resistant to change, focused on maintaining what is. In the midst of flux, Saturn asks us to value what's real.

Saturn is the essence of value as measured by the march of time. Only things of value perdure. All ephemeral things pass away, but those of value persist – if only for the current time. For all is in flux...

Saturn represents a deep paradox. While valuing the past, Saturn is also the march of time, and the essence of releasing those things no longer appropriate for the future. While Saturn represents the desire for preservation, for conservatism and stability, for holding on, ultimately Saturn marks the cycle of time that forces us to release those things no longer of value.

Value itself transforms over time. Saturn represents that cycle of value, how it changes.

Uranus

Uranus is the electric charge, the mutation, the shock of the new. Uranus opens the known to the impact of the unexpected. Uranus points a vision, vast and foreboding, sometimes challenging and often alluring. Uranus pushes us over the edge of the known world to confront the newly birthed as it emerges unlooked-for from the belly of the world. Uranus is the seed that mutates the matrix of the known into the fruit of the future, or into its destruction.

Uranus is unyielding, just as Saturn is unwavering. Uranus' vision cannot be denied. He points to a vastness, then impales us on the narrow transformative spike of mutation and change. Uranus is the unseen visitor, the unlooked-for guest who at a glance transforms the fabric of the familiar to become the dawning of the next age.

This unknown visitor can break things of great value, shattering the values of the past, replacing them with untried and untested visions that shock and dismay. The impulse to launch into the new makes us choose the reckless over the reasonable.

Pluto

Hades abducted Persephone to the Underworld, crafting a gorgeous flower to tempt her. Pluto – the same deity in the Roman pantheon – abducts, tempts with passions, creates obsessions to lure us away from our egocentricity – or to submerge us in our own delusions.

Pluto inspires the masses, or deludes them. The saint that inspires us and the tyrant that enslaves us are both Plutonic manifestations.

Transformation arises from the depth of the earth. These are the Hadean depths, the realm of the underworld. When those energies surface, bubbling up erratically, they destroy things that they touch, and they create completely new lands. The terrain is different once Pluto's eruptions complete. The new and the loss of the old are in the same breath.

When a passion seizes us we are in Pluto's realm. When an obsession draws us to the abyssal edge, we are near to Pluto's depth.

In the Western Mysteries the Ring-Pass-Not encircles the treasure that the heart seeks. To pass the Ring one must master the forces of obsession and power. One must dive deep while retaining the essential core soul/spirit that marks each as an individual spark of the divine.

Focus on value

Saturn often gets an unnecessarily bad rap in astrological circles. Conscious, careful planning and deliberate action bring about the best possible result from any interaction with Saturn. Compared to the unpredictable forces of the other planets, Saturn's a snap: all it takes is time, discipline, and the willingness to release those things that are no longer of value.

How do we value something? Do we automatically assign a monetary value to gauge the importance of something? Stuff that we collect often has less enduring value than we believe it does when we rush out on a quest to acquire. What about relationships: are they economic goods or something more? What of intangible things, like experiences? All things of value connect us back with our core meaning. Saturn wants us to recover that core meaning. The reverse is also true: Saturn wants us to purify ourselves and release the dross that is no longer of any real value.

- If we are what we eat, then most of us are cheap, fast, and easy. It's time to get healthier.
- How do we use time? Take an inventory of time use. How valuable is watching television casually, mindlessly? Is it something to keep the mind from doing something important?

Valuable things change over our lives. We don't think so in the heat of desire for a new bauble, a new fling, or a passionate moment. Chances are the bauble won't fascinate very long – certainly not in proportion to the importance we assign to it in the instant.

Saturn's hardest lessons come when it is time to release something of value. The bauble breaks. The relationship cools when the passion ebbs. Sometimes we lose something we treasure. Suffering arises instantly when we are separated from what we want and love and desire, or when we are forced into contact with something we dislike. Attachment and aversion: these are the poisons that Saturn helps us to uproot.

Saturn's challenge is to understand the attachments that keep you from becoming your true self. Saturn and the Buddha speak the same message. The true self evolves continuously. Change is inevitable: ask your physicist. Saturn both creates the desire for control and forces us to understand that control is always evanescent.

Choosing what is of value is an exercise that everyone does continuously. When you feel too comfortable, when you feel too stable, Saturn awakens in you the desire for deep change. Fixity or rigidity betrays a deadness deep inside. To revitalize the whole organism is to release what is dying and to embrace the living.

In biology *apoptosis* – the controlled, programmed death of cells – guides an organism's life. Death is as important as life. Differentiation of an embryo into complex mature forms requires as much death and release of infantile structures as it does growth and development of new ones. To become something of inestimable value requires leaving behind worthless things. The good that you covet and retain keeps you from clearing the space for the new to emerge.

Dragons hoard wealth and virgins, and they do nothing with either one. It is in the free expression of things, in the gradual evolution of new forms, that genius resides. Saturn is the highest calling of the design of destruction and release. Without it we become undifferentiated, stale, swollen, filled with toxicity.

Value arises only through experience. But you can begin to understand the strands of gold that weave through your life by suspending conscious thought for a moment and registering those things that emerge. What is each telling you? Write them down. Capture the thread of images. Write down five, ten, maybe a hundred images that flit through your mind when you hold the concept of value, of worth.

Comb through that list. As you wrote things down, you doubtless varied in speed: sometimes racing forward, sometimes holding back and wondering if the well was dry. Some are repeated or along a common theme. Jot down that theme and see if it unifies other aspects of your life.

What is the core of your heart? Review your list and then suspend judgment for a time. Open yourself in a relaxed moment and let other images surface. Affirm that you see the most important golden thread for your life going forward.

Now see things that are holding you back from advancing along that thread. Maybe they are little things: losing time in pursuits that are less that good for you. Maybe you are denying yourself health through your habits, your diet, or immobility. Simply note these. Nothing will change, just yet. Change happens in the encounter with the other archetypes of change: Uranus and Pluto.

Break a little glass

Break a little glass... Sound messy? Sound attractive? You get to break a taboo? Maybe you'd like to trash something utterly awful? Uranus wants us to step outside the known world. Uranus is just on the outer side of Saturn's line of reality in the sand. Saturn defines the limits of the possible. Uranus, Neptune, and Pluto want us to step past those limits and to embrace the barely imaginable.

Uranus is the barely imaginable. It is the faculty of mentation, accelerated and pushed beyond semblance to normalcy, that creates the attraction for the next step. Uranus is logical, brilliant, even a genius. But his work is not limited to the logical and computable. Uranus wants us to step beyond the boundaries of the known. If Saturn defines the Ring-Pass-Not separating the world of material condensation from the rarefied world of imagination and potentiation, then Uranus describes where our foot first lands when we step outside that ring. We have transgressed the bounds and we love it.

Uranus spirals out of control very easily. That is its nature, after all. You cannot be a rebel, a mutant, and expect to stay within the bounds of the known and reasonable. Working with Uranus takes a completely different strategy than working with Saturn. With Saturn, being reasonable and responsible is all it takes to have a good life. For Uranus, you do not get the creative flash, the insight that makes everything new again, unless you are ready to step outside the limits of the known. Uranus is the *Shock of the New*.

Physically Uranus can be just what it takes to get out of a rut, but just as easily it can be the energy that ends with a nervous breakdown. Needing to move, needing to get out of confinement, all these are just the first step into Uranian crazy-making. Needing to drop everything known can shatter a relationship. Skipping out on duties may lead to abandoned children.

And the Buddha did all of these things. He left his wife and children behind. (Ultimately they joined him as students.) Jesus, too, instructs us to leave family obligations behind. Maybe it's a mortgage and lots of stuff that you don't need any longer. Maybe you'd like to move and you don't know the right way yet.

Restlessness and chaos may come to mind. But these aren't Uranus's authentic nature. His is the spirit of real genius. Simply shattering something to break it isn't a step to higher consciousness. Uranus wants to create the ground for the higher mind to flower with abandon.

Real rebellion means stepping out beyond the known in a deliberate way. *Start with an experiment.* Experiments are something you do to learn about the world. If you knew how an experiment will turn out in advance, it's not an experiment; it's a recipe – something you do for a purely utilitarian end. Uranus wants more than rote recipes. He wants to transform you.

So pick an experiment. Your experiment should call for you to step outside your comfort zone. It should take a limited amount of time to do, and shouldn't cause your life to be completely disrupted and destroyed. (Warning: further disruptions may follow…)

Try something really new. Get just a bit uncomfortable and uneasy. See how you feel. Check back in with yourself as you go. Keep records, just like a scientist does of her delvings into the nature of things. What if it fails? Who cares. The best thing is that you now *know*. You'll try another experiment and keep things moving.

Direct tension into opening the fabric of your body. Tension is one of Uranus's common side effects. You want to change and you cannot move, and so you fret. Or you feel like splitting from responsibilities and you cannot. (That's Saturn - Uranus in a nutshell.)

Rhythm is the key. It seems odd for Uranus, prince of the unconventional and erratic, to have rhythm as a basic need. The urge to move, the need to shake the body: all these are Uranus calling you outside yourself. Plan an experiment. Try something that helps you move your body. See how taijiquan works for you. Or maybe yoga. How about ecstatic dance – that's a Uranian natural.

Deliberate, planned ecstasy is the trick to pull Uranus out of the tension-producing role and promote him to your personal genius. That's his real role.

Raise a little ruckus

Pluto has a deep story to tell: literally. Pluto / Hades is tied with Persephone and Demeter in one of the greatest of the ancient Greek mystery traditions, the Eleusinian Mysteries. The mystery of cyclic birth and death, of renewal and immersion in the eternal cycle, are all here.

Pluto fashions a lure of unendurable beauty. Persephone seizes it, giving him the chance to seize her. In a way, passion is the key that opens to the underworld. The descent into madness comes through unendurable beauty. Obsession you might call it, but this beauty opens to a depth never before understood. And here is Pluto's first secret: his process happens in secret and in silence before it becomes transformative. The secret is to create a world apart, a world of internal immersion, of silence, and of stillness.

In the dark caverns misty images appear and vanish, like fog rising from a dark lake may take shape and then disappear. Those images are the secrets to your own internal world. You have worlds within you, vastness that you cannot imagine. Busying yourself with the affairs of the day, with electronic distractions, or with religions that keep you fastened to the surface notions of holiness, conformity, conservatism – all these mask the depths. Pluto intends you to go deeper.

You need practice and some diligence. To emerge transformed you must first pick apart the bare essentials to your soul's life. What is your true mission here? Are you open to the deep mysteries of your own life's nature?

You must renounce distractions, at least a bit. Step back from things that serve you little. Embrace silence. See what craziness emerges as you sit with yourself. The inner paths of the heart are known only in treading them carefully, watching for the secrets to inspire and motivate. Pluto seeks to bring you to this interior place. The alchemical transformation begins from examining the discarded fragments of reality. As you release them, begin to burn and putrefy them, you enter a strange space where nature itself begins to transform as a metamorphosing being. In the loss of the interior, a reorganization begins that opens you to a new dawn.

As did Persephone, you will step out of the inner sanctum where you have worked alone and in silence. Pluto rules both the solitary expression and the mass movement. From authentic life a magnetic attraction begins. You begin to draw to you effortlessly what you need, and there are many who need you and your wisdom as never before. Those who have understood the inner depths, who understand the Void that supports and encompasses each instant of reality, only those can lead into a dynamically changing world.

16. References

1. 'A History of World Financial Crises,' http://www.economywatch.com/economy-business-and-finance-news/A_history_of_world_financial_crises_07-14.html.

2. 'Adams-Onís Treaty,' http://en.wikipedia.org/wiki/Adams-On%C3%ADs_Treaty.

3. Addey, John. *Harmonics in Astrology.* (London: Urania Trust, 1996).

4. Addey, John. *A New Study of Astrology.* (London: Urania Trust, 1996).

5. 'American Revolution,' http://en.wikipedia.org/wiki/American_Revolution#1733.E2.80.931763:_Navigation_Acts.2C_Molasses_Act_and_Royal_Proclamation.

6. 'American Revolutionary War,' http://en.wikipedia.org/wiki/American_Revolutionary_War#An_international_war.2C_1778.E2.80.931783.

7. Anderson, Chris. 'What would radical transparency mean for Wired?" http://www.longtail.com/the_long_tail/2006/12/what_would_radi.html.

8. 'Battle of Elchingen,' http://en.wikipedia.org/wiki/Battle_of_Elchingen.

9. 'Battle of Eylau,' http://en.wikipedia.org/wiki/Battle_of_Eylau.

10. 'Benito Mussolini,' http://en.wikipedia.org/wiki/Mussolini.

11. 'Boxer Rebellion,' http://en.wikipedia.org/wiki/Boxer_Rebellion.

12. 'Business Cycle Expansions and Contractions,' http://web.archive.org/web/20071012231548/http://www.nber.org/cycles.html.

13. 'China,' http://en.wikipedia.org/wiki/China.

14. 'Cold War,' http://en.wikipedia.org/wiki/Cold_War.

15. 'Committee of Correspondence,' http://en.wikipedia.org/wiki/Committees_of_Correspondence.

16. 'Communist Party of China,' http://en.wikipedia.org/wiki/Communist_Party_of_China.

17. 'Compromise of 1850,' http://en.wikipedia.org/wiki/Compromise_of_1850.

18. 'Continental System,' http://en.wikipedia.org/wiki/Continental_Blockade.

19. 'Cosimo de' Medici,' http://en.wikipedia.org/wiki/Cosimo_de%27_Medici.

20. 'Cultural Revolution,' http://en.wikipedia.org/wiki/Cultural_Revolution.

21. 'Dates for Banking Crises, Currency Crashes, Sovereign Domestic or External Default (or Restructuring), and Stock Market Crases (Varieties),' http://www.reinhartandrogoff.com/data/browse-by-topic/topics/7/.

22. 'Diplomatic Revolution,' http://en.wikipedia.org/wiki/Diplomatic_Revolution.

23. 'Dissolution of the Monasteries,' http://en.wikipedia.org/wiki/Dissolution_of_the_Monasteries.

24. 'Dumbarton Oaks Conference,' http://en.wikipedia.org/wiki/Dumbarton_Oaks_Conference.

25. 'East Germany,' http://en.wikipedia.org/wiki/East_Germany.

26. Ebertin, Baldur. *Vom kosmischen Symbol zur ganzheitlichen Deutung.* (Freiburg: Ebertin-Verlag, 1998).

27. Ebertin, Reinhold. *The Combination of Stellar Influences.* (Aalen: Ebertin-Verlag, 1972).

28. Ebertin, Reinhold. *Man in the Universe: An Introduction to Cosmobiology.* (Aalen: Ebertin-Verlag, 1973).

29. Ellul, Jacques. *Propaganda: The Formation of Men's Attitudes*, translated by Konrad Kellen and Jean Lerner. (New York: Vintage Books, 1965).

30. Ellul, Jacques. *The Technological Society*, translated by John Wilkenson. (New York: Vintage Books, 1964).

31. 'First Boer War,' http://en.wikipedia.org/wiki/First_Boer_War.

32. 'Frederick V, Elector Palatine,' http://en.wikipedia.org/wiki/Frederick_V,_Elector_Palatine.

33. 'French First Republic,' http://en.wikipedia.org/wiki/French_First_Republic.

34. 'French and Indian War,' http://en.wikipedia.org/wiki/French_and_Indian_War.

35. 'Gemistus Pletho,' http://en.wikipedia.org/wiki/Gemistus_Pletho.

36. 'German Peasants' War,' http://en.wikipedia.org/wiki/German_Peasants%27_War.

37. 'Glorious Revolution,' http://en.wikipedia.org/wiki/Glorious_Revolution.

38. 'Great Depression,' http://en.wikipedia.org/wiki/Great_Depression.

39. 'Great Society,' http://en.wikipedia.org/wiki/Great_Society.

40. 'Greco-Turkish War (1919-1922),' http://en.wikipedia.org/wiki/Greco-Turkish_War_(1919%E2%80%931922).

41. 'Gutenberg Bible,' http://en.wikipedia.org/wiki/Gutenberg_Bible.

42. Hamblin, David. *Harmonic Charts: A New Dimension in Astrology.* (Wellingborough, Northamptonshire: Aquarian Press, 1983), 47 ff.

43. *Ibid.*, 64 ff.

44. *Ibid.* 80 ff.

45. 'Hanseatic League,' http://en.wikipedia.org/wiki/Hanseatic_League.

46. 'Hegemony,' http://en.wikipedia.org/wiki/Hegemony.

47. 'History of the Church of England,' http://en.wikipedia.org/wiki/History_of_the_Church_of_England.

48. 'Huguenot,' http://en.wikipedia.org/wiki/Hugenot.

49. 'Indian Removal Act,' http://en.wikipedia.org/wiki/Indian_Removal_Act.

50. 'Indulgence,' http://en.wikipedia.org/wiki/Indulgence.

51. 'Iran-Iraq War,' http://en.wikipedia.org/wiki/Iran-Iraq_War.

52. 'Irish Civil War,' http://en.wikipedia.org/wiki/Irish_Civil_War.

53. 'Israel,' http://en.wikipedia.org/wiki/Israel.

54. 'Kipper and Wipper: Rogue Traders, Rogue Princes, Rogue Bishops and the German Financial Meltdown of 1621-23,' http://blogs.smithsonianmag.com/history/2012/03/%E2%80%9Ckipper-und-wipper%E2%80%9D-rogue-traders-rogue-princes-rogue-bishops-and-the-german-financial-meltdown-of-1621-23/.

55. 'Ku Klux Klan,' http://en.wikipedia.org/wiki/KKK.

56. Jacobson, Roger A. *The Language of Uranian Astrology*. (Franksville, WI: Uranian Publications, 1975).

57. 'James VI and I,' http://en.wikipedia.org/wiki/James_I.

58. Johnson, Steven. *Emergence: The Connected Lives of Ants, Brains, Cities, and Software*. (New York: Scribner, 2001).

59. Johnson, Steven. *Everything Bad Is Good For You*. (New York: Riverhead Books, 2001).

60. 'List of French monarchs,' http://en.wikipedia.org/wiki/French_monarchy#House_of_Bourbon_.281815.E2.80.931830.29.

61. 'List of Recessions in the United States,' http://en.wikipedia.org/wiki/List_of_recessions_in_the_United_States.

62. 'Long War (Ottoman wars),' http://en.wikipedia.org/wiki/Long_War_(Ottoman_wars).

63. 'Mahatma Gandhi,' http://en.wikipedia.org/wiki/Gandhi.

64. 'Marshall Plan,' http://en.wikipedia.org/wiki/Marshall_Plan.

65. 'Mary, Queen of Scots,' http://en.wikipedia.org/wiki/Mary,_Queen_of_Scots.

66. 'Mexican Revolution,' http://en.wikipedia.org/wiki/Mexican_Revolution.

67. 'Modernism (Roman Catholicism),' http://en.wikipedia.org/wiki/Modernist_Crisis.

68. 'Napoleon,' http://en.wikipedia.org/wiki/Napoleon.

69. 'National Convention,' http://en.wikipedia.org/wiki/National_Convention.

70. 'New Deal,' http://en.wikipedia.org/wiki/New_Deal.

71. 'Night of the Long Knives,' http://en.wikipedia.org/wiki/Night_of_the_Long_Knives.

72. 'Otto von Bismarck,' http://www.ssa.gov/history/ottob.html.

73. 'Pahlavi dynasty,' http://en.wikipedia.org/wiki/Pahlavi_dynasty.

74. 'Partition of India,' http://en.wikipedia.org/wiki/Partition_of_India.

75. 'Pope Innocent X,' http://en.wikipedia.org/wiki/Innocent_X.

76. 'Pope Sixtus IV,' http://en.wikipedia.org/wiki/Sixtus_IV.

77. 'Platonic Academy (Florence),' http://en.wikipedia.org/wiki/Platonic_Academy_(Florence).

78. 'Recession,' http://en.wikipedia.org/wiki/Recession.

79. 'Renaissance Magic,' http://en.wikipedia.org/wiki/Renaissance_magic.

80. 'Republic of Ireland,' http://en.wikipedia.org/wiki/Republic_of_Ireland.

81. 'Romanus Pontifex,' http://en.wikipedia.org/wiki/Romanus_Pontifex.

82. Roubini, Nouriel. 'Is Capitalism Doomed?' Project Syndicate: http://www.project-syndicate.org/commentary/roubini41/English.

83. 'Rudolf II, Holy Roman Emperor,' http://en.wikipedia.org/wiki/Rudolf_II,_Holy_Roman_Emperor.

84. 'Russian famine of 1921,' http://en.wikipedia.org/wiki/Russian_famine_of_1921.

85. 'Russo-Turkish War (1877-1878),' http://en.wikipedia.org/wiki/Russo-Turkish_War,_1877%E2%80%931878.

86. 'Schutzstaffel,' http://en.wikipedia.org/wiki/Schutzstaffel.

87. 'Second Boer War,' http://en.wikipedia.org/wiki/Second_Boer_War.

88. 'Seven Years' War,' http://en.wikipedia.org/wiki/Seven_Years%27_War.

89. 'Siege of Port Royal (1710),' http://en.wikipedia.org/wiki/Siege_of_Port_Royal_(1710).

90. 'Sherman Antitrust Act,' http://en.wikipedia.org/wiki/Sherman_Act.

91. 'Society of Jesus,' http://en.wikipedia.org/wiki/Jesuits.

92. 'Sturmabteilung,' http://en.wikipedia.org/wiki/Sturmabteilung.

93. 'Taiping Rebellion,' http://en.wikipedia.org/wiki/Taiping_Rebellion.

94. Taleb, Nassim Nicholas. *Antifragile: Things That Gain From Disorder*. (New York: Random House, 2012).

95. Tarnas, Richard. *Cosmos and Psyche: Intimations of the New World View*. (New York: Viking, 2006).

96. 'The City of the Sun,' http://en.wikipedia.org/wiki/The_City_of_the_Sun.

97. Thiel, Peter. 'The End of the Future.' http_www.nationalreview.com_blogs_print_278758.pdf.

98. 'Thirty Years' War,' http://en.wikipedia.org/wiki/Thirty_Years%27_War.

99. 'Treaty of New Echota," http://en.wikipedia.org/wiki/Treaty_of_New_Echota.

100. 'United Nations Monetary and Financial Conference,' http://en.wikipedia.org/wiki/United_Nations_Monetary_and_Financial_Conference.

101. 'Union of Brussels,' http://en.wikipedia.org/wiki/Union_of_Brussels.

102. 'United States Bill of Rights,' http://en.wikipedia.org/wiki/United_States_Bill_of_Rights.

103. 'Universal Declaration of Human Rights,' http://en.wikipedia.org/wiki/Universal_Declaration_of_Human_Rights.

104. Vallerion, Alain-Jacques, *et al.* 'Transmissibility and geographic spread of the 1889 influenza pandemic.' *Proceedings of the National Academy of Sciences.* 107:19. pp. 8778-8781.

105. 'Vietnam War,' http://en.wikipedia.org/wiki/Vietnam_War.

106. 'Vladimir Lenin,' http://en.wikipedia.org/wiki/Lenin.

107. 'War of 1812," http://en.wikipedia.org/wiki/War_of_1812.

108. 'War of Devolution,' http://en.wikipedia.org/wiki/War_of_Devolution.

109. 'Wars of the Roses,' http://en.wikipedia.org/wiki/Wars_of_the_Roses.

110. 'Watts Riots,' http://en.wikipedia.org/wiki/Watts_Riots.

111. 'West Germany,' http://en.wikipedia.org/wiki/West_Germany.

112. Williams, Hywel. *Cassell's Chronology of World History.* (London: Weidenfeld & Nicholson: 2005).

113. 'World War I,' http://en.wikipedia.org/wiki/World_war_i.

114. 'World War I reparations,' http://en.wikipedia.org/wiki/World_War_I_reparations.

115. 'World War II,' http://en.wikipedia.org/wiki/World_War_II.

116. 'Yalta Conference,' http://en.wikipedia.org/wiki/Yalta_Conference.

About the author

Thomas O. Sidebottom is a mystical geek. This book combines his deep experience in software design and implementation with a life-long passion for astrology and the Western Mystery Traditions.

The work continues...

The research work described here continues to develop. Please follow the ongoing progress at:

http://www.Beyond2012Astrology.com

www.ingramcontent.com/pod-product-compliance
Lightning Source LLC
Chambersburg PA
CBHW080504110426
42742CB00017B/2994